LONG TRAIL GUIDE

TWENTY-SEVENTH EDITION 2011

Green Mountain Club

LONG TRAIL GUIDE

Hiking Vermont's High Ridge

TWENTY-SEVENTH EDITION

2011

Green Mountain Club
Waterbury Center, Vermont 05677

Editions:

First Edition 1917
Second Edition 1920
Third Edition 1921
Fourth Edition 1922
Fifth Edition 1924
Sixth Edition 1924
Seventh Edition 1928
Eighth Edition 1930
Ninth Edition 1932
Tenth Edition 1935
Eleventh Edition 1937
Twelfth Edition 1940
Thirteenth Edition 1947
Fourteenth Edition 1951

Fifteenth Edition 1956
Sixteenth Edition 1960
Seventeenth Edition 1963
Eighteenth Edition 1966
Nineteenth Edition 1968
Twentieth Edition 1971
Twenty-first Edition 1977
Twenty-second Edition 1983
Twenty-third Edition 1985
Twenty-fourth Edition 1996
Twenty-fifth Edition 2003
Twenty-sixth Edition 2007
Twenty-seventh Edition 2011

The Green Mountain Club, Inc.
4711 Waterbury-Stowe Road, Waterbury Center, Vermont 05677
(802) 244-7037
gmc@greenmountainclub.org
www.greenmountainclub.org

The information in this guide is the result of the best effort of
the publisher, using information available at the time of printing.
Changes resulting from maintenance and relocations are constantly
occurring, and therefore no published route can be regarded as
precisely accurate at the time you read this notice.

Twenty-seventh edition

ISBN 978-1-888021-38-7

Editors
Dave Hardy
Matt Krebs

Map Editing
Megan Duni

It is impossible to list every person who assisted in the production of this edition of the guidebook, but many deserve special recognition. We gratefully acknowledge the creativity, patience, and enthusiasm of all the volunteers who have contributed to each of the twenty-seven editions of this guidebook.

27th Edition Contributors

Richard Andrews
Pete Antos-Ketcham
Dave Blumenthal
Cheryl Byrne
Jen Donley
Karen and Al Fiebig
Marge Fish
Heidi Fleury
Ruth Hare
Ken Hertz
Maisie Howard
Lynda Hutchins
Mary Lou Johnson
Steve Larose
Doug McKain

Andrew and Reidun Nuquist
Herb Ogden
John Page
Mary Lou Recor
Doug Reeves
Gary Sawyer
Roy Schweiker
Susan Shea
Martha Stitelman
Val Stori
Ted Vogt
Kevin Williamson
Will Wiquist
Kathryn Wrigley

Cover and book design: Laughing Bear Associates, Montpelier, VT

Index: Pendragon Productions, Montpelier, VT

Original cartography: Map Adventures, Portland, ME, revised by Dave Blumenthal and Megan Duni

Thanks to Ed Epstein, Clyde Smith, Duncan Wilkie, and Dave Blumenthal for generously allowing use of their illustrations from previous editions.

To all the people working every day
to maintain and promote the Long Trail,
especially to Ben Rose,
former Green Mountain Club executive director,
for his leadership, passion, spirit, and
steady hand, which helped guide the club
for more than a decade.

Contents

Foreword x

Using This Guide xii

Welcome to the Long Trail xiv

Guidelines for the Use of the Long Trail 2

The Green Mountain Club and the Long Trail 29

Division 1:
Massachusetts–Vermont State Line to Vt. 9 43

Division 2:
Vt. 9 to Arlington–West Wardsboro Road 55

Division 3:
Arlington–West Wardsboro Road to
Mad Tom Notch 67

Division 4:
Mad Tom Notch to Vt. 140 81

Division 5:
Vt. 140 to U.S. 4 (Sherburne Pass) 97

Division 6:
U.S. 4 (Sherburne Pass) to Vt. 73 (Brandon Gap) . . 113

Division 7:
Vt. 73 (Brandon Gap) to Cooley Glen Shelter 125

Division 8:
Cooley Glen Shelter to Birch Glen Camp 139

Division 9:
Birch Glen Camp to Bolton Mountain 151

Division 10:
Bolton Mountain to Lamoille River 171

Division 11:
Lamoille River to Tillotson Camp 203

Division 12:
Tillotson Camp to the Canadian Border 215

Appalachian Trail 1:
Long Trail at Maine Junction to Vt. 12 227

Appalachian Trail 2:
Vt. 12 to the Connecticut River 237

Public Campgrounds near the Long Trail 246

Post Offices and Stores 248

Useful Addresses 249

Index 250

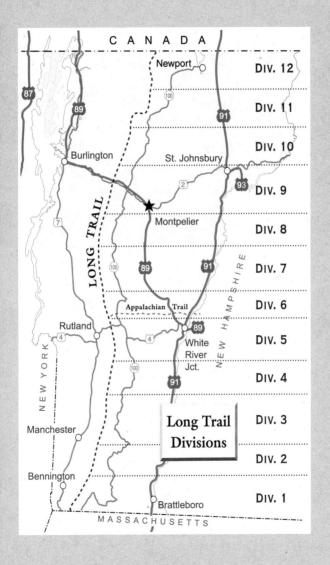

Foreword

In many ways, today's Long Trail is the same as yesterday's Long Trail. For a century, the grandfather of America's long distance hiking trails has traversed Vermont's ridgelines from Massachusetts to the Canadian border.

Yet, every year — and indeed every moment — the Long Trail changes one way or another. With more than 270 miles of trails through woods, mountain ponds, glens, and rocky summits, it is both by nature and by design that the Long Trail changes. Through erosion and beaver activity, nature moves the trail. The trail also moves for a variety of hiker-centric reasons: to avoid treacherous descents and powerful rivers, to integrate new and forgotten trail routes for various reasons, to find a way to previously unutilized viewpoints, and to better realize the goal of a ridgeline path through the Green Mountains.

It is with this balance between constant change and an unchanging mission that the Green Mountain Club produces periodic updates to its historic *Long Trail Guide*. While new technologies have their time and place, we still believe a pocket-sized guidebook is as irreplaceable for the Long Trail experience as worn-in boots and a breeze on a quiet mountain summit.

This guidebook describes the Long Trail as experienced in a traditional south-to-north hike. But things do change on the Long Trail. Please contact the Club and visit our website if you have any questions or note any problems with this book.

Thank you for picking up this, the 27th edition of the *Long Trail Guide*. The Long Trail is an American treasure, and your interest in experiencing its splendor continues a century-old tradition. Whether you are an end to ender or a day hiker, follow the white blazes and, most of all, enjoy your hike.

Marge Fish
GMC President

Will Wiquist
GMC Executive Director

Using This Guide

The *Long Trail Guide* is the official guide to the Long Trail and its network of side trails. It is produced and updated by Green Mountain Club volunteers and staff who maintain and manage the trail. This guidebook and the club's companion publication, the *Day Hiker's Guide to Vermont*, which includes trails on and off of the Long Trail System, together cover the majority of hiking trails in Vermont.

This guide divides the Long Trail into twelve divisions, numbered from south to north. Each division includes a map, elevation profile, division summary, and trail description.

Maps

The scale of the maps is about three miles to the inch. The contour interval is 100 feet. The Long Trail is shown as a heavy red line. Double-dashed lines depict roads that may not be passable; solid lines represent roads that probably are.

Division Summaries

Tables of mileage and elevation information are provided for each division. The northbound hiker will read the tables from the bottom up. Southbound hikers can follow the tables from top to bottom. They are useful for quickly determining the distance and net elevation gain or loss between one point on the trail and the next. The listed features in bold type correspond to features mentioned in the Long Trail descriptions. Mileages are cumulative. Long Trail elevations are given in both feet and meters.

Trail Descriptions

The Long Trail and Appalachian Trail descriptions read from south to north. Distances are cumulative within each division. Distances between shelters are given in both miles and kilometers and include northbound hiking times. Southbound times are in parentheses. Mileage between shelters in the division summaries are based on the Long Trail; mileages in the text include spur trails to the shelters. Cumulative distances to Massachusetts and Canada from the beginning (i.e., the southernmost point) of the division are given at the top of the first page of each division. Many trail features, such as shelters, summits, side trails, and road crossings that appear in bold type in the descriptions, are also listed in bold type in the summary tables. Side trails are noted in the Long Trail description where they intersect the trail. Side trails are described after the Long Trail descriptions. Trailhead elevations of side trails are included in the text.

Mileages used in the division summaries and trail descriptions are actual hiking distances, including twists and turns, based on surveyor's wheel measurements. Bear in mind that road distances are from odometer readings and odometers vary! *Hiking times are based on the age-old formula of one-half hour for each mile plus one-half hour for each 1,000 feet of ascent.* These estimates are for actual walking time; allowances should be made for breaks, ruggedness of terrain, and hiking experience and also for trips to summits and other viewpoints reached via side trails. Of course, everyone has his or her own pace, and your actual pace will probably differ from "book time."

Elevation Profiles

This feature provides a sense of the ups and downs of the Long Trail for each division. It is just a representation, so don't be surprised if there are little ups and downs that don't show in the profiles. Observant readers will notice that a miniature version of each division's elevation profile is at the start of the division trail descriptions.

Abbreviations

ANR. . . . . . Agency of Natural Resources
AT . . . . Appalachian Trail
ATC. . . . . . Appalachian Trail Conference
CCC . . . . . Civilian Conservation Corps
DOC . . . . . Dartmouth Outing Club
ft. . . . . feet
GMC . . . . . Green Mountain Club
GMNF . . . . Green Mountain National Forest
hr. . . . . hour(s)
km. . . . . kilometer(s)
LT . . . . Long Trail
LTP . . . . . . Long Trail Patrol
m. . . . . meter(s)
mi. . . . . mile(s)
Mt. . . . . . . Mount
Mtn. . . . . . Mountain
Rev. . . . . . . Reverse time for side trails
SB . . . . southbound
USFS . . . . . U.S. Forest Service
DFPR . . . . Vermont Department of Forests,
Parks and Recreation
VYCC . . . Vermont Youth Conservation Corps

Key to Division Maps

▬▬▬▬▬	paved road
═══════	unpaved road
▬ ▬ ▬ ▬ ▬	hiking trail
◪	shelter
■	four-sided lodge
▲	campsite
▮▮	public land
▬▬▬▬	federal wilderness boundary
──────	100-foot contour interval
▬▬▬▬	500-foot contour interval

Welcome to the Long Trail

Vermont's Long Trail System, with its 272-mile footpath, 185 miles of side trails, and approximately seventy backcountry campsites, many featuring shelters, offers endless hiking opportunities for the day hiker, weekend overnighter, and extended backpacker. The Long Trail follows the main ridge of the Green Mountains from the Massachusetts-Vermont state line to the Canadian border, crossing Vermont's highest peaks.

On its way to Canada, this "footpath in the wilderness" climbs rugged peaks and passes pristine ponds, alpine sedge, hardwood forests, and swift streams. It is steep in places, muddy in others, and rugged in most. Novice and expert alike will enjoy the varied terrain of the trail as it passes through the heart of Vermont.

Built by the Green Mountain Club between 1910 and 1930, the Long Trail is the oldest long-distance hiking trail in the country. It was the inspiration for the Appalachian Trail, which coincides with the Long Trail for over one hundred miles in southern Vermont. As maintainer and protector of the Long Trail, the Green Mountain Club works in partnership with the Green Mountain National Forest, state of Vermont, Appalachian Trail Conservancy, and private landowners to offer a world-class hiking trail.

Guidelines for the Use of the Long Trail

With proper care, a hiker of almost any ability and experience can enjoy an excursion on the Long Trail. Hikers are encouraged to plan their hikes with both their ability and weather conditions in mind. For the latest information on trail and shelter conditions, contact GMC or visit www.greenmountainclub.org.

Please treat all trail lands with respect. Portions of the Long Trail in northern Vermont cross private land. You may encounter logging in a few places — please remember that you are a guest on somebody's property. It only takes one inconsiderate hiker to cause a landowner to close the trail. Park so as not to block access to roads or driveways. Practice Leave No Trace (see pages 11 to 12). Carry out all trash. Landowners may be farming, grazing, maple sugaring, or logging on lands adjacent to the trail, activities that are an integral part of Vermont's economy and way of life. In certain seasons, you may encounter hunters. They are welcome on the Long Trail too.

Trail Marking

The Long Trail is marked by two-by-six-inch white blazes. Intersections usually have signs. Double blazes may mark important turns. In open areas or on rocky summits, blazes are often painted on rocks; cairns and scree walls may also define the trail. Property lines, snowmobile routes, and cross-country ski trails marked in various colors occasionally cross the route, but the well-worn footpath and standard white blazes distinguish the

Long Trail from these. Nearly all side trails are blazed in blue. Hikers should always pay special attention at trail intersections as signs may be missing and blazes fade.

Camping and Fires

Because the Long Trail System passes through private, state, and federal lands, regulations vary from one part of the trail to another. Guidelines for each type of land ownership are described below. Camping at designated sites is strongly encouraged. The division trail descriptions provide information about where dispersed camping is allowed.

Private Lands. Camping on private lands is limited to designated sites. Fires are only allowed in permanent fireplaces. Use of these areas is permitted through the generosity of the landowners. Abuse of our long-standing arrangements could result in closure of the Long Trail on private lands.

State Lands. Primitive camping is permitted below 2,500 feet, 200 feet from water, and 200 feet from any trail, in accordance with Leave No Trace practices. Fires are permitted below 2,500 feet. See page 13 for information regarding group use permits.

Federal Lands. Camping between shelters is permitted along much of the trail in the Green Mountain National Forest between the Massachusetts border and Vt. 140 and between Sherburne Pass and Mount Ellen if Leave No Trace principles are followed. Exceptions are noted in each division. Small wood fires are allowed unless noted in trail descriptions. See page 18 for information regarding Outfitter-Guide Special Use Permits.

Overnight Sites

There are nearly six dozen Long Trail overnight sites spaced no more than a moderate day's hike apart. These range from fully enclosed lodges to three-sided lean-tos and tenting areas. All sites, although primitive, have a water source nearby (purity and reliability cannot be guaranteed) and a privy. Visitors must carry their own food, backpacking stove, and overnight gear.

The overnight structures along the trail are designated as shelters, camps, or lodges. Shelters usually have open fronts. Some camps are enclosed and have doors and glazed windows. Larger enclosed structures are lodges. Any exceptions to these classifications are noted.

These facilities are used on a first-come, first-served basis until filled to their stated capacity. Please make room for other hikers. Overnight hikers should carry tents as shelter space is not guaranteed. Use of any overnight facility is limited to three consecutive nights. Shelters are intended for individual or small group use. Larger groups of more than six should not plan to use shelters and should carry tents or tarps. Organized groups should follow group hiking guidelines on pages 13 to 17. Anticipated shelter changes are noted in each division.

To improve toilet efficiency, please follow the guidelines posted on the outhouse doors. If no guidelines are present, please urinate in the woods well away from water sources to reduce odors. As part of its waste management efforts, the Green Mountain Club (GMC) composts sewage at nineteen overnight sites.

Caretakers: Who Are They and Why Are They There?

Each year from Memorial Day weekend until October, GMC hires caretakers for selected sites along the trail: the fragile alpine summits of Mount Mansfield, Camel's Hump, and Mount Abraham; a ridgerunner for the Coolidge Range (Killington and Pico); popular sites on the AT in southern Vermont such as Stratton Pond, Little Rock Pond, and Griffith Lake; and high-use overnight destinations such as Montclair Glen and Butler and Taft lodges, where composting of sewage is necessary. Caretakers talk with hikers about the fragile summit ecosystems, local camping and fire regulations, and provide first aid.

Through informal conversation and example, the caretakers educate hikers about Leave No Trace principles and perform trail and shelter maintenance. The caretakers compost sewage, so be nice to them!

GMC caretakers are experienced hikers. They are happy to provide backpacking suggestions and tips as well as basic information about the trail and the club. Caretakers and their field supervisors also work up and down the trail with volunteers, taking care of backcountry privies and addressing other maintenance and management problems that crop up each season. This important program is partially funded by a modest overnight use fee charged at caretaker sites. Site fees cover a quarter of the cost of the caretakers' program. If a caretaker is present at your overnight site, you should pay the fee. This applies to tent sites (e.g., Hump Brook) as well as shelter sites.

Water

Although the GMC makes every effort to locate shelters and campsites near water sources, the quality and quantity of water cannot be guaranteed. During dry weather, water sources may fail. Areas particularly prone to water shortages are noted in the trail description.

Contamination of water supplies is a problem, even in remote areas. Water may look and taste clean but still be unsafe to drink. Giardiasis, caused by the intestinal parasite *Giardia lamblia*, is just one of many illnesses caused by drinking contaminated water. Other bacteria and viruses may also be present in water sources. If giardiasis symptoms such as severe cramping and diarrhea occur, consult your physician.

Hikers and dogs are probably the main carriers of *Giardia*. Often, they carry the parasite and unknowingly contaminate water supplies through the careless disposal of waste. People can pass it on to others by failing to wash their hands after making a pit stop.

The best way to prevent illness is to treat all drinking water. To kill *Giardia*, water must be brought to a rolling boil, filtered with a water purifier guaranteed to remove the *Giardia* parasite (filters may not remove all contaminants, such as viruses), or treated with a chemical purifier (follow the directions on the bottle). To kill all viruses and bacteria, water must be chemically treated or boiled for ten minutes.

Spring and Fall Mud Seasons

The GMC and its agency partners encourage hikers to avoid higher elevation trails during the spring and late fall mud seasons (usually late March through the end of May and late October until the ground freezes or the snowpack forms).

Please help protect the fragile alpine tundra and prevent soil erosion by staying off the trails during mud season! This will allow the trails to dry out and reduce the amount of maintenance required each year to keep them safe and enjoyable. We know everyone is just itching to get out and enjoy the wonders of spring — we are, too!

Rain and melting snow at higher elevations keep many of Vermont's hiking trails wet and muddy. When hikers tramp on saturated soils, they cause irreversible erosion and damage to the trail and surrounding vegetation. The GMC, Vermont Department of Forests, Parks and Recreation, and Green Mountain National Forest advocate responsible use of the state's hiking trails between maple sugaring season (usually early March to early April) and Memorial Day weekend.

Higher elevation soils take longer to dry out, and their higher content of organic material slows the drying process. A trail may be dry at the trailhead, but it will get muddy if you climb very high this time of year. Trails at lower elevations, dirt roads, and recreation paths provide excellent opportunities for early spring walking.

Note: Trails on state lands are closed from April 15 through the Friday of Memorial Day Weekend: Coolidge State Forest, Camel's Hump State Park, Mansfield State Forest, Long Trail State Forest, and Jay State Forest.

Guidelines

- If a trail is so muddy that you need to walk on the vegetation beside it, turn back and seek another place to hike.
- Plan spring hikes in hardwood forests at lower elevations.
- Avoid spruce-fir (conifer) forest at higher elevations and on north slopes before late May and from the end of October until frozen or snow covered.

• The state of Vermont closes trails in Camel's Hump and Mount Mansfield areas from snowmelt until late May. Please do not hike here. Stay below 3,000 feet during these times of year.

Mud Season Hiking Alternatives

Here are a few mud season hiking suggestions:

Northern Vermont:
> Burlington Bike Path
> Missisquoi Valley Rail Trail
> Stowe Bike Path
> Cotton Brook Area/Moscow/Stowe
> Alburg Recreation Trail
> Mallets Bay Causeway
> Cambridge Greenway Recreation Path
> Mount Philo

Central Vermont:
> Austin Brook Trail in Warren/Granville
> Thresher Hill and Pine Brook Trails
> Cross Vermont Trail (runs west to east across Vermont)
> Liberty Hill & Contest Trails
> Lefferts Pond
> Robert Frost Interpretive Trail
> Trail Around Middlebury (TAM)

Southern Vermont:
> Emerald Lake State Park Trail
> Harriman Trail
> Delaware and Hudson Rail Trail
> Woodford State Park Trails
> West River Trail
> Jamaica State Park Trails

With the trails in state parks, you should check in with the Vermont Department of Forests, Parks and Recreation to see if the park and trails are open. Their phone number is (802) 241-3655.

If you know of other hikes or walks in your region that are suitable for foot traffic during mud season, please contact the GMC at www.greenmountainclub.org so that they can be added to this list.

Hiking descriptions for many of these trails can be found in the *Day Hikers Guide to Vermont* and the *Walker's Guide to Vermont*, available for sale from the GMC at greenmountainclub. org. Descriptions for some of the central Vermont trails can be found at the recreation page for the Green Mountain National Forest. You should contact the Rochester Ranger Station at (802) 767-4261 to make sure these trails are open during mud season.

Special Natural Areas and Wildlife

Alpine Areas

Vermont is fortunate to be home to three arctic-alpine areas. These fragile ecosystems, found on the summits of Mount Mansfield, Camel's Hump, and Mount Abraham, contain plant communities similar to those found 1,500 miles to the north. Although these plants are hardy enough to survive the harsh climate of mountain summits, they are vulnerable to trampling. Please protect these special natural areas by staying on marked trails, walking only on bare rock, leashing your dog(s) to limit wandering off the trail, and packing out dog waste. Camping and fires are prohibited above timberline.

Wilderness Areas

In parts of the Green Mountain National Forest, the Long Trail passes through federally designated Wilderness Areas. These generally remote areas were established by the U.S. Congress as places where human impact is minimal. Hiking, hunting, and fishing are allowed, but logging, roads, and mechanical equipment (including mountain bikes and chain saws) are not. In time, the forest will regenerate from past clearing, and the wilderness will approximate the primeval lands early European explorers first encountered. The Long Trail crosses six wilderness areas: Glastenbury (Division 2), Lye Brook (Division 3),

Big Branch and Peru Peak (Division 4), Joseph Battell (Division 7), and Breadloaf (Divisions 7 and 8).

Trail blazing and brush cutting are limited. Signs are less frequent, and they often omit mileage figures. There may be more downed trees across the trail, reflecting a reduced intensity of trail maintenance. Bridges, if any, are generally primitive, and there are occasional stream fords.

Peregrine Falcons

After almost a thirty-year absence, peregrine falcons have returned to nest in Vermont. Thirty-one nesting pairs were reported in 2010. Peregrines prefer high cliffs and outcrops. With many of these locations on or near the Long Trail, such as Smugglers' Notch and Mount Horrid, they are easily disturbed, especially by hikers above their cliffside nests.

During the nesting season, from mid-March to mid-August, hikers may encounter spur trails off the Long Trail that have been closed during this time. Please stay away from such areas until young falcons have fledged. For information, call the Vermont Department of Fish and Wildlife at (802) 241-3700.

Animals

Mice, raccoons, and squirrels gnaw through packs in search of food. Take food, trash, and items resembling food (toothpaste, peppermint soap) out of your pack and hang them in waterproof sacks from a nearby tree. Think of hanging your food bag as campsite entertainment.

Porcupines enjoy gnawing on shelters and outhouses. Close and latch privy doors and lodge doors to keep porkies from chomping on the interior. They love salt; never leave your boots where porcupines can reach them. Hang boots to keep porcupines away and also to help them dry out. Hang packs: the animals will chew sweaty pack straps and belts, too.

Although there are roughly 6,300 black bears in Vermont, they are generally shy and seldom seen. Don't feed them, and please follow Leave No Trace practices so bears do not begin to associate hikers with food and become a problem (as has happened elsewhere in the Northeast).

Dogs

Many Long Trail hikers bring their dogs along. The GMC and public land managing partners strongly recommend keeping dogs under control at all times. If you bring your dog along with you on the trail, you should bring a pair of pliers in case you meet a porcupine. Sad experience has shown that dogs don't learn from their first porcupine encounter.

Leash your dog when hiking in alpine zones, near roads, at overnight campsites, and at drinking water sources. Please don't allow your pet to muck up a small water source! Properly manage your dog's waste. Above treeline, dog waste should be packed out. Below treeline, dog waste should be treated the same as human waste using Leave No Trace principles (see pages 11 to 12). Please also leash dogs at other hikers' request; not everyone is comfortable around your lovable pet.

Hunting

Hunting is a time-honored Vermont tradition, and hunters and hikers have coexisted peaceably for generations. All land crossed by the Long Trail is open to hunting. Hikers should be aware of the various hunting seasons from September 1 through mid-December. In particular, note deer rifle season, from mid- to late November. Wear blaze orange!

Late fall offers some of the best bug-free hiking of the year, with leafless trees affording greater long-range visibility; but hunting season necessitates that hikers take certain precautions during this time of year. Dress loudly but hike quietly. Remember that hunters only get a few weeks each year, so please be considerate if hiking during hunting season. Consider leaving your pet at home to limit disturbance of wildlife. Avoid wearing brown, tan, black, or patches of white that might be mistaken for the white tail of a deer. For information on hunting seasons, write or call the Vermont Department of Fish and Wildlife at 103 South Main Street, Waterbury, Vermont 05671; (802) 241-3700.

Leave No Trace

Leave No Trace is a nationwide effort to educate backcountry travelers about low-impact camping and travel techniques to reduce impacts on land, water, wildlife, and other visitors. Leave No Trace promotes sustainable use of the backcountry. The GMC offers a variety of Leave No Trace workshops. We encourage you to contact the GMC to find out more or visit the Leave No Trace website at www.lnt.org. The Leave No Trace principles are:

Plan Ahead and Prepare. Familiarize yourself with local regulations. Bring appropriate hiking clothing, sturdy footwear, and ample food and water. Repackage food to minimize waste; camp meals should be prepared to minimize leftovers. Prepare adequately for extreme weather, hazards, and emergencies. Trails can be difficult and travel slower than it appears on a map, especially in northern Vermont. Be prepared to purify drinking water. Carry and know how to use a map and compass. Bring enough tents for everyone.

Travel and Camp on Durable Surfaces. Stay on the trail; avoid shortcuts that erode soil and damage vegetation. Camp at designated sites. Use tent platforms if available to avoid compacting soil. Avoid camping where impact is just beginning. Walk single file in the middle of the trail, even when wet or muddy, to avoid widening the treadway. Walk on rocks whenever possible, especially in fragile areas such as shorelines and alpine zones.

Dispose of Waste Properly. If you pack it in, pack it out! Use outhouses when possible. Otherwise, bury human and pet waste in six- to eight-inch-deep cat holes at least 200 feet away from water sources. Pack out all trash including hygiene products (opaque bags are helpful). To wash yourself or your dishes, carry water 200 feet (about seventy steps) away from streams or ponds and use little or no soap. Strain food particles from dishwater and pack out. Keep pets away from water sources to protect water quality. Above timberline, pack out human and animal wastes.

Leave What You Find. Take only pictures, leave only foot-prints. Flowers and other natural wonders are best enjoyed in their natural states. Leave natural and cultural artifacts as you originally found them for others to enjoy. Please don't carve into trees or shelters along the trail. Leave your campsite cleaner than you found it.

Minimize Campfire Impact. Know local regulations — wood fires may be prohibited. Campfires cause lasting impacts to the backcountry and are discouraged along the Long Trail. Use a portable stove for cooking instead of a fire. Where permitted, if you choose to build a fire, use only preexisting fire rings. Keep fires small, using only dead, downed wood. To minimize im-pacts to the campsite, collect wood on the way in. Burn all wood and coals to ash, extinguish completely, then scatter cool ashes. Pack out all foil and plastic packaging — these don't burn!

Respect Wildlife. Observe wildlife from a distance. Feeding animals damages their health, alters behavior, and exposes them to predators. Protect wildlife and your food by storing food securely. If you must bring a dog, keep it leashed and dispose of its waste in a privy or a cat hole, especially in fragile areas and at campsites. Consider leaving your pet at home.

Be Considerate of Other Visitors. Respect other trail users and the quality of their experience. Be courteous and yield to others on the trail. Take breaks on durable surfaces without intruding on others or blocking the trail. Travel and camp quietly.

Cell Phone Use Guidance. Many outdoor recreationists carry cell phones for safety and emergencies. Be considerate of other visitors: carry and use cell phones out of sight and sound of other people. Keep them turned off until needed or left in a pocket on the vibrate or silent ringer setting. Be self-reliant, whether car-rying cell phones or not. Don't leave ill-prepared or engage in risky actions just because you have a cell phone to call for rescue. Remember that in many remote areas, cell-phone coverage is limited or nonexistent. Many people go to the out-of-doors to get away from technology. Please respect their desire for solitude and be considerate when using a cell phone.

Group Use

Group use of hiking trails in the Northeast is on the rise; more than 280 groups hiked on the Long Trail in 2010. It is estimated that more than 200,000 people hike on the Long Trail annually, with 40,000 visiting Mount Mansfield alone.

Groups come in various shapes and sizes. A group may be comprised of children, teenagers, or adults led by camp counselors, teachers, scout masters, professional guides, or responsible, experienced adults. A group may also be an informal gathering of friends. Groups exert a disproportionate impact on water quality, alpine vegetation, wildlife habitat, trail treadway, backcountry campsites, and the experiences of other hikers. Groups can minimize their impacts by following these guidelines.

Leadership

Group leaders are responsible for their group members' safety and behavior. The recommended leader-to-participant ratio is one to four. GMC's *Trip Leader's Handbook* provides helpful information on leading successful group trips. It is available via GMC's website or by contacting the director of membership and volunteer services at the GMC for a paper copy.

Group Size Guidelines for Day Hikes

GMC strongly discourages group sizes in excess of twenty, including leaders, on day hikes in most areas. In fragile areas such as exposed alpine summits, pond shorelines, high-use areas, and designated wilderness areas, the recommended group size is ten. These numbers have been endorsed by the National Outdoor Leadership School, Appalachian Trail Conservancy, Green Mountain National Forest, and Vermont Department of Forests, Parks and Recreation.

Larger groups should hike in less-frequented areas off the Long Trail. Large groups may break into smaller parties and use different trails to get to the same destination or hike on the same trail but leave at staggered times.

Overnight Use

Most Long Trail campsites were originally intended for solitary hikers or small, informal groups. Overall annual use of the trail in the 1930s is easily exceeded in a single weekend in the twenty-first century. Over the past forty years, trail use has soared, putting pressure on the Long Trail's shelter system and threatening water quality. Blast zones, where vegetation ceases to grow, have expanded around shelters, increasing soil erosion. To prevent further blast-zone damage, groups should carry tents and/or tarps and use them at designated tent sites, using tent platforms where available.

Group Size Guidelines for Overnight Trips

On overnight trips the recommended maximum group size is eight, although fewer are preferable. Do not plan to use shelters. Come prepared with tarps and tents for everyone in your group. Groups should use recommended group use campsites (see pages 16 to 17).

Group Trip Planning

When planning a trip during a busy time of year, particularly weekends, holidays, or during the college orientation season (the weeks before and after Labor Day), GMC strongly recommends using a state park as a base camp instead of overcrowding a Long Trail backcountry campsite. Vermont state parks are equipped to handle large groups for overnights and can provide other amenities. Find out more about camping in state parks by visiting www.vtstateparks.com.

The table on pages 16 to 17 will help you plan your group trip. It includes recommended group campsites, their capacities, the guidebook divisions in which they are located, and if an overnight camping fee is required. *Note:* This is not a permit fee, which is separate.

High-use sites on the Long Trail are staffed by caretakers during the hiking season to assist and educate hikers, help maintain local trails and campsites, and compost sewage to protect water quality. Additionally, caretakers work with volunteers, including groups, on needed trail projects. The per-person site fee is charged for overnight use to help fund the GMC's caretaker and site maintenance programs and covers only a fraction of the program's annual cost. GMC encourages prepayment for group use; contact the group outreach coordinator at GMC or visit www.greenmountainclub.org.

Note: Prepayment does not constitute a reservation and does not imply exclusive rights or access to a site, which cannot be guaranteed. Overnight use fees are separate from use permit fees.

GMC strongly encourages groups to use the Group Notification System to prevent overcrowding at Long Trail campsites. Whether visiting a summit for an afternoon or planning a multiday backpacking adventure, groups should notify GMC of their itineraries at least two weeks in advance of their trips.

This system enables GMC to track backcountry use and assist caretakers with effective site management. And it allows GMC to recommend alternate routes or destinations to limit overcrowding and minimize negative impacts to backcountry resources.

GMC caretakers are trained by Leave No Trace master educators. Caretakers provide written feedback on group skills and performance. Feedback forms include observations of group strengths and suggestions for improvements in the areas of preparedness, practice of Leave No Trace skills, and leadership. A copy of this form is sent to your organization with a letter containing seasonally updated resource information. Caretaker feedback aids groups in evaluating their impacts and helps GMC measure the effectiveness of its education programs.

Before You Go

- Evaluate your skills and seek instruction or refresher courses if needed.

- Contact GMC or check the website for trail updates and seasonal information.

- Determine if you need a state or federal permit for your hike.

- Call the GMC group outreach specialist to use the Group Notification System. Call (802) 244-7037, ext. 27.

Division	Group Use Campsite*	Capacity	Fee
1	Seth Warner Shelter tenting area	16	no
1	Congdon Shelter tenting area	16	no
1	**Woodford State Park Campground**		yes
2	Caughnawaga tenting area	12	no
2	Story Spring Shelter tenting area	16	no
2	**GMNF Grout Pond Campground** (includes 2 lean-tos)		yes
3	Stratton Pond North Shore tenting area and platforms	24	yes
3	Spruce Peak Shelter tenting area	12	no
3	**GMNF Hapgood Pond Campground**		yes
3	Bromley Shelter	16	no
3	Bromley Mtn. ski area warming hut (contact GMC to confirm availability)	10	no
4	Griffith Lake tenting area and platforms	20	yes
4	Old Job Shelter tenting area	12	no
4	Lost Pond Shelter tenting area	10	no
4	Big Branch Shelter tenting area	10	no
4	**Emerald Lake State Park Campground**		yes
4	Little Rock Pond tenting area and platforms	28	yes
5	Minerva Hinchey Shelter tenting area	10	no
5	Clarendon Shelter tenting area	20	no
5	Cooper Lodge tent platforms and ski slope	20	no
5/AT 1	**Gifford Woods State Park Campground**	48	yes
6	Rolston Rest tenting area	10	no
6	David Logan Shelter tenting area	10	no
6	**GMNF Chittenden Brook Campground**		yes
7	USFS primitive campsite at Sucker Brook Trail trailhead	10	no
7	Worth Mtn. Lodge (lodge only; no tenting)	18	no
7	USFS primitive campsite at	10	no

*Campgrounds listed in bold charge per site, not per person. Call for info.

Division	Group Use Campsite*	Capacity	Fee
	Skylight Pond Trail trailhead		
7	Emily Proctor Shelter tent platforms	10	no
7	USFS primitive campsite at Clark Brook Trail trailhead	20	no
7	USFS primitive campsite at Cooley Glen Trail trailhead	10	no
7	Cooley Glen Shelter tenting area	10	no
8	Stark's Nest, Mad River Glen warming hut (contact GMC to confirm availability)	20	no
8	Birch Glen Camp tenting area	14	no
9	Hump Brook tenting area and platforms	20	yes
9	Bamforth Ridge Shelter tent platforms	15	no
9	**Little River State Park Campground**		yes
9	Duck Brook Shelter tenting area	10	no
9	Buchanan Shelter tenting area	10	no
10	Taylor Lodge tenting area and platforms	10	no
10	Twin Brooks tenting area and platforms	24	no
10	**Underhill State Park Campground**		yes
10	Taft Lodge (lodge only; no tenting)	24	yes
10	**Smugglers' Notch State Park Campground**		yes
10	Sterling Pond (on ski slope)	20	yes
10	Bear Hollow Shelter tenting area	10	no
10	Beaver Meadow Lodge tenting area	8	no
10/11	**Elmore State Park Campground**		yes
11	Corliss Camp tenting area	10	no
11	Spruce Ledge Camp tenting area	10	no
11	Tillotson Camp tenting area	10	no
12	Hazen's Notch Camp tenting area	10	no
12	Jay Camp tenting area and platforms	10	no
12	Laura Woodward Shelter tenting area	10	no
AT 2	Happy Hill Shelter tenting area	10	no
AT 2	**Silver Lake State Park Campground**		yes

Permits

Both the Green Mountain National Forest and Vermont Department of Forests, Parks and Recreation require permits for day or overnight use by certain groups on their lands. Permits are not required on private land, but please respect landowners and camp only at designated overnight sites.

To determine whether or not you need a permit, first you need to know where you plan to hike. Each division lists the managing agency to contact for a permit under the heading "Group Use." To apply for a permit, contact the appropriate land managing agency listed below.

Federal Lands: Green Mountain National Forest

Much of the Long Trail south of Mount Ellen (with the exception of some trail corridor over Killington Peak) and nearly all the Appalachian Trail east to Norwich, lies within the Green Mountain National Forest. Although the Appalachian Trail is actually part of the national park system, in Vermont it is managed by the U.S. Forest Service. You may need an Outfitter-Guide Special Use Permit if you or the organization you work for is:

- charging a fee for profit above the cost of basic trip expenses (i.e., food, travel) (*Note:* if the leader is paid, then it is considered a fee-for-profit operation);

- providing equipment for profit as part of the trip (any fee for equipment rental is considered fee for profit); or

- collecting plants, animals, historic artifacts, or other items.

Permits are required regardless of trip length. No outfitter-guide use may occur in the national forest without a valid permit. Processing permits takes time, especially during the hiking season, so obtain permits well in advance of your trip.

Contact Green Mountain National Forest at (802) 747-6700 or visit www.fs.fed.us/r9/gmfl for information on Outfitter-Guide Special Use Permits on the National Forest. Their mailing address is:

Realty Specialist
Green Mountain National Forest
231 North Main Street
Rutland, VT 05701

State Lands: Vermont Department of Forests, Parks and Recreation

The Long Trail north of Mount Ellen to Canada is mostly on state land. Group use of state lands may require a commercial use permit if the use:

• is organized or publicized;

• involves a fee to participants (or requests a donation);

• alters the site in any way; or

• could conflict with other established uses.

Permit applications are available by mail:

ANR Lands Director
Vermont Department of Forests, Parks and Recreation
103 South Main Street, Building 10 South
Waterbury, VT 05671-0601
Or call (802) 241-3693;
or visit www.vtfpr.org/lands/licenses.cfm

Trip Planning

When planning your hike, consider the experience and conditioning of all members of your group, the terrain you plan to cover, the season, the weather, and available hours of daylight. Leave a copy of your itinerary with a reliable person.

Try out your equipment at home, new or old; it's always better to learn you need to fix something before you carry it into the woods. Learn basic first aid and how to deal with emergencies.

For long hikes, plan conservatively, allowing at least one day's leeway in case of unforeseen weather conditions. Start your hike slowly to get accustomed to your pack and minimize your risk of blisters and other injuries.

Going light is critical to a pleasant backpacking trip. Beginning hikers tend to take along more than they need. Few hikers can comfortably carry more than one-fourth of their body weight. On the other hand, even experienced hikers often forget something they wished they remembered to pack. Below are some basic items to make a hike safe and comfortable.

Day Hikes for Spring, Summer, and Fall

- guidebook or map
- lunch, snacks, water (and plenty of it)
- sturdy boots or hiking shoes (some people now prefer hiking sandals)
- wind jacket or rain gear with a breathable shell (remember it's colder on summits than in valleys)
- warm layer (wool or synthetic fleece)
- hats and mittens
- flashlight or headlamp (extra bulb and batteries)
- compass
- first-aid kit
- matches or other reliable fire starter
- insect repellent and sunscreen
- toilet paper and trowel
- whistle
- leash for Fido

Overnight Hikes

Add the following items to those carried on a day hike:

- backpacking stove and fuel
- cook kit and eating utensils
- additional food
- sleeping bag and pad (in a waterproof sack)
- tent and ground cloth or tarp
- extra clothes and socks (in a waterproof sack)

- garbage bags
- water filter or purifier
- repair kit (include duct tape)
- sturdy cord to hang your food overnight

Reduce pack weight on long-distance hikes by forwarding parcels marked "General Delivery, hold for Long Trail hiker, arriving about [date]" to post offices near the trail (see list of post offices on page 248), or by caching supplies out of sight in critterproof containers near road crossings. People making an extended backpacking trip on the Long Trail may want to purchase GMC's *Long Trail End-to-Ender's Guide*, which is updated biennially.

Safety

Simply put, it is safer to hike with others. There are risks associated with hiking the Long Trail, but considering how many people hike each year and how few bad things happen, the risks are small. Hikers should be aware of their surroundings and exercise reasonable caution when dealing with strangers. If you're not comfortable with someone you meet on the trail or at a campsite, pack up and move on.

Most Long Trail campsites are at least two miles in from the nearest road. Some of the older sites were established before high-clearance four-wheel-drive and all-terrain vehicles made them accessible to visitors other than hikers. The farther in from a road, the less likely you are to encounter nonhikers at your campsite.

Unless you are a hunter, carrying a gun on the trail is probably unnecessary. Plus, they are really heavy!

Staying Found

Should the next blaze ahead not be visible within a ten-minute walk at a brisk pace, stop, look, and backtrack if necessary. It is better to lose a moment looking for the correct route than to forge ahead on the wrong route. We recommend carrying a topographic map and compass if you are not familiar with the trail. The guidebook maps are not suitable for map and compass work. GMC publishes the *Waterproof Hiking Map of Vermont's Long Trail*, a nice companion to this guidebook.

Weather

Although summers in the Green Mountains are usually pleasant, hot humid days are common. Never underestimate the variability of Vermont weather. Conditions along the crest of the Green Mountains are not the same as in the lowlands; temperatures often vary dramatically, sometimes as much as 5 degrees Fahrenheit per 1,000 feet. There is also a marked increase in the amount of precipitation at higher elevations. The annual average precipitation in Vermont is forty inches. Other conditions, such as rain, fog, and sudden drops in temperature, can occur at any time, even in the summer. Always carry a warm layer, a hat, and wind gear when hiking to higher elevations. On the higher peaks, the annual precipitation exceeds 100 inches. Summer nights can be cool, so hikers should always carry layers and be prepared for rain.

Hypothermia

The threat of hypothermia, a dangerous and potentially deadly condition, exists year-round. Hypothermia is the cooling of the body's core temperature caused by heat loss and the body's inability to keep its internal temperature constant. This condition is not limited to winter. In fact, what is often referred to as hypothermia weather is not minus 20 degrees Fahrenheit, but those rainy, windy 40- to 50-degree or even 60-degree Fahrenheit days that occur in Vermont's mountains at any time of the year.

Symptoms of hypothermia include poor judgment, forgetfulness, and confusion. Motor control may suffer, leading to problems with coordination (such as being unable to fasten one's clothing), an unsteady gait, or slurred speech. Other warning signs include being unable to keep one's fingers and toes warm, uncontrollable shivering, or extreme unexpected fatigue. If untreated, hypothermia can result in coma and even death.

Prevention is the key to avoiding hypothermia. Always eat and drink plenty. Dress in layers, including, as needed, wicking underwear, an insulating layer, and a wind- and waterproof shell. Wear wool or synthetics like polypropylene or pile, or if it's warm, keep some of these in your pack, just in case. Regulate body temperature by adding and removing layers as needed. Keep your pace steady when it is cold. Keep rest stops brief so as not to cool off too much. We recommend packing at least one sleeping bag per group on winter day hikes.

When spotted early, hypothermia is easy to treat. Immediately get the chilled person out of the wind and into dry and warm clothing, including a hat. Give him or her food and water and keep the person moving. If a chilled person is walking, keep walking. If this doesn't work and you must rewarm the person, put him or her in a prewarmed sleeping bag. For more information about hypothermia or other backcountry emergencies, consult *Medicine for the Backcountry* by Buck Tilton and Frank Hubbell or take a course in wilderness first aid.

Lightning

Injury from lightning, although fortunately rare, is a serious risk to hikers. Whenever there is a threat:

- avoid open summits, ridges, and fields;
- if in the forest, seek an area amid shorter trees;
- avoid wet gullies and crevices and stay out of small depressions where ground currents may travel;
- stay out of small caves (large, dry ones are usually good, however);
- sit or crouch on insulating objects, such as a dry sleeping bag or mattress, making yourself as small as possible; and
- set aside exposed metal objects (things inside a pack are usually all right).

About 70 percent of people hit by lightning survive. If a person is still conscious and breathing after being struck, the chance of survival is excellent. Even if a lightning victim is not breathing or has no pulse, prompt and effective CPR may save him or her. Continue CPR as long as possible; there is a much greater chance of survival in this situation than in most other cases of cardiac arrest.

Bug Season

Blackflies and mosquitoes can make hiking in the Green Mountains uncomfortable and at times unbearable. Blackflies breed in running water and are most abundant in early summer. They usually fade away by mid-July. Mosquitoes buzz around most of the summer. A headnet is helpful. Be sure your tent has no-see-um-proof netting. Almost nothing works against blackflies, but long-sleeved shirts and pants can help. Although insect repellent containing Deet is most effective, there is some concern about its safety. If you do choose to use it, apply it to clothing rather than directly to the skin and avoid using it on children. Alternative repellents are available.

Lyme disease is making its way north, so hikers should be on the lookout for deer ticks and protect themselves from bites with clothing or repellent.

If you are allergic to bees, carry the appropriate medication prescribed by your doctor and know how to use it.

Rabies

The danger of rabies remains greater at home than on the trail. Take precautions. Beware of any animal that is acting strangely. Leave dead animals alone. Live ones, too, actually.

If bitten by an animal, wash the wound thoroughly with soap and water and get to a doctor as soon as possible. Rabies today is preventable as long as medical treatment is received soon after contact; otherwise, it is 100 percent fatal.

Snakes

There are no poisonous snakes on the Long Trail or Appalachian Trail in Vermont. In Vermont, snakes have more to fear from humans than vice versa.

Winter Use

Winter hiking can be rewarding and challenging, with clear skies and breathtaking views. It can also be dangerous. A winter trip must be planned and conducted with care—the margin for error is small.

The Long Trail and its shelters are not designed for winter use. The white blazes that mark the Long Trail are usually painted four to five feet from the ground, a height that may be at knee-level or even completely buried under snow. Overhanging branches, well out of reach during summer hiking, may obstruct a winter hiker's way.

Vermont winters are harsh, with abrupt temperature changes. Changing weather conditions, deep snow, short daylight, and the need to carry extra warm clothing and safety gear all need to be considered. Breaking trail is strenuous, sometimes exhausting. Conditions at higher elevations will be much more severe, and wind may make winter travel impossible. On open ridges and summits, hikers may encounter icy, windswept conditions. Crampons may be needed. Hypothermia, always a threat, can happen fast in winter weather. (See more about hypothermia on page 22.) Carry a map and compass and know how to use them. Be prepared to spend the night in the woods, if necessary.

Long Trail shelters are uninsulated and unheated. All Long Trail hikers should be prepared to spend the night in a shelter without a stove for warmth. The presence of a stove at a shelter on a summer trip is not a guarantee it will be there on a winter trip. Shelters may be covered or filled with snow. An open-faced lean-to provides little protection against the elements and is no substitute for a winter tent and below-zero-rated sleeping bag.

Winter conditions occur from October to May in the Green Mountains, with snow lasting until early June at higher elevations just below treeline. At 3,800 feet, snow can linger for eight to twelve weeks longer than at 1,800 feet. Maximum snow depth usually occurs in March.

If you are new to winter outings, gain some experience before you set out on your own. Go on winter hikes with friends who have experience, take a class, or join a guided hike. GMC offers volunteer and staff-led winter trips, as do many outdoor gear stores.

Each trail division includes a note about winter use. Some divisions are better suited for snowshoeing and require more technical equipment, while the rolling terrain of other sections make them ideal for cross-country skiing. Always give yourself extra time; the estimated hiking times in the guidebook do not apply during the winter months.

Use Skis or Snowshoes. Please think of other hikers and those who come after you. Avoid post-holing through the snow. Also, knee-deep holes can make the trail unpleasant, even dangerous for the hiker who comes next. Wear (or bring) snowshoes or skis! Post-holing is exhausting and time consuming, potentially turning a pleasant hike into a cold, wet, miserable outing.

Winter Sanitation. Carry a shovel and dig out the outhouse door whenever possible. Be aware of the locations of streams and avoid making pit stops near them. It is *not OK* to leave toilet paper in the snow.

Catamount Trail. The Catamount Trail provides a full range of skiing opportunities. Founded in 1984, it is fashioned after the Long Trail, traversing the length of Vermont from Massachusetts to Canada, linking cross-country ski areas with stretches of backcountry trail. For more information about the Catamount Trail and its latest guidebook (9th edition, 2009), contact the Catamount Trail Association, 1 Mill Street, Suite 350, Burlington, Vermont 05401; (802) 864-5794; www.catamounttrail.org.

Trail Access

The Long Trail is easily reached from many major roads. This guide gives directions to all Long Trail road crossings at the beginning of each division. Directions to side trails are included in side trail descriptions. For a road map, hikers may request the "Official Vermont Road Map" from Vermont Attractions Association, Box 1284, Montpelier, Vermont 05601; (802) 229-4581 or attractions@vtchamber.com.

The trail is also shown in many road atlases. *Vermont Road Atlas and Guide*, and *Vermont Atlas & Gazetteer* are excellent resources and can be useful for locating access points to the Long Trail as well as side trails.

Transportation

Bus. Public transportation in the vicinity of the Long Trail is provided primarily by Greyhound Lines. Timetables are available from Greyhound Lines, Inc. P.O. Box 660362, Dallas, Texas 75266; 800-231-2222; www.greyhound.com. For details on a daily bus between Middlebury and Middlebury Gap, check www.actr-vt.org or call (802) 388-1946.

Air. The Burlington International Airport and Manchester Airport in New Hampshire are served by several major carriers, while smaller companies provide air service to Rutland.

Rail. Amtrak provides passenger rail service to Rutland and central Vermont from Washington, D.C., New York, and many other cities. Although Amtrak crosses the trail at Jonesville, it does not stop closer than Waterbury or Essex Junction. For more information, see www.amtrak.com.

Parking. There are many small and some larger parking areas at trailheads on both the Long Trail and its side trails. Parking information is included with road directions to trailheads. When parking vehicles at trailheads, take special care to avoid obstructing traffic or blocking access to homes, farms, or woodlots.

Vandalism

Each year, vandalism becomes a problem at a few trailheads. The best option is to find a way to avoid leaving your vehicle at a trailhead overnight. If possible, leave your vehicle in town or arrange to be shuttled to and from the trail. Police and service stations will usually provide a place to park (in the case of the latter, usually for a small fee), and the Long Trail may then be reached by walking, taxi, or other public transportation. The *Long Trail End-to-Ender's Guide*, updated biennially, lists available shuttle services.

Leave valuables at home, or, at the very least, keep them locked in the trunk or otherwise hidden. Remove your stereo if possible. Don't leave a note on the car advising of your plans. Some folks empty their glove compartment and leave it open. If you do that, remember to unscrew the glove box light, or you may return to a dead battery. Park in the open in plain view. If you have a problem at a trailhead, call the local or state police immediately. GMC would like to be notified as well, but your highest priority is to notify law enforcement as soon as possible.

Public Campgrounds near the Trail

State and U.S. Forest Service campgrounds make ideal base camps for hikers. They are inexpensive and often located near trailheads. Many are on lakes or ponds with excellent swimming. For a list of campgrounds and the closest trailheads, see pages 246 to 247.

The Green Mountain Club
and the Long Trail

I n 1910, the Green Mountain Club (GMC) began
building the Long Trail with the mission "to make
the mountains of Vermont play a larger part in the
life of the people." Although GMC's mission has remained
essentially unchanged since the club was founded, its responsibilities have increased. In the twenty-first century, we face
pressures of encroaching development and resource damage
from overuse.

Membership

GMC membership is an important way to support hiking opportunities in Vermont. Today, the club has more than 10,000 members. New members are always welcome. Membership dues fund trail protection and maintenance, corridor management, and education programs.

Members may choose to join one of the club's local sections, which offer outings and organized trail maintenance opportunities. Sections provide four-season schedules of outings, including hiking, biking, cross-country skiing, and canoeing. They also maintain specific sections of the Long Trail and shelters.

The club offers an at-large membership category for those who wish to support the work of GMC but are not interested in affiliating with a specific section. Both section and at-large members receive the club's quarterly magazine, the *Long Trail News*, which provides updates on trail and shelter conditions, club news and history, events, and feature articles. Members receive discounts on club publications and items carried in the GMC store and discounts on admission to GMC events. Section members also receive their section's newsletters and activity schedules.

There are currently fourteen GMC sections. Twelve are based in Vermont: Bennington, Brattleboro, Bread Loaf (Middlebury), Burlington, Killington (Rutland), Laraway (Northwestern Vermont), Manchester, Montpelier, Northern Frontier, Northeast Kingdom, Ottauquechee (Woodstock and the Upper Valley), and Sterling (Stowe-Morrisville). Two sections are based out of state: Connecticut and Worcester (eastern Massachusetts). Turn to pages 40 and 41 for a description of section maintenance responsibilities.

To join GMC, visit www.greenmountainclub.org or call (802) 244-7037. Thank you for supporting the trail!

Publications

The GMC publishes a number of books, maps, and brochures, including the *Day Hiker's Guide to Vermont*, which contains descriptions of trails that are not part of the Long Trail system. Visit www.greenmountainclub.org for more information.

Headquarters

The GMC's headquarters is on the west side of Vt. 100 in Waterbury Center, Vermont, midway between Waterbury and Stowe. To reach GMC from I-89 in Waterbury (exit 10), head north on Vt. 100 for four miles and turn left on Cabin Lane. If coming from Stowe, GMC headquarters is six miles south of the intersection of Vt. 108 and 100. Safest access is via Cabin Lane, a few hundred yards south of headquarters.

Information and Education

The Marvin B. Gameroff Hiker Center at GMC headquarters is open seven days a week (9 a.m. to 5 p.m.) from Memorial Day to Columbus Day. Business hours the rest of the year are Monday through Friday from 10 a.m. to 5 p.m. Hikers and members are encouraged to stop by the club for trail information. During the winter months, the club hosts the James P. Taylor Winter Series—a slide show and lecture series celebrating outdoor recreation. Check the website for listings.

The Short Trail

GMC's headquarters is located on an attractive campus of more than fifty acres, acquired in 2001. It is worth visiting to take a walk on "The Short Trail: A Footpath in the Backyard." This pleasant 0.5 mile loop features interpretive displays, examples of trailwork, views of the Worcester Range, and the original 1931 Journey's End Camp. The Short Trail is open year-round.

End-to-End

On average, more than 100 people hike the Long Trail end-to-end each year. Since the Long Trail opened, more than 3,396 hikers have completed the trail. Although many hike the trail in a continuous trip, the majority complete it in sections, one person having taken as long as fifty-two years to finish. Many have hiked the trail more than once. Any hiker who has completed the Long Trail—in one season or many—is entitled to an end-to-ender's certificate. Guidelines for certification are available from the GMC office or online.

Side-to-Side

In September 2006, the GMC board of directors approved establishment of a "side-to-side" certification program for hikers who complete all eighty-four side trails of the Long Trail system. The ad-hoc committee that proposed this new recognition created a patch and award certificate for those who report completing the designated side trails, patterned after the end-to-end certificate program. Check the website for details.

Long Trail History

The Early Years: 1910 to 1920

The Long Trail is the oldest long-distance hiking trail in the United States. It was conceived by James P. Taylor as he waited for the mist to clear from Stratton Mountain.

Taylor, headmaster of Vermont Academy for Boys at Saxtons River, envisioned a footpath linking the state's highest summits. Unlike the mountains in neighboring states, the Green Mountains remained largely unappreciated and unused for recreation.

The trail took its first step toward reality when twenty-three people gathered in Burlington on March 11, 1910, to found the Green Mountain Club. Taylor promised that the new organization would "make the Vermont Mountains play a larger part in the life of the people."

Work began almost immediately in the Camel's Hump and Mount Mansfield areas; by the end of 1912 Burlington members had cleared a path from Sterling Pond to Camel's Hump. Early the following season, a Vermont Forestry Department crew cut a route from Killington Peak to Brandon Gap and from Camel's Hump south to Lincoln Gap. Later that summer, trail builders were busy between Lincoln and Brandon Gaps. Concurrently, the trail expanded in the north from Sterling Pond to Johnson.

In 1914 the slogan was "Killington to Massachusetts," and by 1917 that goal had been reached. Also that year the first *Guide Book of the Long Trail* guide, was published. It listed fourteen overnight accommodations, including private camps, the Mount Mansfield Hotel, abandoned lumber camps, and five new GMC shelters. Nine farmhouses near the trail were available for lodging and meals.

The second edition of the guidebook, published in 1920, showed the trail running from Johnson to the Massachusetts line, with another nine GMC shelters and twelve more farms or other lodgings along the way. Thus, in the first decade members built 209 miles of trail and provided forty-four overnight facilities, fourteen of which were built by GMC.

Completion of the Long Trail

The next decade saw the extension of the Long Trail north from Johnson, culminating at Jay Peak in 1927. Many club members felt Jay was "almost to Canada" and far enough, but Bruce Buchanan of Brattleboro vowed, "We better get rid of the 'almost.'" Two years later Bruce and his brother, Roy O. Buchanan, professor of electrical engineering at the University of Vermont, marked the remaining ten-odd miles to the Canadian border. In 1930, Charles G. Doll and Phillips D. Carleton cut the final link to Canada.

On its twenty-first birthday, GMC could celebrate the completion of Taylor's footpath from Massachusetts to Canada. The occasion was marked by a large gathering at the club's headquarters, the Long Trail Lodge at Sherburne Pass. The lodge was a gift from the Proctor family, early and dedicated supporters of the Long Trail. The highlight of the celebration was the lighting of flares from mountaintop to mountaintop along the spine of the Green Mountains.

Besides regularly updating the *Guide Book of the Long Trail*, (now titled, *Long Trail Guide*) GMC began publishing a bimonthly newsletter, the *Green Mountain News*, in 1922. It was later retitled the *Long Trail News*. Today, the *Long Trail News* is a quarterly magazine for GMC members.

Many GMC members associate with one of GMC's local sections. Each of the 14 sections is responsible for maintaining a designated portion of the trail and overnight shelters (except for the Northeast Kingdom section, which focuses on hiking trails in that region of the state). The oldest section is the Burlington

Section, first known as the Mount Mansfield Section when it was formed in 1910. Other sections have also existed for many decades, while still others have come and gone as local interest has waxed and waned.

Long Trail Patrol and End-to-End

With the trail completed, the club continued to expand its network of shelters. A prime mover in this effort was Roy Buchanan. In 1930, the club's board of trustees authorized formation of a salaried Long Trail Patrol (LTP) with Buchanan taking on the role of crew leader in 1931. Each summer through the mid-1960s, he assembled groups of students and worked with them on trail maintenance, construction of new shelters, and repairs to existing ones. From 1930 to 1940, the LTP, sections, and other groups built or rebuilt twenty-nine shelters and lodges.

Not surprisingly, the World War II years saw reductions in trail use and trail work. One GMC program, however, began during this period. In 1942 the club trustees authorized formal recognition of GMCers who had tramped the full length of the trail and awarded thirty-two special certificates that began the long roster of end-to-enders.

Back to the Woods

Shelter construction and reconstruction resumed at a modest rate through the 1950s, then accelerated in the next decade. The reason for the renewed activity was a significant increase in the number of hikers, especially young people, who sought recreation in the backcountry as part of a new back-to-the-land movement. Between 1966 and 1975, responding to heavy trail traffic, the club launched a variety of initiatives, including removal of dumps at shelters and promotion of a "carry-in, carry-out" policy; dissemination of information on responsible hiking and camping practices; and stationing caretakers at popular shelters and ranger-naturalists (now called summit caretakers) on the fragile alpine summits of Mount Mansfield and Camel's Hump. The caretaker program was the revival of an informal program from the 1920s and 1930s when caretakers were stationed at Taft Lodge, Butler Lodge, and Killington Peak's Porky Lodge.

During most of its history, GMC has chosen not to become involved in national conservation causes, concentrating its energy on preserving the wilderness character of the Long Trail. In the mid-1930s, however, when a scenic highway, called the Green Mountain Parkway (similar to Shenandoah National Park's Skyline Drive) was proposed for the length of the Green Mountains, the club mounted energetic opposition. Vermonters ultimately rejected the idea in a statewide referendum. Similarly in 1958, when the U.S. Air Force dropped its plan to erect a missile communications facility on the Chin of Mount Mansfield, it was due in part to GMC objection.

Founder, Sponsor, Defender, and Protector

On the GMC's fiftieth anniversary in 1960, the Vermont General Assembly adopted a resolution "expressing its gratitude and recognition to the Green Mountain Club" for its role in establishing and maintaining the Long Trail. In 1971, the legislature passed yet another resolution, recognizing the club as "the founder, sponsor, defender, and protector" of the Long Trail System and delegating to it responsibility for developing policies and programs for "the preservation, maintenance, and proper use of hiking trails for the benefit of the people of Vermont."

In 2010 the United States Senate passed resolution 460 to commemorate the 100th anniversary of the Green Mountain Club. The resolution stated the Green Mountain Club "has delivered 100 years of conservation, community education, and outreach on local ecology" and has "worked to maintain, manage, and protect the Long Trail for the benefit of the people of the State of Vermont."

Protecting Vermont's Mountain Lands

Although the club's fundamental responsibility remains the same—maintaining and protecting the Long Trail—the challenges have changed since the early days of pioneer trail blazing. Recent generations of GMC members have taken

up the challenges of land acquisition and stewardship of the Long Trail's corridor.

The Long Trail protection effort began in the 1980s when the GMC learned that land crossed by almost 30 miles of the Long Trail in northern Vermont was up for sale, threatening the continuity of the trail. An additional 30 miles were in private ownership and potentially at risk due to rapidly changing ownership patterns, development, clear-cutting, and logskidding on the trail and posting by some private landowners. A protracted economic slump in the timber industry made it difficult for forest owners to hold onto their land, and large landholdings were coming onto the market at an alarming rate.

For the first time in the history of the Long Trail, a simple handshake wasn't enough to ensure passage for hikers or permanence of the trail corridor. Much of the southernmost 200 miles of the trail had been protected through acquisition for the Green Mountain National Forest and the Appalachian Trail. But between Mount Ellen and the Canadian border, in areas outside the Camel's Hump, Mount Mansfield, and Jay State Forests, over 60 miles of the Long Trail and 22 miles of side trails were unprotected and vulnerable to landowner closure.

In 1986, GMC launched the Long Trail Protection Campaign, an ambitious effort to acquire land or easements where the trail crossed private land. By 2011, the club had protected 60.6 miles of the Long Trail and 18 miles of side trails, thanks to more than eighty willing sellers and donors. Over 24,922 acres of backcountry land with important wildlife habitat, recreational, and scenic value has been safeguarded. The state of Vermont has been a leading partner, appropriating more than $4 million for Long Trail land acquisitions. The Vermont Housing and Conservation Board has also been a consistent funder of the program. Governor Howard Dean, an end-to-end hiker, was a strong supporter of the effort during his eleven-year tenure.

The 265-Mile Club (named for the length of the trail in the early 90s prior to relocations which made the trail slightly longer), honors the 650-plus people, foundations, businesses, schools, civic groups, GMC sections, and other organizations that have contributed $1,000 or more toward Long Trail protection. Since 1992, three granite plaques have been erected outside club headquarters in Waterbury Center, listing 265-Mile Club supporters. There is still room for names on the fourth plaque, which will be completed when the trail is fully protected.

Much of the land acquired has gone into state ownership, and the new Long Trail State Forest has been created as a result of GMC's work. During the early years of the campaign, the Vermont field office of The Nature Conservancy assisted GMC with real-estate closings and interim capital when needed. As of 2011, there are 6.5 miles of the Long Trail and 4.5 miles of side trails that are privately owned and without permanent protection.

Headquarters and the Short Trail

In 1992, the club purchased five acres on Route 100 in Waterbury Center, between Interstate 89 and Stowe. The property was once part of the 1836 May Farm and featured two historic barns. The club had sold its original clubhouse at Sherburne Pass in 1955. Since then, it had rented office space, first in Rutland then in downtown Montpelier. Finally, GMC was its own landlord again.

In 2000, the club acquired an additional forty-eight acres of woods and fields on the west side of Route 100. The Short Trail opened in 2003, is a pleasant 0.5 mile walking loop through the heart of GMC's campus. The Short Trail leads visitors to the original Journey's End Camp, constructed in 1931 by Professor

Roy Buchanan and his crew. When a new Journey's End Camp was built on the Long Trail in 2004, the old one was disassembled and moved to the Short Trail as a piece of GMC history.

The Second Century Campaign

Starting in 2005, GMC volunteers and staff began asking members and supporters to help the club establish a solid financial base for the Long Trail's second century. Over 700 donors answered that call, and by 2008, the GMC's Second Century Campaign reached its $5.25 million goal.

Never before had GMC undertaken such an ambitious campaign. In years to come, the Second Century Campaign will be remembered as a magnificent gift from the club members of today to Vermont and to future generations. When all pledge payments are received, we will have successfully:

- secured more than $1 million toward land and easements necessary to guarantee public access for the remaining 6.5 miles of the Long Trail;
- increased GMC's trails and shelters endowment by nearly $1.5 million;
- raised $1.25 million for a new Visitor Center to replace the South Barn, which was lost to fire in 2003; and
- increased the Aldie Gannett Stewardship Endowment Fund by $500,000.

The success of the Second Century Campaign can be largely credited to the tireless, inspiring leadership of its cochairs, former GMC presidents Andrew S. Nuquist of Montpelier and Joseph E. Frank of South Burlington. More than sixty campaign volunteers invested their time and energy, doing everything from hosting "awareness gatherings" in the living rooms of their homes to visiting with friends and colleagues to ask for their support.

Commented campaign chair Joe Frank, "Early in its first century, the ultimate mission articulated for the Green Mountain Club was to 'make the Vermont mountains play a larger part in the life of the people.' I can say with confidence, based on a half century of personal participation, that this mission is being accomplished magnificently. With the conclusion of our Second Century Campaign, the club has achieved a more secure financial footing for sustaining its mission in its second century. Hallelujah!"

Management of the Long Trail

A Private-Public Partnership

Managing the Long Trail System is a complex task, involving volunteers and staff, federal and state agencies, organizations and businesses. Over the years, as use of the Long Trail and outside pressures such as development have increased, management of the trail has expanded from trail building and maintenance to include protecting natural resources from overuse, upholding easements, protecting the trail from development, and educating hikers.

The Long Trail is maintained by the GMC in cooperation with the Vermont Agency of Natural Resources, the U.S. Forest Service, the National Park Service, the Appalachian Trail Conservancy, and private landowners. The cooperation and assistance of these agencies, organizations, and individuals is indispensable. In the Green Mountain National Forest, the U.S. Forest Service actively manages the Long Trail and its side trails with the GMC, providing funding for trail crews, managerial expertise, and staff support. On state lands, the Vermont Department of Forests, Parks and Recreation works in a similar way on matters pertaining to the Long Trail System. The department provides grants from the Vermont Recreational Trails Fund. The GMC is a maintaining club of the Appalachian Trail Conservancy and, together with the ATC, U.S. Forest Service, and National Park Service, manages the Long/Appalachian Trail in Vermont from Massachusetts to Route 12.

Ongoing financial support for GMC's alpine caretakers on the Mount Mansfield ridgeline is provided by the broadcasters who use telecommunications towers on the Nose, through the Mount Mansfield Colocation Association.

The GMC also works with private landowners who allow access to the trail on their lands and with Vermont ski areas, which, in some instances, provide financial and logistical support for Long Trail projects and operations.

Volunteers

Volunteers are the backbone of the GMC. Without them, the Long Trail would never have been built nor would it be managed as it is today. Volunteers serve on committees, and as board members, section officers, leaders of maintenance outings and other trips, trail and shelter adopters, and corridor monitors. Maintenance of the Long Trail is an annual miracle of volunteer generosity.

The GMC welcomes new volunteers, members or not. To volunteer or to learn about gaining trailwork skills through GMC workshops, contact the GMC.

Each GMC section maintains a portion of trail, side trails, and shelters. They host work parties throughout the year. Anyone wishing to join a section or its maintenance activities may contact the GMC. Portions of the Long Trail maintained by GMC sections are listed below.

Bennington	Harmon Hill to Glastenbury Mountain
Brattleboro	Winhall River to Vt. 11 and 30
Bread Loaf	Sucker Brook Shelter to Emily Proctor Shelter
Burlington	Jonesville to Smugglers Notch
Connecticut	Glastenbury Mountain to Stratton-Arlington Road
Killington	Vt. 140 to Maine Junction
Laraway	Lamoille River to Vt. 118
Manchester	Vt. 11 and 30 to Mad Tom Notch
Montpelier	Camel's Hump to Jonesville and Smugglers' Notch to Chilcoot Pass
Northeast Kingdom	Bald Mountain* and other trails in northeastern Vermont
Northern Frontier	Hazen's Notch to Canada
Ottauquechee	Appalachian Trail: Maine Junction to Vt. 12
Sterling	Chilcoot Pass to Lamoille River
Worcester	Stratton-Arlington Road to Winhall River

With Northwoods Stewardship Center and Westmore Trails Association.

Section maintenance efforts are supplemented by the club's Trail and Shelter Adopter Program. Independent individual adopters agree to care for a shelter or portion of the trail and do inspections, basic maintenance, and cleanup. Volunteers also assist GMC field staff throughout the hiking season as site and summit caretakers, with trail management, and on special projects.

Long Trail Patrol

The LTP is the GMC's seasonal paid trail crew. Directed by University of Vermont professor Roy O. Buchanan nearly from its inception in 1930 until the mid-1960s, the LTP is GMC's oldest continuous nonvolunteer program. Patrol crews, supported primarily by the U.S. Forest Service and Vermont Department of Forests, Parks and Recreation, concentrate on trail relocation and reconstruction projects such as installing rock waterbars and steps. Crews typically live under primitive conditions for five days a week near the work sites.

From midsummer to early fall, the Volunteer Long Trail Patrol spends an intensive five days a week doing trail maintenance and construction. This successful program draws volunteers from far and wide, recruited by the ATC, as well as local GMCers.

Appalachian National Scenic Trail

Vermont and the Long Trail hold a prominent place in the history of the Appalachian Trail. It may have been on or near the summit of Stratton Mountain, after construction of the Long Trail was begun, that the idea of an extended footpath linking the scenic ridges of the East crystallized in the mind of AT visionary Benton MacKaye.

First proposed in 1921 by MacKaye, a forester, author, and philosopher, the Appalachian Trail was completed in 1937. It extends for 2,175 miles from Katahdin in Maine to northern Georgia's Springer Mountain. The Appalachian Trail Conservancy, founded in 1925, works with its member clubs and federal and state agencies to preserve and maintain the Appalachian Trail, the world's longest linear national park.

In Vermont, the Appalachian Trail coincides with the Long Trail from the Massachusetts border to Maine Junction at Willard Gap just north of U.S. 4, and then swings east to cross the Connecticut River near Hanover, New Hampshire, a distance of 149.8 miles. The GMC maintains the AT from the Massachusetts border to Vt. 12. From there to Norwich, the AT in Vermont is maintained by the Dartmouth Outing Club. For more information about the Appalachian Trail, contact the Appalachian Trail Conservancy, 799 Washington Street, P.O. Box 807, Harpers Ferry, WV 25425-0807; (304) 535-6331; fax: (304) 535-2667; www.appalachiantrail.org.

Looking south from Jay Peak

Division 1
Massachusetts–Vermont
State Line to Vt. 9

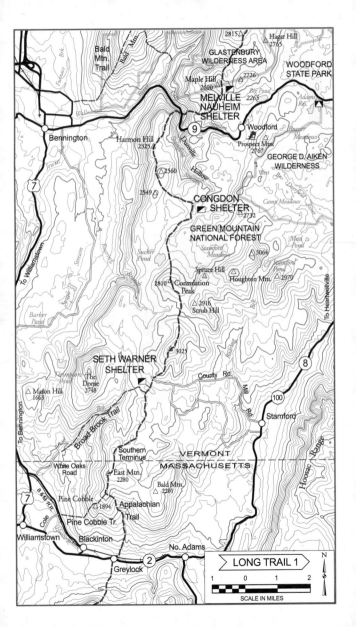

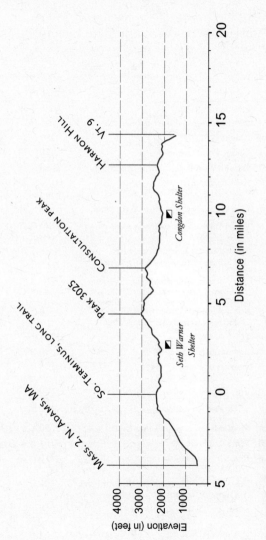

Division 1 Profile

Elevation (in feet)

Distance (in miles)

MASS. 2, N. ADAMS, MA

SO. TERMINUS, LONG TRAIL

PEAK 3025

CONSULTATION PEAK

HARMON HILL

VT. 9

Seth Warner Shelter

Congdon Shelter

Massachusetts–Vermont State Line to Vt. 9

miles northbound	▲ NORTH	elevation at Long Trail (feet/meters)	miles southbound
14.3	**Vt. 9**	1360/415	0.0
12.5	**Harmon Hill**	2325/709	1.8
10.6	**Old Bennington–Heartwellville Road**	2220/677	3.7
10.0	**Congdon Shelter**	2080/634	4.3
8.4	**Sucker Pond Outlet Brook**	2180/665	5.9
7.0	**Consultation Peak**, northwest summit	2810/857	7.3
5.8	**Roaring Branch**	2470/753	8.5
3.1	**County Road**	2290/698	11.2
2.8	**Seth Warner Shelter**, 900 ft W via spur	2200/671	11.5
2.6	**Broad Brook Trail** to **White Oaks Road**, 4.0 mi. SW	2130/649	11.7
0.0	**Massachusetts-Vermont state line**, southern terminus of **Long Trail**	2330/710	14.3

WILLIAMSTOWN APPROACH VIA PINE COBBLE AND APPALACHIAN TRAILS

3.3	**Massachusetts-Vermont state line**, southern terminus of **Long Trail**	2330/710	0.0
2.5	**Eph's Lookout**	2254/687	0.8
2.1	**Appalachian Trail** to **Mass. 2**, 2.6 mi S	2010/613	1.2
1.5	**Summit of Pine Cobble** (1894 ft/577 m), 0.1 mi S via spur	1850/564	1.8
0.0	**Pine Cobble Road** in Williamstown	630/192	3.3

NORTH ADAMS APPROACH VIA APPALACHIAN TRAIL

3.8	**Southern terminus** of **Long Trail**	2330/710	0.0
3.0	**Eph's Lookout**	2254/687	0.8
2.6	**Pine Cobble Trail** to **Pine Cobble Road**, 2.1 mi W	2010/613	1.2
1.4	**Pete's Spring, Sherman Brook Primitive Campsite**, 0.1 mi W via spur	1300/396	2.4
0.0	**Mass. 2** in **North Adams**	660/201	3.8

SOUTH
▼

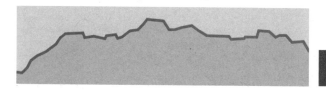

Division 1

Massachusetts–Vermont State Line to Vt. 9

Massachusetts: 0.0 miles   **Canada: 272.7 miles**

The southern terminus of the Long Trail (LT) is at the Massachusetts-Vermont boundary, northwest of North Adams, Massachusetts. The Appalachian Trail (AT) and Pine Cobble Trail provide access to the start of the LT. The AT approach description begins on page 49. The Pine Cobble Trail is found on page 51.

The LT and the AT coincide throughout this division.

The future maintenance of 2 of the 14 trail miles in this division has been endowed by Ed Mazdzer and Marty Lawthers, Frederick P. Clark, and David Rubin.

Camping and Fires

Although this division of the LT crosses the Green Mountain National Forest (GMNF) and the Stamford Meadows Wildlife Management Area, it follows a narrow, publicly owned trail corridor surrounded by private property. Camping is limited to shelters. Small wood fires, although discouraged, are permitted at the shelters' established fire rings. Refer to Leave No Trace principles (pages 11 to 12) to minimize your impact.

Note: Camping at Sucker Pond is prohibited to protect the city of Bennington public water supply.

Group Use

Groups hiking on this division of the LT may need an Outfitter–Guide Special Use Permit from the GMNF. Group tenting space is available at both Seth Warner and Congdon Shelters. Woodford State Park is available east of the LT on Vt. 9 for base camp hiking. Refer to group use guidelines (pages 13 to 19) to determine whether your group needs a permit.

Winter Use

Harmon Hill via the LT and Bald Mountain via the Bald Mtn. Trail from Woodford provide rewarding snowshoe destinations with good views. The AT and Pine Cobble Trail out of Williamstown also make good snowshoe hikes.

Suggested Day Hikes

PINE COBBLE. This pleasant climb on the Pine Cobble Trail leads to a vista of the tri-state region's rugged terrain. Round trip, 3.2 mi., 2¼ hr.

HARMON HILL. A steep climb on the LT south from Vt. 9, this hike boasts expansive hilltop views. A steep rock staircase may be challenging to some hikers. Round trip, 3.6 mi., 2¾ hr.

ROARING BRANCH. This hike on the LT north from County Road out of Stamford leads to a sizable beaver dam beneath Scrub Hill. County Road may not be passable all the way to the LT, so some walking along the road may be necessary. Round trip, 5.4 mi., 3½ hr.

Access to the Long Trail

COUNTY ROAD. Turn west onto Mill Road from Vt. 8 and Vt. 100, 0.5 mi. north of Billmont's Country Store in Stamford, or 6.8 mi. south of the junction of Vt. 8 and Vt. 100 in Readsboro. Follow the paved and then gravel road 2.0 mi. to a left turn onto County Road. Follow County Road beyond the last residences at 3.3 mi. where it becomes an unimproved gravel road. In dry conditions, the road is passable another 0.9 mi. west to the LT where there is parking for four cars on the south side just beyond the trail. If the road is not passable, park cars so that no woods roads are blocked. This road is not passable from the Pownal side where it is also known as County Road. The last mile to the LT is not plowed in winter.

VT. 9. This LT crossing is 5.0 mi. east of U.S. 7 in downtown Bennington or 8.8 mi. west of the junction of Vt. 9 and Vt. 8 South. There is a U.S. Forest Service parking lot on the north side of the highway just west of the trail.

Approach Trails

APPALACHIAN TRAIL (NORTH ADAMS APPROACH). This trail begins on Mass. 2 opposite Phelps Avenue at a traffic light 3.0 mi. east of the U.S. 7/Mass. 2 traffic circle in Williamstown and 2.4 mi. west of the center of North Adams. There is no parking at the trailhead, so hikers should obtain permission to park at the Greylock Community Club 0.1 mi. east of the trail on Mass. 2 or at the Holy Family Catholic Church adjacent to the AT.

Proceed north on the white-blazed AT from **Mass. 2 in North Adams (0.0 mi., 660 ft.)** opposite Phelps Ave. east of the church, and cross over the railroad and Hoosic River on a footbridge. Turn right and follow the AT along Massachusetts Avenue east. Just before a stone bridge, turn left off the road and cross two footbridges before reaching a small reservoir on Sherman Brook (0.2 mi.). Follow Sherman Brook upstream, and then climb away from the brook. Descend to **Pete's Spring (1.4 mi.)** and a spur leading west 0.1 mi. to **Sherman Brook Primitive Campsite** and continuing another 0.1 mi. to loop back to the AT.

WINTER HIKING?

- The Long Trail is marked with white blazes, which are difficult to see against a snowy background and frequently buried beneath the snow.
- Deep snow may obscure all signs of the trail. Topographical maps and a compass are helpful.
- Daylight is short in the winter. Darkness may come suddenly.
- Stay alert to the dangers of hypothermia and frostbite. Know the signs and how to treat them.
- Keep group size between four and ten people.
- Be prepared to keep warm and sheltered with nothing more than the equipment you carry. Never count on a campfire or wood stove to keep you warm.
- You may encounter winter weather at higher elevations during the fall and spring.
- Use skis or snowshoes. Post-holing makes the trail unpleasant and dangerous for the next person.

Continue on the AT and return to Sherman Brook at some old bridge abutments. Pass the north end of the campsite spur. Ascend and join an old woods road (1.7 mi.). Follow the woods road before swinging to the west and climbing through an old rock slide from which there are views to the south and east (2.3 mi.). There is a bad weather alternate route around the rockfall to the west. Skirt a boggy pond and climb a rocky knoll where the **Pine Cobble Trail (2.6 mi.)** enters from the west.

This junction is located near the south end of an extensive area on East Mtn. that is recovering from old forest fires. There are views of the Berkshire Hills to the south, including the Hoosac Range (left), the Taconics (right), and, between them, Mt. Greylock (3491 ft.), the highest peak in Massachusetts. Bear right at the Pine Cobble junction and ascend to the north along the ridge to another rocky clearing, **Eph's Lookout (3.0 mi.)**, named after Ephraim Williams, founder of Williams College. Reenter the woods and continue north to the Class of 98 Trail, which leads west to the Pine Cobble Trail near Bear Spring, and then pass a blue diamond–blazed trail that also leads west. Follow the AT north to the **south terminus of the LT (3.8 mi.) at the Massachusetts-Vermont state line. Mass. 2 to LT, 3.8 mi., 6.1 km., 2²⁄₃ hr. (Rev. 2 hr.).**

PINE COBBLE TRAIL (Williamstown Approach). From its junction with U.S. 7 in Williamstown, follow Mass. 2 east 0.6 mi. to Cole Avenue Turn left and follow Cole Avenue 0.8 mi. to its end at North Hoosac Road. Turn right onto this road and proceed 0.3 mi., then take a left onto Pine Cobble Road. Follow this road 0.2 mi. to the trailhead. Pine Cobble Road is 2.1 mi. west of the AT on Massachusetts Avenue/North Hoosac Road. Parking is available opposite the trail.

From **Pine Cobble Road in Williamstown (0.0 mi., 630 ft.),** follow the blue-blazed Pine Cobble Trail up the hillside and into the woods. After passing a side trail on the right leading 350 ft. to Bear Spring, ascend steadily to the ridge where a **spur (1.5 mi.)** leads south 0.1 mi. to the **summit of Pine Cobble.** Here there is a wide view of the Hoosic Valley with Mt. Greylock and other Berkshire and Taconic peaks.

Continuing from the junction, follow gentle grades through scrub oak, pitch pine, and stunted white pines to a rocky knob and the **junction with the AT (2.1 mi.)**. From here, follow the AT (described in the North Adams Approach) north (left) to the **south terminus of the LT (3.3 mi.) at the Massachusetts-Vermont state line**. Pine Cobble Road to LT, 3.3 mi., 5.3 km., 2½ hr. (Rev. 1¾ hr.).

Long Trail Description

From the **Massachusetts-Vermont state line (0.0 mi.)**, descend to a brook crossing (0.4 mi.). Climb to the east side of a low ridge, pass over a bedrock ridge (1.7 mi.), and continue to a woods road (2.4 mi.). Cross the road and proceed to a dirt road **(2.6 mi.)**, which to the west is the **Broad Brook Trail**. This trail leads southwest 4.0 mi. to White Oaks Road out of Williamstown.

Cross the road and ascend to the junction with a **spur (2.8 mi.)** leading 900 ft. west to **Seth Warner Shelter**. This frame lean-to was built by carpenter trainees of the Manpower Development Training Act in 1965 and has space for eight. A brook, which may fail in dry seasons, is 450 ft. to the west. A primitive tenting area is located 400 ft. south of the shelter. **North Adams to Seth Warner Shelter, 6.8 mi., 10.9 km., 4¼ hr. (SB 3½ hr.). Pine Cobble Road to Seth Warner Shelter, 6.3 mi., 10.1 km., 4 hr. (SB 3¼ hr.).**

Hike north from the shelter spur, crossing **County Road (3.1 mi.)** just beyond a power line. Under favorable conditions, this road may be driven 4.2 mi. east to Vt. 8 and Vt. 100 in Stamford.

Begin a steady ascent from the road and, after passing a view south to Mt. Greylock, continue to the south summit of a nameless ridge (4.5 mi.). Here there are views to the south and west. Return to the woods and continue north along the ridge. After passing under a power line (4.9 mi.), descend to an old beaver pond, where there is a view of nearby Scrub Hill. Cross **Roaring Branch (5.8 mi.)** on stepping-stones just below the beaver dam.

Beyond the brook crossing, pass over several minor knobs and, remaining on or just below the ridge most of the way, continue to the wooded northwest summit of **Consultation Peak**

(**7.0 mi.**), so named by volunteer trail workers because of its strategic location for planning maintenance activities. Descend to a well-traveled woods road (**8.0 mi.**), which leads 0.1 mi. west to a clearing on the east shore of Sucker Pond. **Note:** To protect the Bennington public water supply, no swimming or camping is allowed at Sucker Pond.

From the woods road crossing, descend gently and cross the **Sucker Pond Outlet Brook (8.4 mi.)**. Then, after passing over beaver-challenged puncheon through a wetland in Stamford Meadows, climb a wooded knoll, passing the stone foundation of a nineteenth-century tavern (**8.9 mi.**). Continue uphill to the ridge and, after crossing a woods road, descend to picturesque Stamford Stream (**9.4 mi.**), following it downstream before bearing left to **Congdon Shelter (10.0 mi.)**.

This open-front frame cabin, with bunks for eight, was built by the Long Trail Patrol in 1967 and modified by Pioneer Valley Section volunteers in 1994. It is named for Herbert Wheaton Congdon, an LT pioneer, trail builder, guidebook editor, and cartographer and was a gift of the Congdon family. A small brook east of the shelter furnishes water; overflow campsites are located on the ridge above the outhouse. **Seth Warner Shelter to Congdon Shelter, 7.4 mi., 11.9 km., 4½ hr. (SB 4½ hr.).**

Continue north from the shelter to ascend the ridge, skirt an area of beaver activity, and then arrive at the **Old Bennington–Heartwellville Road (10.6 mi.)**. This woods road can be followed west 4.0 mi. to Vt. 9 via Burgess Road, 1.0 mi. east of U.S. 7 in Bennington. To the east, this road leads to Stamford Stream and the woods roads of Dunville Hollow.

From the woods road, cross a small stream, climb steadily past two more woods roads, and then traverse a small clearing (**11.4 mi.**). Beyond this point, after fairly level going, cross a brook and climb to the open summit of **Harmon Hill (12.5 mi.)**, where controlled burns are used as a management tool by the U.S. Forest Service to retain vistas and provide wildlife clearings. There is a view to the west including Mt. Anthony, the historic village of Bennington, and the monument that commemorates the American Revolution's Battle of Bennington. To the north are views of Bald Mtn. and Glastenbury Mtn.

From the summit, bear east across the clearing, enter the woods, and begin to descend. The descent steepens (13.7 mi.), following extensive rock staircases, ending at a pullout on the south side of **Vt. 9 (14.3 mi.)**. *Use caution when crossing Vt. 9; traffic moves at high speeds.*

Vt. 9 leads west 5.0 mi. to U.S. 7 in Bennington. Old Bennington, the town center of colonial days, is a mile west of the present center. Many historical buildings and sites, including the Bennington Museum and the Bennington Battle Monument, are located there. To the east it is 2.8 mi. to Woodford and 4.8 mi. to Woodford State Park.

Side Trail

BROAD BROOK TRAIL. This trail begins on White Oaks Road in Pownal, Vermont, near the state line. Refer to the Pine Cobble Trail directions in this division to the junction of Cole Avenue and North Hoosac Road. From there, proceed 0.8 mi. west on North Hoosac and Bridges Road to White Oaks Road. Continue on White Oaks Road 1.2 mi. north to the Vermont border and the crossing of Broad Brook. The parking lot is on the east side of the road just beyond the Massachusetts-Vermont state line. Long-term parking is not recommended.

From the east side of the parking lot (0.0 mi., 900 ft.), skirt the south side of the North Adams waterworks. Once past the waterworks, follow an old woods road east and north. Parallel Broad Brook, and cross it several times. These crossings can be challenging in the spring. Ascend northeasterly to a dirt road (3.7 mi.), and follow it east to the LT (4.0 mi., 2100 ft.). **White Oaks Road to LT, 4.0 mi., 6.4 km., 2½ hr. (Rev. 2 hr.).**

Bromley and Stratton from Glastenbury

Division 2
Vt. 9 to Stratton–Arlington (Kelley Stand) Road

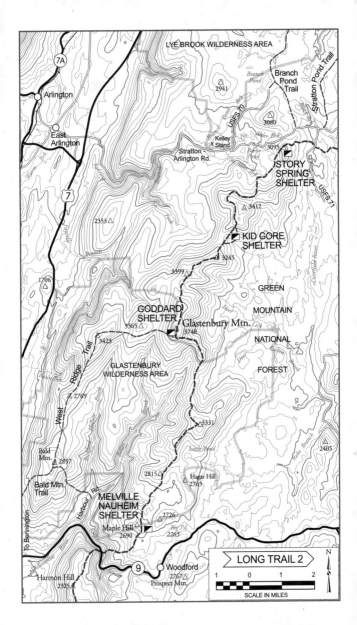

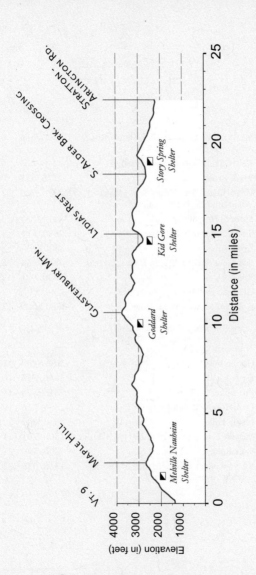

Division 2 Profile

Vt. 9 to Stratton–Arlington
(Kelley Stand) Road

miles north-bound	▲ NORTH	elevation at Long Trail (feet/meters)	miles south-bound
22.6	**Stratton–Arlington (Kelley Stand) Road,** Stratton Mtn. parking lot	2230/680	0.0
22.5	**Kelley Stand Road,** south junction	2240/683	0.1
21.7	**Black Brook bridge**	2220/677	0.9
20.6	**USFS Road 71** to Kelley Stand Road and Stratton Pond Trail, 0.75 mi N	2380/726	2.0
19.0	**Story Spring Shelter**	2810/857	3.6
18.1	**South Alder Brook,** crossing	2600/793	4.5
15.1	**Lydia's Rest**	3300/1006	7.5
14.2	**Kid Gore Shelter,** 0.1 mi E via loop trail	2800/854	8.4
13.7	**Big Rock**	3250/991	8.9
10.4	**Glastenbury Mtn. fire tower**	3748/1143	12.2
10.1	**Goddard Shelter: West Ridge Trail** to Woodford Hollow via Bald Mtn. Trail east branch, 9.7 mi S; to Branch Street in Bennington via Bald Mtn. Trail west branch, 11.3 mi S	3560/1085	12.5
7.6	**Glastenbury Lookout**	2920/890	15.0
5.8	**Little Pond Lookout**	3060/933	16.8
4.4	**Porcupine Lookout**	2815/858	18.2
3.2	**Hell Hollow Brook bridge**	2350/716	19.4
2.1	**Maple Hill**	2630/802	20.5
1.6	**Melville Nauheim Shelter,** 250 ft E via spur	2300/701	21.0
0.7	**Split Rock**	1900/579	21.9
0.0	**Vt. 9; William D. MacArthur Memorial bridge** over **City Stream**	1360/415	22.6

SOUTH
▼

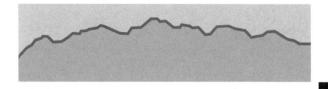

Division 2

Vt. 9 to Stratton–Arlington (Kelley Stand) Road

Massachusetts: 14.3 miles   **Canada 258.4 miles**

From the power-line crossing on Maple Hill to just south of Goddard Shelter, the Long Trail (LT) crosses the Glastenbury Wilderness. Refer to wilderness information on pages 8 to 9. The LT and the Appalachian Trail (AT) coincide throughout this division.

The following people have contributed to endow the future maintenance of 2 miles of the LT within this division: Mary Ann Carlson and Bob and Karen Allen.

Camping and Fires

This division of the LT crosses the Green Mountain National Forest (GMNF). Primitive off-trail camping with small wood fires is allowed. Refer to Leave No Trace principles (pages 11 to 12) to minimize your impact.

Note: Camping between Maple Hill and Porcupine Lookout is prohibited to protect the city of Bennington public water supply (Hell Hollow Brook).

Group Use

Groups hiking this division of the LT may need an Outfitter Guide Special Permit from the GMNF. Group tenting space is available just south of the north end of the Kid Gore Loop on the LT and at Story Spring Shelters. Woodford State Park is available east of the LT on Vt. 9 for base camp hiking. GMNF Grout Pond Campground is also available east of the LT on the Stratton-Arlington Road for base camp hiking. Refer to group use guidelines (pages 13 to 19) to determine whether your group needs a permit.

Winter Use

The remoteness of this section of trail cannot be overemphasized. Snowshoeing north from Vt. 9 provides views south to Harmon Hill.

Access to the Long Trail

Vt. 9. Refer to directions on page 49 in Division 1.

Stratton–Arlington (Kelley Stand) Road. *Western approach via U.S. 7:* From U.S. 7 take exit 3 (Arlington) and proceed 0.1 mi. west on Vt. 313 to a right turn onto South Road. Follow South Road 0.6 mi. to its end on Kansas Road. Turn right and

Suggested Day Hikes

Split Rock. This short hikes leads to a large glacial erratic on the LT north of Vt. 9. Round trip, 1.4 mi., 1 hr.

Porcupine Lookout. A full day's trip on the LT north from Vt. 9 to a lookout that offers fine views. Round trip, 8.8 mi., 5½ hr.

proceed 0.7 mi. to a fork just after crossing a bridge. The right-hand fork is Kelley Stand Road, which continues east 10.8 mi. to the LT. Parking is on the north side of the road just beyond the bridge over the East Branch of the Deerfield River.

Western approach via Vt. 7A: From Vt. 7A, follow East Arlington Road east for 1.0 mi. and turn right just before a bridge onto Old Mill Road. Follow Old Mill Road, which becomes Kansas Road at the Sunderland town line, 2.4 mi. to a fork just after crossing a bridge over Roaring Brook. The right-hand fork is Kelley Stand Road, which continues east 10.6 mi. to the LT. Parking is available on the north side of the road just beyond the bridge over the East Branch of the Deerfield River.

Eastern approach: From Vt. 100 in West Wardsboro, 0.5 mi. south of the post office, 8.5 mi. south of Vt. 30 in East Jamaica and 13.6 mi. north of Wilmington, follow Stratton-Arlington Road west 3.4 mi. to the town of Stratton and another 3.4 mi. farther to the LT parking lot on the north side of the road just before crossing the bridge over the East Branch of the Deerfield River.

Kelley Stand Road maintenance is a contract service paid by the GMNF to the town of Sunderland; regular maintenance begins June 1 and ends on November 1. The road is unplowed between a major snowmobile parking lot west of Roaring Brook and another snowmobile parking lot east of the LT parking lot. The unmaintained portion of the road is a snowmobile trail.

Long Trail Description

Cross **Vt. 9 (0.0 mi.).** *Use caution when crossing Vt. 9; traffic moves at high speeds.* North of the highway, follow the LT past a spur leading west to a paved parking lot with a trailhead privy and cross the **William D. MacArthur Memorial Bridge over City Stream**. The bridge, built by the U.S. Forest Service, honors the memory of a dedicated volunteer trail maintainer with the Pioneer Valley and Bennington Sections.

From the bridge, follow City Stream's north bank downstream, and then turn right to begin a steady climb with several switchbacks to a lookout with a view to the northwest. Above the lookout, pass between the upright halves of **Split Rock (0.7 mi.)**. After crossing a woods road, ascend at an easier grade, cross another woods road, and then continue to a **spur (1.6 mi.)** leading east 250 ft. to **Melville Nauheim Shelter**. This frame shelter, constructed in 1977, has bunk space for eight. It was built with funds contributed by Mrs. Melville Nauheim of New York City in memory of her husband. The stream the LT crosses just north of the spur junction provides water. **Congdon Shelter to Melville Nauheim Shelter, 5.9 mi., 9.5 km., 3¾ hr. (SB 4 hr.).**

Continue north, crossing the stream and then climbing gradually, crossing a power line on **Maple Hill (2.1 mi.)**. Here there are views of Bennington and Mt. Anthony to the west and of Mt. Snow, Haystack Mtn., and the north end of the Hoosac Range to the east. After cresting a rise, descend to cross a small stream, and then continue with little change in elevation to cross the **Hell Hollow Brook Bridge (3.2 mi.)**. Just beyond, cross the original route of the LT (circa 1920), long since obliterated, which followed Hell Hollow Brook upstream from Woodford Hollow. *Camping is prohibited in this area to protect the city of Bennington public water supply.*

North of the brook, climb gradually and, after passing through a balsam and spruce swamp on puncheon, climb steadily to a ridge leading to **Porcupine Lookout (4.4 mi.)**, with views to the east and south, and then drop to the first of several sags in the ridge. After some gradual climbing, ascend moderately to the wooded summit of **Little Pond Mtn. (5.5 mi.)**, descend a short distance, and then continue along a narrow ridge to Little Pond Lookout (5.8 mi.) with a view east over the pond. Proceed with only minor elevation changes, and then climb steadily to a point just below the summit (3331 ft.) of an unnamed peak. Remaining somewhat below the ridge to

SIGN IN AND OUT OF TRAIL REGISTERS
It builds support for funding for maintenance
on public lands.

the west, descend steadily, and then continue on easier grades for nearly a mile before regaining the ridge a short distance south of **Glastenbury Lookout (7.6 mi.)**, from which there is a view of Glastenbury Mtn. and West Ridge.

Beyond the lookout, drop to a shallow sag and cross an old woods road (8.1 mi.). From the woods road, ascend gradually, then climb steadily to a large rectangular boulder (8.8 mi.) near an unnamed summit (3150 ft.). Continue along the ridge with little change in elevation before beginning a moderate ascent. Climb steadily over rock and log stairs, and then level off and pass a spring just before entering the clearing for **Goddard Shelter (10.1 mi.)**, where there is a view of Mt. Greylock to the south.

This timber frame lean-to, with space for twelve, was built by Erik and Laurel Tobiason with GMC volunteers, friends, the U.S. Forest Service, and the Keenan family in 2005. The fourth LT facility on this site, it replaces a similar log structure built by GMC Bennington Section in 1985. The name honors Ted Goddard, former president and treasurer of the GMC and past president of the Bennington Section. Funds were contributed by the family of Shaun P. Keenan, a local hiker who inspired friends and family to enjoy the trails. The spring just to the south on the LT provides water. **Melville Nauheim Shelter to Goddard Shelter, 8.5 mi., 13.7 km., 4¾ hr. (SB 5 hr.).**

Beyond the west wall of the shelter, the **West Ridge Trail** enters the woods and follows Glastenbury Mtn.'s southwest ridge 11.3 mi. to Bennington and 9.7 mi. to Woodford Hollow. Combined with one of the branches of the **Bald Mtn. Trail**, this is an alternate route to the summit of Glastenbury Mtn. from the south.

Ascend north of Goddard Shelter past the remains of the old fire warden's cabin to the densely wooded summit of **Glastenbury Mtn. (10.4 mi.)**. Here, a **fire tower** built in 1927 and most recently renovated in 2005 by U.S. Forest Service and GMC Long Trail Patrol (LTP) led by Matt Wels, serves as an observation deck for hikers. It affords a 360-degree view, which includes more wild forest than can be seen from any other point on the LT. Beyond the nearby ridges are the Berkshires to the south, the Taconics to the west, Mt. Equinox and Stratton Mtn.

to the north, and Somerset Reservoir, Mt. Snow, and Haystack Mtn. to the east.

From the tower, descend gently, crossing a snowmobile trail one mile north of the summit, and then follow the rugged ridge with minor changes in elevation to **Big Rock (13.7 mi.)**. Drop steadily to the south end of a loop trail **(14.2 mi.)** leading east 0.1 mi. to **Kid Gore Shelter**. Pass the north end of the loop in Glen Haven. Via the north loop it is 180 ft. to Kid Gore Shelter. Just beyond and to the west is the former site of Caughnawaga Shelter. Kid Gore Shelter is a log lean-to with bunks for eight. It was built by Connecticut Section volunteers and Camp Najerog alumni in 1971 and is named in memory of Harold M. (Kid) Gore, who ran Camp Najerog. Its water source is a spring 30 ft. north of the shelter (unreliable in dry seasons). There is a reliable brook and overflow campsites next to the one-time Caughnawaga site. **Goddard Shelter to Kid Gore Shelter, 4.2 mi., 6.8 km., 2½ hr. (SB 3 hr.).**

Cross the brook, ascend to a small ridge, and then descend to another brook. Beyond the brook crossing, begin to climb and bear to the west of an unnamed summit (3412 ft.), passing a vista to the west near **Lydia's Rest (15.1 mi.)**. Descend to the west side of the ridge, and follow gentle terrain before descending to cross two adjacent branches of **South Alder Brook (18.1 mi.)**. Then, after passing several beaver ponds, climb a hill to **Story Spring Shelter (19.0 mi.)**. This frame lean-to with space for eight was built by the U.S. Forest Service in 1963. It is named in honor of George F. Story, for many years an active trail worker in the Worcester Section. The spring beside the trail 135 ft. north of the shelter provides water. **Kid Gore Shelter to Story Spring Shelter, 4.9 mi., 7.9 km., 3 hr. (SB 3 hr.).**

Pass the spring, and then following a rugged climb from the shelter, descend gradually through an old logged-over area to reach **USFS Road 71 (20.6 mi.)**, 0.75 mile south of Kelley Stand Road and the Stratton Pond Trail parking lot. After crossing the road, pass a series of beaver ponds, ascend a low knoll, and descend to a woods road. Cross **Black Brook Bridge (21.7 mi.)**, rebuilt by the Volunteer LTP in 2002 and follow a woods road to a clearing with a view of Little Stratton Mtn. After bearing northeast across the clearing and entering the woods, continue along a low ridge above the Deerfield River. Cross another brook and gradually ascend to the gravel **Kelley Stand Road (22.5 mi.)**. Turn right to follow the road east over the East Branch of the Deerfield River. Just beyond the river is trailhead parking on the north side of **Stratton-Arlington (Kelley Stand) Road (22.6 mi.)**.

West along Kelley Stand Road it is 0.9 mi. to Stratton Pond Trail parking, 2.1 mi. to the Branch Pond Trailhead, 4.9 mi. to the site of Kelley Stand, an eighteenth-century overnight stage-coach stop, and 13.0 mi. to Arlington on Vt. 7A. To the east, it is 3.4 mi. to Stratton village and 6.7 mi. to West Wardsboro (store has a public phone) and Vt. 100.

Side Trails

WEST RIDGE TRAIL. This trail links the Bald Mtn. Trail to Glastenbury Mtn. and the LT. From its junction with the Bald Mtn. Trail (0.0 mi., 2720 ft.), follow the West Ridge Trail over the summit of Bald Mtn. (0.1 mi.) with views north to Glastenbury Mtn., Mt. Equinox, and Dorset Peak. Descend from the summit, and then continue north on or near the ridge toward Glastenbury Mtn. Swinging to the west of an unnamed summit (3423 ft.), descend to an old woods road (5.3 mi.) and follow it a short distance south. Reenter the woods, pass a beaver pond, and after climbing near another unnamed summit (3365 ft.), slab the southwest slope of Glastenbury Mtn. to arrive at the LT(7.8 mi., 3560 ft.) at Goddard Shelter. **Bald Mtn. Trail to LT, 7.8 mi., 12.6 km., 4¾ hr. (Rev. 4¼ hr.)**

BALD MTN. TRAIL. *West trailhead:* The west branch of this trail begins at a power-line crossing of Branch Street Extension in Bennington. Follow U.S. 7 north from the junction of U.S. 7 and Vt. 9 in Bennington. At 1.0 mi. turn east on Kocher Drive, then continue straight past a traffic light about 1.0 mi. to the power-line crossing (blue-blazed utility pole). The parking space is minimal.

From Branch Street (0.0 mi., 700 ft.) ascend on old woods roads, cross a brook (0.6 mi.), then bear left off the road (0.9

mi.). Cross and follow several brooks for the next mile before turning right to begin a steady climb out of the hollow (1.9 mi.). Ascend on several long switchbacks, and cross some old rock slides before reaching White Rocks (2.6 mi.) with a view to the west. Continue climbing, passing a spring (3.1 mi.), to the junction with the West Ridge Trail (3.5 mi., 2720 ft.) just below the summit of Bald Mtn. **Branch Street to West Ridge Trail, 3.5 mi., 5.6 km., 2¾ hr. (Rev. 1¾ hr.).**

East trailhead: To reach the east branch of the Bald Mtn. Trail, continue 1.0 mi. west of the LT crossing on Vt. 9. From here, turn north onto Harbour Road in Woodford Hollow. Follow the road 0.8 mi. north just past a large water storage tank. There is limited parking near the trail sign. Care should be taken not to block any access roads. The trail follows a woods road west uphill beyond the water tank. From the road (0.0 mi., 1260 ft.), ascend a series of old woods roads to a spur (1.6 mi.) leading 0.1 mi. to a spring at Bear Wallow, then climb switchbacks to the junction with the West Ridge Trail (1.9 mi., 2720 ft.). **Woodford Hollow trailhead to West Ridge Trail, 1.9 mi., 3.1 km., 1½ hr. (Rev. 1 hr.).**

Additional distances: Branch Street in Bennington to Woodford Hollow via the Bald Mtn. Trail is 5.4 mi.; Branch Street in Bennington to Goddard Shelter on the LT via the Bald Mtn. (west branch) and West Ridge Trails is 11.3 mi.; and Woodford Hollow to Goddard Shelter on the LT via the Bald Mtn. (east branch) and West Ridge Trails is 9.7 mi.

Brick tops mushrooms

Division 3
Stratton-Arlington (Kelley Stand) Road to Mad Tom Notch

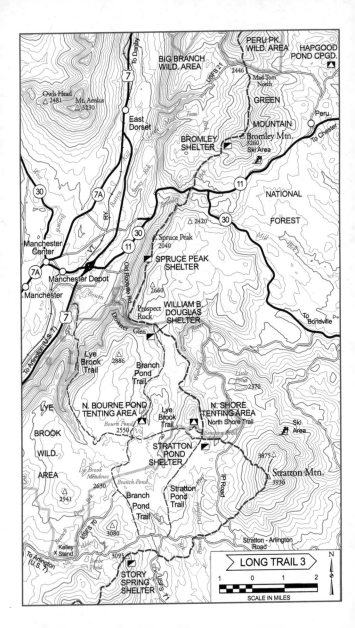

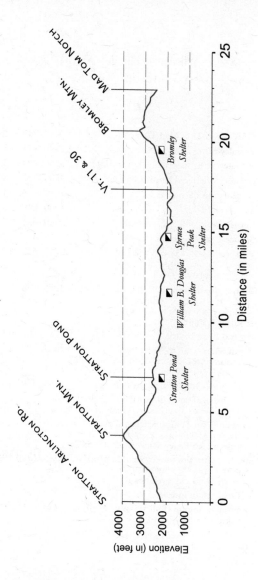

Division 3 Profile

Elevation (in feet)

Distance (in miles)

STRATTON - ARLINGTON RD.

STRATTON MTN.

STRATTON POND

Stratton Pond Shelter

William B. Douglas Shelter

Spruce Peak Shelter

VT. 11 & 30

Bromley Shelter

BROMLEY MTN.

MAD TOM NOTCH

Stratton–Arlington (Kelley Stand) Road to Mad Tom Notch

miles north-bound	▲ NORTH	elevation at Long Trail (feet/meters)	miles south-bound
23.0	**USFS Road 21 at Mad Tom Notch**	2446/746	0.0
21.0	**Bromley Mtn.**, north summit	3120/951	2.0
20.5	**Bromley Mtn.**, observation tower, 100 ft E	3260/994	2.5
19.5	**Bromley Shelter**, 110 yd E via spur	2500/762	3.5
18.2	**Bromley Brook bridge**;	2080/634	4.8
17.5	**Vt. 11** and **30**	1800/549	5.5
15.1	**Spruce Peak**, 300 ft W via spur	2040/622	7.9
14.7	**Spruce Peak Shelter**, 0.1 mi W via spur	2200/671	8.3
12.6	**Prospect Rock**, 150 ft W via spur; Old Rootville Road: to paved public road, 1.8 mi W	2150/655	10.4
11.7	**Branch Pond Trail** to **William B. Douglas Shelter**, 0.5 mi S; to **Bourn Pond Shelter**, 4.0 mi S; to Kelley Stand Road, 8.3 mi S	2280/695	11.3
8.9	**Winhall River bridge**	2175/663	14.1
7.1	**North Shore Trail** to **North Shore Tenting Area**, 0.5 mi W; to Lye Brook Trail, 0.7 mi W	2555/779	15.9
7.0	**Willis Ross Clearing at Stratton Pond**; **Lye Brook Trail** to **Bourn Pond Shelter**, 2.4 mi W; to Manchester, 9.7 mi W	2555/779	16.0
6.9	**Stratton Pond Trail** to **Stratton Pond Shelter**, 450 ft S via Stratton Pond Trail and spur; to Kelley Stand Road, 3.7 mi S	2620/799	16.1
3.8	**Stratton Mtn. fire tower**; **Stratton Mtn.**, north peak (3875 ft/1181 m), 0.7 mi N via old service road	3936/1200	19.2
1.4	**IP Road**, south intersection	2520/768	21.6
0.0	**Stratton–Arlington (Kelley Stand) Road**; Stratton Mtn. parking lot	2230/680	23.0

SOUTH

▼

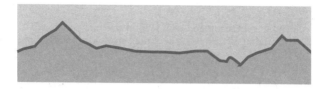

Division 3

Stratton–Arlington (Kelley Stand) Road to Mad Tom Notch

3

Massachusetts: 36.9 miles   **Canada: 235.8 miles**

From just north of Stratton Pond to the Branch Pond Trail, the Long Trail (LT) crosses the Lye Brook Wilderness. Refer to wilderness information on pages 8 to 9.

Bromley Ski Area generously allows hikers to use their ski patrol warming hut on the summit; this use depends on respect for the facility, and its availability is subject to change.

The LT and the Appalachian Trail (AT) coincide throughout this division.

The following people have contributed to endow the future maintenance of 2 miles of the LT within this division: Bob and Marge Fish.

Camping and Fires

This division of the LT is within the Green Mountain National Forest (GMNF). Primitive off-trail camping with small wood fires is allowed. Refer to Leave No Trace principles (pages 11 to 12) to minimize your impact.

Exceptions: Camping at Stratton Pond is limited to designated sites and prohibited on Stratton Mtn. to protect vulnerable vegetation and soils. Wood fires are prohibited at Stratton Pond Shelter to protect the surrounding vegetation; wood fires are permitted at Stratton Pond's North Shore Tenting Area.

Suggested Day Hikes

SPRUCE PEAK. This rock outcrop with views of the Battenkill Valley, Mt. Equinox, and Dorset Peak is located on a spur off the LT south from Vt. 11 and Vt. 30. Round trip, 4.8 mi., 2½ hr.

BROMLEY MTN. This summit, reached from either the south or the north via the LT, features 360-degree views from its observation tower. LT north from Vt. 11 and Vt. 30: round trip, 6.0 mi., 3¾ hr.; LT south from Mad Tom Notch: round trip, 5.0 mi., 3 hr.

STRATTON MTN. This summit also offers a 360-degree view from its fire tower. Round trip via LT north from Kelley Stand Road, 7.6 mi., 4⅔ hr.

LYE BROOK WILDERNESS. The LT/AT and its side trails offer a number of day hike and backpack/loop opportunities featuring highland ponds, wetlands, and scenic views. One such hike is a circuit from Kelley Stand Road north to Stratton Pond, then west to Bourn Pond, then south back to Kelley Stand Road using the Stratton Pond, Long, Lye Brook, and Branch Pond Trails. It requires a 1.2 mi. road walk on the Kelley Stand Road between the Stratton Pond Trail and Branch Pond Trail. This loop can be done as a day hike or a backpack. Round trip, 11.7 mi., 6 hr.

Group Use

Groups hiking this division of the LT may need an Outfitter-Guide Special Permit Permit from the GMNF. Group tenting space is available at Stratton Pond's North Shore Tenting Area, Spruce Peak Shelter, and, if available, Bromley's ski patrol warming hut. GMNF Grout Pond Campground is available east of the LT on the Stratton-Arlington Road for base camp hiking. GMNF Hapgood Pond Campground is also available (refer to LT access directions for USFS Road 21 below) for base camp hiking. Refer to group use guidelines (pages 13 to 19) to determine whether your group needs a permit.

Winter Use

Much of the terrain between Stratton Pond and Vt. 11 and Vt. 30 is suitable for intermediate level cross-country skiing. Both Stratton Mtn. and Bromley Mtn. make challenging snowshoe trips. Spruce Peak via the LT from Vt. 11 and Vt. 30 is also a good winter destination. It offers fine views without exposing winter hikers to the more severe conditions of the high summits. The LT intersects the Catamount Trail (a cross-country ski trail that runs the length of Vermont) at Stratton Pond. See Catamount Trail information on page 27.

Access to the Long Trail

STRATTON-ARLINGTON (KELLEY STAND) ROAD. Refer to directions on pages 60 to 61 in Division 2.

VT. 11 AND VT. 30. This LT crossing is 5.9 mi. east of Vt. 7A in Manchester Center, 4.5 mi. east of the U.S. 7 interchange east of Manchester Center, and 0.5 mi. west of the junction of Vt. 11 and Vt. 30 south. There is a large paved parking lot on the north side of the road. *Use caution when crossing this highway.*

USFS ROAD 21 AT MAD TOM NOTCH. This LT intersection is 4.0 mi. west of Peru. From Peru's J. J. Hapgood Store (0.3 mi. north of Vt. 11, 3.5 mi. east of the junction of Vt. 11 and Vt. 30 south or 4.4 mi. west of the junction of Vt. 11 and Vt. 100 south), follow the Hapgood Pond Road 1.0 mi. to North Road. Take the initially paved North Road 0.5 mi. beyond the end of the pavement to the second left, which is the gravel-surfaced Mad Tom Notch Road. Follow this road 2.1 mi. to the height of land in Mad Tom Notch and the LT. A gravel parking lot on the south side of the road is just beyond the trail crossing. USFS Hapgood Pond campground, a good base for day hikes in the region, is on Hapgood Pond Road, 0.7 mi. north of North Road.

The last mile of USFS Road 21 to the LT is not plowed in winter. A large parking lot is maintained at the end of the plowed portion of the road. It is a popular snowmobile trailhead and is open for all winter recreation activities.

Long Trail Description

From the parking lot on the north side of **Stratton-Arlington (Kelley Stand) Road (0.0 mi.)**, at the site of Grout Job, an old lumber camp, head north into the woods and travel over gently rolling terrain toward Stratton Mtn. After crossing the gravel **International Paper (IP) Road (1.4 mi.)**, begin to climb gradually, then ascend switchbacks to a vista to the south (2.0 mi.).

Climb to the col (2.7 mi.) between Stratton and Little Stratton Mtns., and then ascend another series of switchbacks. Pass a spring (3.2 mi.), and continue to climb to the **fire tower** on the **south peak of Stratton Mtn. (3.8 mi.)**. A renovation of the tower was started in 2010 by the Long Trail Patrol (LTP) led by Matt Wels, with completion expected in 2011. Straight ahead from the tower, the old service road follows the ridge 0.7 mi. to the **north peak of Stratton Mtn.** and provides access to Stratton Ski Area. Stratton Mtn. claims a unique role in hiking trail history. James P. Taylor was on this mountain when the idea of the LT was born, and the AT was conceived by Benton MacKaye near its summit.

The fire tower on the summit provides views of the surrounding mountains and countryside. Somerset Reservoir and Mt. Snow are to the south, Glastenbury Mtn. is southwest, and the Taconics, including Mt. Equinox, the highest peak of the range, lie to the west. Mt. Ascutney is to the northeast and Grand Monadnock in New Hampshire is to the southeast. To the north is Stratton's north peak with its gondola station. On clear viewing days, Killington Peak is visible to the north. A GMC summit caretaker may be on duty to assist hikers. *Camping is prohibited on Stratton Mtn. to protect vulnerable vegetation and soils.*

At the summit, bear left beyond the tower. Descend a series of switchbacks, pass a short spur (4.0 mi.) to a spring, and continue to a view (4.5 mi.) west to Stratton Pond, the Lye Brook Wilderness and Mt. Equinox. Continue downhill at a gradual grade to the IP Road (5.8 mi.). Beyond the road, descend gently to cross a bridge (6.4 mi.) over a brook.

Beyond the brook, ascend past a beaver pond, then level out before reaching a junction with the **Stratton Pond Trail (6.9 mi.).** This trail leads 150 ft. south to a **spur** and 3.7 mi. south to Kelley Stand Road and provides an alternate route between Kelley Stand Road and Stratton Pond. The spur leads 300 ft. east to **Stratton Pond Shelter**. This post-and-beam structure, built by Erik and Laurel Tobiason and the GMC Worcester Section in 1999, is dedicated to the memory of Robert Humes, longtime Worcester Section volunteer and past GMC president. Future maintenance of Stratton Pond Shelter has been endowed by Lee and Sunny Allen. It has room for twenty campers. Wood fires are prohibited at Stratton Pond Shelter to protect the surrounding vegetation. There is a composting privy on the shelter spur. The water source is Bigelow Spring, just west of Willis Ross Clearing on the Lye Brook Trail. **Story Spring Shelter to Stratton Pond Shelter, 10.6 mi., 17.1 km., 6¼ hr. (SB 6 hr.).**

Descend from the junction to reach **Willis Ross Clearing** and the junction with the Lye Brook Trail at the southeast shoreline of **Stratton Pond (7.0 mi.).** The foundation stones of Willis Ross Camp, which burned in 1972, are visible at the east end of the clearing. To the south of the clearing, the Lye Brook Trail follows the south shore of the pond to piped **Bigelow Spring** (unreliable in drought) and continues west 2.4 mi. to **Bourn Pond** and ultimately 9.7 mi. to Manchester.

Stratton Pond is the largest body of water on the LT. It also receives the most annual overnight use of any location on the trail. This heavy use was once concentrated at the pond's shoreline, which is particularly prone to erosion, adding sediment to the pond. A GMC caretaker stays near Willis Ross Clearing during the hiking season to assist and educate hikers, help maintain the local trails and campsites, and compost sewage to protect water quality. Hikers are strongly urged to safeguard this natural area by using the shelter and designated campsites. A fee is charged for overnight use at the shelter and all campsites near the pond.

From Willis Ross Clearing, head north, pass an intermittent spring on the right, and reach a junction with the **North Shore Trail (7.1 mi.)**. This trail leads west 0.5 mi. to the **North Shore Tenting Area**, which has tent platforms and a composting privy, and 0.7 mi. to the Lye Brook Trail. From the junction, bear right and leave the shoreline on the Catamount Trail following a woods road. After a short distance, bear left from the woods road, enter the Lye Brook Wilderness, and continue with minor changes in elevation, before descending to the **Winhall River (8.9 mi.)**. Cross the river on a bridge and proceed, again with little change in elevation, along the northeast edge of the plateau above the Winhall River Valley. The LT may be more challenging to follow in the Wilderness Area due to minimal brushing and blazing. Continue to the junction with the **Branch Pond Trail (11.7 mi.)**, at the north boundary of the Lye Brook Wilderness. The Branch Pond Trail leads 0.5 mi. south to **William B. Douglas Shelter** and 8.3 mi. south to **Kelley Stand Road**. Douglas Shelter is a log lean-to, built in 1956 and renovated in 2004 by the GMC Brattleboro Section, and has space for ten. There is a spring 50 ft. south of the shelter on the Branch Pond Trail. **Stratton Pond Shelter to William B. Douglas Shelter, 5.4 mi., 8.7 km., 2¾ hr. (SB 2¾ hr.).**

From the junction, cross a brook over a bridge and turn left into a clearing. After following the Old Rootville Road for nearly a mile, arrive at a **spur (12.6 mi.)** leading west 150 ft. to **Prospect Rock**, perched high above Downer Glen. It offers a view of Manchester below and Mt. Equinox. The LT leaves the road opposite the spur, turning right and climbing a rock staircase out of the roadbed to proceed north. The **Old Rootville Road** continues downhill 1.8 mi. to a paved public road, which leads 0.2 mi. to Vt. 11 and Vt. 30, 1.8 mi. east of Manchester Center.

After passing west of a summit (14.3 mi.), descend to a **spur (14.7 mi.)** leading west 0.1 mi. to **Spruce Peak Shelter**. This enclosed log structure, with bunk space for sixteen, was built by the Brattleboro Section in cooperation with the U.S. Forest Service in 1983. A reliable piped spring is located 100 ft.

beyond the shelter. A composting privy is just northwest of the shelter. **William B. Douglas Shelter to Spruce Peak Shelter, 3.6 mi., 5.8 km., 2¼ hr. (SB 2¼ hr.).**

From the shelter spur, travel to a junction where a **spur (15.1 mi.)** leads west 300 ft. to **Spruce Peak**, offering a view of the Taconic Range and valley below. Continue north from the junction, drop to a brook, cross a power line (15.6 mi.) and, just beyond, a woods road. After a gradual ascent, crest the top of a ridge, pass two vistas to the west, and begin a winding descent to a stream crossing. A short distance beyond, cross abandoned old Vt. 30, and a bridge over a stream (17.1 mi.), and then pass through large boulders to **Vt. 11 and Vt. 30 (17.5 mi.).** From here it is 5.8 mi. west to Vt. 7A in Manchester Center and 4.1 mi. east to Peru. *Use caution when crossing Vt. 11 and Vt. 30; traffic moves at high speeds.*

Cross the highway and bear right through a large, paved parking lot to follow abandoned old Vt. 11, before turning sharply left (17.6 mi.) to enter the woods. Cross a brook over an I-beam bridge, pass under a power line, and climb gently to **Bromley Brook (18.2).** Cross over a bridge and continue along an old logging road.

Turn left off the logging road and ascend toward the ridgeline. A spur **(19.5)** leads east 100 yds. to **Bromley Shelter**. This post-and-beam structure was built by Erik and Laurel Tobiason and the GMC Manchester Section in 2003 after extensive site work by the volunteer LTP. Funding for this shelter was provided by the family of Debby Edelstein. Future maintenance of the shelter has been endowed by Marge and Bob Fish. Its two decks can sleep twelve. There is an accessible composting toilet and four tent platforms at the site. The water source is a spring just below the shelter on an extension of the spur. **Spruce Peak Shelter to Bromley Shelter, 5.0 mil, 8.0 km., 2¾ hr. (SB 2¾ hr.).**

Upon reaching a ski trail (20.3 mi.), bear left and follow it to the **south summit of Bromley Mtn. (20.5 mi.).** It is 100 ft. east to the facilities of Bromley Mtn. Ski Area including a warming hut and an **observation tower** that offers views in all directions, notably of Stratton Mtn. and Mt. Equinox. Camping at the warming hut may be allowed.

Continuing straight ahead along the west edge of the clearing, the trail turns sharp left, passing to the right of an outhouse. Descend to a col, then climb over **Bromley's north summit (21.0 mi.)**. Descend steadily, passing a vista near the north summit, and then continue downhill to **USFS Road 21 (Mad Tom Notch Road) at Mad Tom Notch (23.0 mi.)**. A parking area is located just west of the trail. The U.S. Forest Service maintains a water pump at the trail crossing, however occasional breakdowns make it unreliable as a water source.

Side Trails

STRATTON POND TRAIL. This trail provides an alternate lowland route between Kelley Stand Road and Stratton Pond. Refer to LT access directions for Stratton-Arlington (Kelley Stand) Road on pages 60 to 61. There is parking for the Stratton Pond Trail opposite USFS Road 71, 0.9 mi. west of the LT parking lot and 1.2 mi. east of the Branch Pond Trailhead and 12.1 mi. east of East Arlington. In winter, Kelley Stand Road is not plowed west of the LT crossing.

Gradually ascend from Kelley Stand Road (0.0 mi., 2380 ft.), passing through wet areas on puncheon and cross a gravel road (2.2 mi.), which is also the Catamount Trail. From the road travel northeast with little change in elevation over more puncheon to the spur to Stratton Pond Shelter and, just beyond, the junction (3.7 mi., 2620 ft.) with the LT, 0.1 mi. east of Stratton Pond. **Kelley Stand Road to LT, 3.7 mi., 6.0 km., 2 hr. (Rev. 2 hr.).**

LYE BROOK TRAIL. Linking Manchester and Bourn Pond to the LT, this trail is within the Lye Brook Wilderness from near its trailhead in Manchester to its crossing of the Winhall River west of Stratton Pond. From Vt. 7A in Manchester Center follow Vt. 11 and Vt. 30 1.9 mi. east and then turn right onto East Manchester Road. Follow the road 1.2 mi. to Glen Road and turn left. Continue straight on a short access road to the trailhead where Glen Road bears left at 0.1 mi. A parking lot and the trailhead are about 0.4 mi. from that junction. This access road is not plowed in winter.

From the parking lot (0.0 mi., 760 ft.), travel east and enter the Lye Brook Wilderness (0.5 mi.), following old railroad grades and woods roads uphill along the west side of Lye Brook

Hollow. Shortly after entering the wilderness, the trail traverses a large blowdown area associated with a wind shear event from a 1997 thunderstorm; GMC and GMNF are minimally clearing this area to minimize human alteration of the landscape. A spur (2.3 mi.) leads south 0.4 mi. to a small stream and one of the higher waterfalls in Vermont. From the waterfall to Bourn Pond, this trail may be more challenging to follow as it is minimally maintained in the Wilderness Area. A compass and topographic map (USGS) are strongly recommended. From the spur, continue along an old woods road; the grade eases, crossing a series of low ridges. Pass some beaver ponds, and reach the junction with the Branch Pond Trail (7.3 mi.) at a stream crossing just beyond the former site of the South Bourn Pond Shelter (removed in 2005). **Manchester to Bourn Pond, 7.3 mi., 11.8 km., 4½ hr. (Rev. 3½ hr.).**

From Bourn Pond, pass over a low ridge and cross a shallow ford of the headwaters of the Winhall River (8.5 mi.), Lye Brook Wilderness's east boundary. Cross this outlet stream of Stratton Pond and ascend along the stream to a junction (9.1 mi.) with the North Shore Trail at Stratton Pond. Bearing right to cross the pond's outlet on puncheon, follow the south shore of Stratton Pond to piped Bigelow Spring and, just beyond, the GMC caretaker tent platform and the junction (9.7 mi., 2555 ft.) with the LT at Willis Ross Clearing. **Manchester trailhead to LT, 9.7 mi., 15.6 km., 6¼ hr. (Rev. 5¼ hr.).**

NORTH SHORE TRAIL. This trail links the Lye Brook Trail near the outlet at the west end of Stratton Pond with the LT at the east end, and together with the Lye Brook Trail and LT completes a 1.4-mi. loop around the pond. Bear east from the Lye Brook Trail (0.0 mi., 2555 ft.) and follow the shoreline past a clearing (0.1 mi.), the former site of Stratton View Shelter, with a view of Stratton Mtn. Paralleling the shoreline, a spur turns left at a beaver-dammed stream to follow puncheon to its headwaters, Stratton View Spring.

Continuing to hug Stratton Pond's shoreline, arrive at a spur (0.2 mi.) leading north 200 ft. to the North Shore Tenting Area, which has tent platforms and a composting privy. Stratton View Spring is the site's water source. Follow the increasingly rugged shore, crossing an arm of the pond on a massive double log bridge, to the junction (0.7 mi., 2555 ft.) with the LT, where the Catamount Trail enters Stratton Pond on a woods road from the east. **Lye Brook Trail to LT 0.7 mi., 1.1 km., ½ hr. (Rev. ½ hr.).**

BRANCH POND TRAIL. Traversing the east half of the Lye Brook Wilderness, this trail connects Branch and Bourn Ponds with the LT near the Old Rootville Road. Refer to LT access directions for Stratton–Arlington (Kelley Stand) Road on pages 60 to 61. The trailhead is 1.2 mi. west of the Stratton Pond parking lot, 2.1 mi. west of the LT crossing, and 11.0 mi. east of East Arlington. There is space for one car on the north side of the road at the trailhead and space for four cars farther west on the north side of the road. In winter, Kelley Stand Road is not plowed west of the LT parking lot.

From Kelley Stand Road (0.0 mi., 2767 ft.), travel north over rolling terrain to a spur (1.8 mi.) leading west 0.3 mi. to USFS Road 70 where there is a boat access ramp to Branch Pond. Continue east of Branch Pond, and enter the Lye Brook Wilderness (2.5 mi.). The trail may be more challenging to follow in the Wilderness Area due to minimal brushing and blazing. Traverse Lye Brook Meadows on an old railroad grade, and reach the junction (4.3 mi.) with the Lye Brook Trail just south of Bourn Pond. **Kelley Stand Road to south shore of Bourn Pond, 4.3 mi., 6.9 km., 2¼ hr. (Rev. 2¼ hr.).**

Follow the west shore of Bourn Pond, reaching a spur (4.8 mi.) leading east 300 ft. to North Bourn Pond Tenting Area. From there, a path leads to the shoreline where there is a view of Stratton Mtn. Continuing north from the spur junction, skirt an area of beaver activity and follow an old lumber railroad grade to a ford (5.6 mi.) of Bourn Brook. This crossing can be difficult during snowmelt or heavy rains. After crossing an overgrown clearing (7.0 mi.), arrive at William B. Douglas Shelter (7.8 mi.). **South shore of Bourn Pond Shelter to William B. Douglas Shelter, 3.5 mi., 5.6 km., 1¾ hr. (Rev. 1¾ hr.).**

Follow an old, sunken woods road from the shelter to the junction (8.3 mi., 2280 ft.) with the LT at the Lye Brook Wilderness's north boundary. **Kelley Stand Road to LT, 8.3 mi., 13.4 km., 4½ hr. (Rev. 4¾ hr.).**

Afternoon sun at White Rocks

Division 4
Mad Tom Notch to Vt. 140

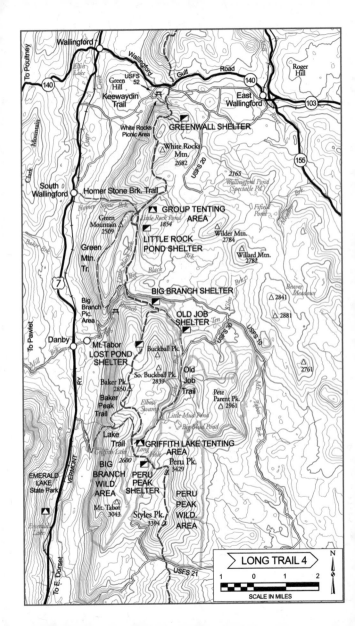

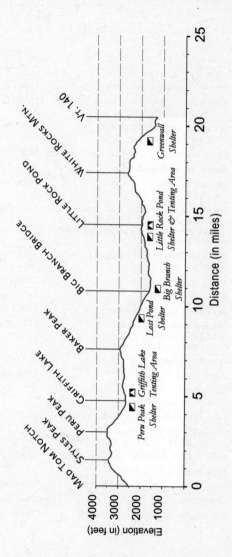

Division 4 Profile

Mad Tom Notch to Vt. 140

miles north-bound	NORTH ▲	elevation at Long Trail (feet/meters)	miles south-bound
20.6	Vt. 140; Roaring Brook bridge	1160/354	0.0
19.8	Keewaydin Trail to White Rocks Picnic Area, 0.4 mi N	1380/421	0.8
19.1	Greenwall Shelter (2020 ft/616 m), 0.2 mi E via Greenwall Spur	2300/701	1.5
18.6	White Rocks Cliff Trail to vista, 0.2 mi W	2400/732	2.0
15.6	Homer Stone Brook bridge	1900/579	5.0
14.6	Green Mtn. Trail to USFS Road 10, 4.1 mi N	1854/565	6.0
14.3	Little Rock Pond; Little Rock Pond Loop to Green Mtn. Trail, 0.4 mi N; Little Rock Pond Shelter and Tenting Area, 100 ft E via spur	1854/565	6.3
12.3	Big Black Branch; USFS Road 10, west junction	1500/457	8.3
12.1	USFS Road 10, east junction	1530/466	8.5
11.0	Big Branch Shelter	1470/448	9.6
10.9	Big Branch suspension bridge	1500/457	9.7
10.8	Old Job Trail, north junction to Old Job Shelter, 1.1 mi SE; to USFS Road 30, 2.0 mi SE	1525/465	9.8
9.3	Lost Pond Shelter, 100 ft W via spur	2150/655	11.3
7.3	Baker Peak	2850/869	13.3
7.2	Baker Peak Trail to South End Road via Lake Trail, 2.9 mi W	2760/841	13.4
5.4	Lake Trail to South End Road, 3.3 mi W	2620/799	15.2
5.3	Old Job Trail, south junction to USFS Road 30, 3.4 mi NE	2600/793	15.3
5.1	Griffith Lake; Griffith Lake Tenting Area	2600/793	15.5
4.6	Peru Peak Shelter	2550/777	16.0
3.3	Peru Peak	3429/1045	17.3
1.6	Styles Peak	3394/1034	19.0
0.0	USFS Road 21 at Mad Tom Notch	2446/746	20.6

SOUTH
▼

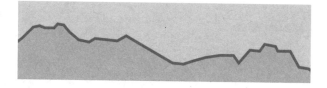

Division 4
Mad Tom Notch to Vt. 140

Massachusetts: 59.9 miles   **Canada: 212.8 miles**

4

From Mad Tom Notch to USFS Road 10, the Long Trail (LT) traverses Peru Peak Wilderness and Big Branch Wilderness. Refer to wilderness information on pages 8 to 9. The LT and the Appalachian Trail (AT) coincide throughout this division.

From Mad Tom Notch to Bully Brook, the LT passes through the Robert Stafford White Rocks National Recreation Area, where the U.S. Forest Service emphasizes management of the forest to provide recreation opportunities.

The following people and organizations have contributed to endow the future maintenance of 4 miles of the LT within this division: the Vermont County Store; Henry Kammerer in memory of Granget Kammerer; and a donation in honor of Leonard and Marguerite Keyes and their children Carolyn, Leonard, and John.

Camping and Fires

This division of the LT crosses the Green Mountain National Forest (GMNF). Primitive off-trail camping with small wood fires is allowed. Refer to Leave No Trace principles (pages 11 to 12) to minimize your impact.

Note: Camping at Griffith Lake and Little Rock Pond is limited to designated sites to protect vulnerable vegetation and soils.

Group Use

Groups hiking this division of the LT may need an Outfitter-Guide Special Use Permit from the GMNF. Group tenting space is available at Griffith Lake and Little Rock Pond Tenting Areas, and Lost Pond, Old Job, and Big Branch Shelters. GMNF Hapgood Pond Campground is available (refer to LT access directions for USFS Road 21) for base camp hiking. Emerald Lake State Park Campground, south of Danby on U.S. 7, is also available for base camp hiking. Refer to group use guidelines (pages 13 to 19) to determine whether your group needs a permit.

Suggested Day Hikes

STYLES PEAK. This climb on the LT north from Mad Tom Notch provides views of southeast Vermont from the summit rock outcrop. Round trip, 3.2 mi., 3¼ hr.

GREEN MOUNTAIN AND LITTLE ROCK POND. A loop using the Long, Green Mtn., and Green Mtn. Connector Trails from USFS Road 10 combines scenic Little Rock Pond with views from the ledges of Green Mtn. Round trip, 7 mi., 4¾ hr.

BAKER PEAK. This loop hike from U.S. 7 follows the Lake, Baker Peak, and Long Trails and features views from the open summit. Round trip, 8.1 mi., 5 hr.

BIG BRANCH WILDERNESS. The Old Job Trail and the LT create a loop hike to Griffith Lake, Baker Peak, Big Branch, and Old Job. This circuit is suitable for a day hike or a backpack. Round trip, 10.4 mi., 6 hr.

Winter Use

Many of the trails in this division, in combination with unplowed USFS roads, provide good cross-country ski opportunities. A suggested loop includes USFS Roads 10 and 30 with the Old Job Trail (north branch) and the LT. Little Rock Pond via the Homer Stone Brook Trail makes a fine snowshoe destination. Styles Peak from Mad Tom Notch provides good views for a 5.2 mi. round trip from the winter parking lot on USFS Road 21.

Access to Long Trail

4

USFS ROAD 21 AT MAD TOM NOTCH. Refer to directions on pages 73 to 74 in Division 3.

USFS ROAD 10. LT parking is available at two trailheads, 0.2 mi. apart. From U.S. 7 in Danby, follow USFS Road 10 3.2 mi. to the primary parking lot (paved) at the west trailhead or continue to a smaller, pull-off parking area at the east trailhead. Because of the risk of vandalism, parking lots in this area are not recommended for long-term parking.

These sites are also accessible from Peru to the east. Refer to LT access directions for Mad Tom Notch, USFS Road 21 on pages 73 to 74 in Division 3. From Peru's J. J. Hapgood General Store follow the Hapgood Pond/Landgrove Road 3.6 mi. to an intersection. Turn left and follow USFS Road 12 0.6 mi. to USFS Road 10 on the right. USFS Road 10 leads 10.6 mi. west to the Trail.

USFS Road 10 between the bridge over Big Black Branch (0.9 mi. east of Danby) and the LT is not plowed in winter, a distance of 2.3 mi. The road is also not plowed between the LT and Landgrove to the east.

VT. 140. The LT intersects this highway 2.7 mi. east of Wallingford and U.S. 7, and 3.3 mi. west of Vt. 103 and Vt. 155 in East Wallingford. The parking lot is off a steep driveway on the north side of Vt. 140, 0.2 mi. east of the trail crossing.

Long Trail Description

From USFS Road 21 at Mad Tom Notch (0.0 mi.), enter the Peru Peak Wilderness and the White Rocks National Recreation Area (0.1 mi.). The LT may be more challenging to follow in the Wilderness Area due to minimal brushing and blazing. Climb steadily to the summit of **Styles Peak (1.6 mi.)**, with views extending from the northeast to the south. Follow the ridge passing over several knobs, to the summit of **Peru Peak (3.3 mi.)**, where a short spur leads east to a lookout.

Beyond the summit, descend past a piped spring (3.7 mi.) and then leave the Peru Peak Wilderness. Just beyond is **Peru Peak Shelter (4.6 mi.)**. This log structure, with space for ten, was built by the Civilian Conservation Corps in 1935 and rebuilt by the Youth Conservation Corps and U.S. Forest Service in 1979. The shelter was rebuilt by the Long Trail Patrol (LTP) with the assistance of the U.S. Forest Service to replace rotten logs in 2000. Repairs to fix sill logs and the sleeping deck were started in 2010 by the LTP led by Jason Snell and Tony Stoltzfus. Future maintenance of Peru Peak Shelter has been endowed by family and friends in loving memory of Bernard Godfrey. Water is found at the nearby brook. There is a composting privy to the north of the shelter. **Bromley Shelter to Peru Peak Shelter, 8.2 mi., 13 km., 4¼ hr. (SB 5 hr.).**

Proceed west from Peru Peak Shelter and cross three bridges before arriving at the shore of **Griffith Lake (5.1 mi.)**, and follow extensive puncheon to **Griffith Lake Tenting Area** with tent platforms and a composting privy. To protect this shoreline and preserve its natural beauty, all camping in the vicinity of Griffith Lake is limited to tent platforms. A GMC caretaker is in residence to assist and educate hikers, help maintain the local trails and campsites, and compost sewage to protect water quality. A fee is charged for overnight use at these designated sites and at Peru Peak Shelter.

Follow more puncheon north, paralleling the shore of the lake, to the south junction with the **Old Job Trail (5.3 mi.)**, which leads northeast 3.4 mi. to USFS Road 30. From the trail junction, continue straight ahead and leave the shoreline of Griffith Lake. Enter Big Branch Wilderness, where the LT may be more challenging to follow due to minimal brushing and blazing. Pass the **Lake Trail (5.4 mi.)**, which descends 3.3 mi. west to South End Road, 0.5 mi. east of U.S. 7.

Follow the ridge northward and descend to cross an old woods road (6.2 mi.). Cross another woods road, and begin to ascend Baker Peak. Reach the junction with the **Baker Peak Trail (7.2 mi.)**, which joins the Lake Trail to lead 2.9 mi. west to South End Road. Bear right for the final scramble up the exposed ledges to the summit of **Baker Peak (7.3 mi.)**. Should adverse weather conditions make the ascent over open rocks treacherous, there is a parallel by-pass route to the east. Baker Peak offers views of the valley. Danby and the north-flowing Otter Creek are directly below. Across the valley is Dorset Peak with its famous marble quarry. Emerald Lake and Mt. Equinox are to the south, and the fire tower on Stratton Mtn. can be seen just behind the ridge of Peru Peak. Pico and Killington Peaks are to the north, and the Adirondacks are visible to the northwest on clear days.

Leave the summit of Baker Peak, enter the woods, and bear north, keeping east of a ridge. After crossing over a height of land (7.8 mi.), descend along the west side of the ridge. Reach a wide, grassy woods road (9.1 mi.) and follow the road to the right for 250 ft., before turning left into the woods. Continue north on an old woods road to a **spur (9.3 mi.)** leading west 100 ft. to Lost Pond Shelter. The original **Lost Pond Shelter**, built by Louis (Sandy) Stare Jr. in 1965, burned in November 2001. It was rebuilt by Tom Abbott and GMC volunteers coordinated by Marge Fish in 2002 and burned again in 2006. It was rebuilt for the second time by John Ogden and GMC volunteers in 2009. The water supply is a stream in the ravine west of the shelter. **Peru Peak Shelter to Lost Pond Shelter, 4.7 mi., 7.6 km., 2¼ hr. (SB 2¾ hr.).**

Continue north from the shelter spur along the woods road. Descend steadily to Big Branch and the north junction with the **Old Job Trail (10.8 mi.)**. This trail leads southeast 1.1 mi. to Old Job Shelter and 2.0 mi. to USFS Road 30. Turn left to follow the river downstream, and then cross the **Big Branch suspension bridge (10.9 mi.)**. This bridge was replaced in 2010 by U.S. Forest Service contractors. Continue following the river

JOIN THE CLUB!

PLEASE DO YOUR PART TO ENSURE THE FUTURE
OF THE LONG TRAIL: BECOME A MEMBER OF
THE GREEN MOUNTAIN CLUB!

By joining GMC, you will:

- Help to conserve Vermont's high-mountain country.

- Support trail and shelter maintenance.

- Sustain hiking opportunities for generations to come.

To join or make a gift to the GMC, contact:

Green Mountain Club
4711 Waterbury-Stowe Road
Waterbury Center, Vermont 05677
(802) 244-7037
gmc@greenmountainclub.org
www.greenmountainclub.org

Thank you!

on an old road, pass a stone mill foundation, and arrive at **Big Branch Shelter (11.0 mi.)**. This frame lean-to, with floor space for eight, was built by the USFS in 1963. Big Branch furnishes water. The outhouse is up the hill behind the shelter. Future maintenance of Big Branch Shelter has been endowed by Marge and Bob Fish. **Long Pond Shelter to Big Branch Shelter, 1.7 mi., 2.7 km., 1 hr. (SB 1½ hr.).**

From the shelter follow Big Branch downstream for a short distance, and then turn right and ascend gradually, crossing the north boundary of the Big Branch Wilderness. Continue a gentle ascent to **USFS Road 10 (12.1 mi.)** and a small parking area. To the east it is 10.6 mi. to Landgrove via USFS Road 10. Descend on the road west to the crossing of **Big Black Branch (12.3)**. Turn north to reenter the woods at the trailhead just beyond the bridge. A paved parking lot is to the south of the trailhead. USFS Road 10 continues west down the mountain 3.2 mi. to U.S. 7 in Danby.

Leave the pavement and follow an old woods road north. Cross Little Black Branch (12.9 mi.) over an I-beam bridge, then recross it over large rocks (13.1 mi.). Travel over numerous puncheon to a spur (14.0 mi.) leading east 100 ft. uphill to the former site of Lula Tye Shelter. *No camping or wood fires are permitted at this site to allow the area to recover from nearly forty years of use.*

Proceed to the south end of **Little Rock Pond (14.3 mi.)** and the **Little Rock Pond Loop Trail**. The loop trail follows the former route of the LT 0.4 mi. around the west side of Little Rock Pond and rejoins the LT north of the pond. Just beyond lies the new **Little Rock Pond Shelter**. This timber frame structure, with space for eight was built by GMC volunteers led by Erik and Laurel Tobiason. Future maintenance of Little Rock Pond Shelter has been endowed in memory of John Kidder. There is a group tenting area at this site with a composting privy on a low shelf 100 ft. east of the pond. This popular pond is one of the most visited sites on the LT, and careful management is required to preserve its beauty and fragile shoreline. Camping in the vicinity of the pond's shoreline is limited to designated sites. A GMC caretaker is in residence to assist and educate hikers, help maintain the local trails and campsites, and compost sewage to protect water quality. A fee is charged for overnight use. **Big Branch Shelter to Little Rock Pond Shelter, 3.3 mi., 5.3 km., 1½ hr. (SB 1⅓ hr.).**

Hug the east shore of the pond and pass the spring (14.4 mi.), which is the water source for all campsites in the vicinity of Little Rock Pond. Arrive at the trail junction near the pond's outlet with the **Green Mtn. Trail (14.6 mi.)**, which ascends Green Mtn. and continues south 4.1 mi. to USFS Road 10. It also leads west 2.3 mi. to South Wallingford via the Homer Stone Brook Trail. From the junction, descend an old woods road to a spur (14.7 mi.) leading east to the site of the Old Little Rock Pond Shelter, which still allows camping on existing tent platforms. Both Lula Tye and the old Little Rock Pond Shelters were removed in 2010 by the Volunteer LTP and the LTP.

Continue with little change in elevation to the long-abandoned Aldrich Job clearing (15.4 mi.). Cross the **Homer Stone Brook Bridge (15.6 mi.)**, before intersecting with the old South Wallingford–Wallingford Pond Road. Begin a steady ascent, passing just to the west of the summit of White Rocks Mtn. (17.8 mi.), then descend to the **White Rocks Cliff Trail (18.6 mi.)**, which leads west downhill 0.2 mi. to a vista from the top of the cliffs. Continue north to the **Greenwall Spur (19.1 mi.)**, which descends east 0.2 mi. to **Greenwall Shelter** just outside the north boundary of the White Rocks National Recreation Area. This frame lean-to, with floor space for eight, was built by the U.S. Forest Service in 1962. A spur leads 600 ft. northeast behind the shelter to a spring, which may fail during droughts. **Little Rock Pond Shelter to Greenwall Shelter, 5.0 mi., 8.0 km., 3⅓ hr. (SB 3 hr.).**

From the Greenwall Spur, continue downhill to a trail junction with the **Keewaydin Trail (19.8 mi.)**, which leads north

IN CASE OF EMERGENCY, CALL 911.
KNOW WHERE YOU ARE!

0.4 mi. to the White Rocks Picnic Area. At the junction, turn right and cross Bully Brook (19.9 mi.). Leave the White Rocks National Recreation Area just past the brook. Descend beside a dramatic gulch to Sugar Hill Road (20.5 mi.), cross the road and drop to cross the **Roaring Brook Bridge (20.6 mi.)**, built by the Volunteer LTP in 2000, and then reach **Vt. 140**. To the east, it is 3.3 mi. to Vt. 103 and Vt. 155 in East Wallingford; to the west, 2.7 mi. to U.S. 7 in Wallingford.

Side Trails

OLD JOB TRAIL. Formerly the route of the LT, this trail provides an alternate lowland route between Griffith Lake and Big Branch. An old woods road, this trail links the LT at both Griffith Lake and Big Branch with USFS Road 30. Follow USFS Road 10 for 6.9 mi. east out of Danby, passing the LT crossing, and turn right onto USFS Road 30 for 2.3 mi. to its end. USFS Road 30 and most of USFS Road 10 are not plowed in winter.

South branch: From the end of USFS Road 30, bear south (left) onto a gated woods road. From the gate (0.0 mi., 2000 ft.), ascend gradually, paralleling the east side of Lake Brook, to cross two tributary brooks on snowmobile bridges (0.6 mi. and 2.1 mi.) before crossing Lake Brook (2.4 mi.) on a large bridge. Follow a woods road around Long Hole, and join the LT (3.4 mi., 2600 ft.) at the north end of Griffith Lake. **USFS Road 30 to LT at Griffith Lake, 3.4 mi., 5.5 km., 2 hr. (Rev. 1¾ hr.).**

North branch: From the end of USFS Road 30, travel north (right) and descend the road embankment (0.0 mi., 2000 ft.). Follow Lake Brook, which leads to Old Job Shelter (0.9 mi.) in an extensive clearing where the village of Griffith once stood. The shelter is a log structure with space for eight, built by the Civilian Conservation Corps in 1935. The shelter was renovated by the Volunteer LTP led by Tony Stoltzfus in 2009. Lake Brook provides water. Cross Lake Brook on a suspension bridge, which was replaced by U.S. Forest Service contractors in 2010, and head northwest through the clearing, passing first a large sawdust pile and then an old jeep road on the right (1.1

mi.). The trail can be difficult to follow in the late summer when the meadow is overgrown. Continue west, entering the Big Branch Wilderness, and parallel Big Branch to the LT junction (2.0 mi., 1525 ft.), 0.1 mi. south of the Big Branch suspension bridge. **USFS Road 30 to LT at Big Branch, 2.0 mi., 3.2 km., 1 hr. (Rev. 1¼ hr.). Griffith Lake to Big Branch via the Old Job Trail is 5.4 mi., 8.7 km., 2¾ hr. (Rev. 3¼ hr.).**

LAKE TRAIL. Take U.S. 7 south from Danby. At 2.1 mi., turn east onto South End Road and follow it 0.5 mi. east to a parking lot and the trailhead. This trail was once a bridle path leading from the valley to Griffith Lake (formerly Buffum Pond).

Enter the woods (0.0 mi., 720 ft.) from the parking lot and gently ascend the old road. Switch back to the left and enter the Big Branch Wilderness (0.9 mi.), where the climb steepens. Cross a bridge (1.5 mi.) anchored to a rock face where the old trestle supports are still visible. Reach a spur to the right, which climbs to an open rock with views of Dorset Peak and the valley. Ascend to cross McGinn Brook at the junction with the Baker Peak Trail (1.9 mi.). From the junction, the climb moderates, leading to the LT (3.3 mi., 2620 ft.) just north of Griffith Lake. **South End Road to LT, 3.3 mi., 5.3 km., 2½ hr.**

BAKER PEAK TRAIL. This trail connects the Lake Trail with the LT near the summit of Baker Peak. From its junction with the Lake Trail (0.0 mi., 1920 ft.), gradually ascend on an old woods road before climbing a steeper grade over ledges to join the LT (0.9

mi., 2760 ft.), 0.1 mi. south of the summit of Baker Peak. **Lake Trail to LT, 0.9 mi., 1.5 km., 1 hr. (Rev. ½ hr.). South End Road to Baker Peak via the Lake, Baker Peak and Long Trails is 2.9 mi., 4.7 km., 2½ hr. (Rev. 1½ hr.).**

LITTLE ROCK POND LOOP TRAIL. This shoreline trail, formerly the LT, follows the west side of Little Rock Pond. From the LT (0.0 mi., 1854 ft.) at the south end of Little Rock Pond, bear left and skirt the south shore of the pond. Climb away from the shore to pass above the ledges of the west shore and reach the Green Mtn. Trail junction (0.4 mi., 1854 ft.), 0.1 mi. west of the LT at the north end of the pond. **LT to Green Mtn. Trail, 0.4 m., 0.6 km., ¼ hr. (Rev. ¼ hr.).**

GREEN MOUNTAIN TRAIL. This trail links USFS Road 10 with the LT at the north end of Little Rock Pond. Follow USFS Road 10 2.7 mi. east from Danby to the USFS Big Branch Picnic Area. USFS 10 is plowed in winter only to the silver bridge, 1.8 mi. west of this trailhead.

Enter the woods opposite the picnic area (0.0 mi., 1550 ft.), and ascend to the junction (0.1 mi.) with the Green Mtn. Connector, which leads east paralleling the road 0.6 mi. to the LT parking lot at Big Black Branch. Take a sharp right and climb to a lookout (0.3 mi.) to the west. Continue to ascend on an old woods road, traverse an impressive, mature stand of hemlock and white pine, before joining another woods road and crossing a brook (1.3 mi.). Cross a shallow saddle (2.1 mi.) before climbing a spruce-covered ridge to a spur leading east 50 ft. to a lookout near the summit of Green Mtn. Cross ledges and reach another spur, which leads east 200 ft. to an outlook with limited views. From the spur, descend steadily to the Little Rock Pond Loop Trail junction (4.0 mi.), and then the junction with the Homer Stone Brook Trail, before continuing over the pond outlet to the north end of Little Rock Pond (4.1 mi., 1854 ft.) and the LT. **Big Branch Picnic Area to LT, 4.1 mi., 6.6 km., 2½ hr. (Rev. 2¼ hr.).**

HOMER STONE BROOK TRAIL. This trail provides an alternate route from the Otter Creek Valley to Little Rock Pond. From U.S. 7 in South Wallingford, just north of Charlie's Market or 4.2 mi.

south of Vt. 140 in Wallingford, turn east onto the south end of Hartsboro Road and cross Otter Creek and the railroad tracks, then bear right onto Homer Stone Road.

Hiker parking is to the left 0.25 mile beyond the school-house. Enter the woods (0.0 mi., 680 ft.) and climb steadily, keeping to the right at all forks, and follow the old South Wallingford–Wallingford Pond Road until it reaches a ford of Homer Stone Brook (1.7 mi.). This ford can be challenging in high water. From the brook crossing, ascend on an old woods road southeast to its junction with the Green Mtn. Trail (2.3 mi., 1854 ft.), which leads west uphill to Green Mtn. and east over the pond outlet to the LT just north of Little Rock Pond. **Homer Stone Road to LT, 2.3 mi., 3.7 km., 1¾ hr. (Rev. 1¼ hr.).**

WHITE ROCKS CLIFF TRAIL. This path descends west from the LT to an outlook on the very brink of White Rocks Cliff. **LT to White Rocks Cliff, 0.2 mi., 0.3 km., 10 min. (Rev. 5 min.).**

KEEWAYDIN TRAIL. This trail links the USFS White Rocks Picnic Area with the LT near its crossing of Bully Brook. From Wallingford, travel 2.3 mi. east on Vt. 140, turn south on Sugar Hill Road for 0.1 mi., then turn right onto USFS Road 52. Continue on this road 0.6 mi. to the picnic area and parking. Overnight parking at the picnic area is not permitted. USFS Road 52 is not maintained in winter.

From the far end of the picnic area and parking lot (0.0 mil, 1140 ft.), climb steadily to the LT (0.4 mil, 1380 ft.), 0.1 mi. from Bully Brook. **USFS White Rocks Picnic Area to LT, 0.4 mi., 0.6 km., ½ hr. (Rev. ¼ hr.).** Other hiking trails from the picnic area include the White Rocks Trail leading 0.2 mi. to a viewpoint on a knoll below White Rocks Cliff and the 0.8 mi. Ice Bed Trail.

Mt. Pico from Killington

Division 5
Vt. 140 to U.S. 4

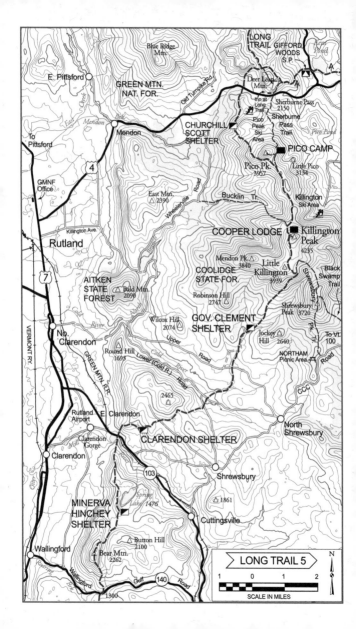

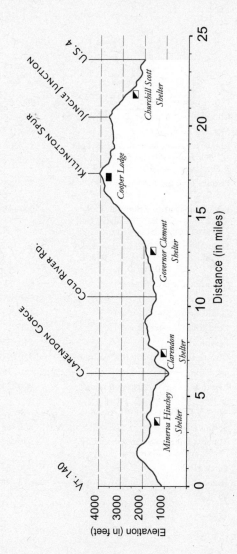

Division 5 Profile

Vt. 140 to U.S. 4

miles northbound	▲ NORTH	elevation at Long Trail (feet/meters)	miles southbound
23.7	**U.S. 4** west of Sherburne Pass	1880/573	0.0
21.8	**Churchill Scott Shelter**, 0.1 mi W via spur	2560/780	1.9
21.5	**Mendon Lookout**	2890/881	2.2
19.9	**Jungle Junction, Sherburne Pass Trail** south end to **Pico Camp**, 0.4 mi N; to Sherburne Pass, 3.1 mi N	3480/1061	3.8
17.6	**Bucklin Trail** to Wheelerville Road, 3.3 mi W	3770/1149	6.1
17.4	**Killington Spur** to Killington Peak (4235 ft/1291 m), 0.2 mi. E; **Cooper Lodge**, 100 ft north via Long Trail	3900/1189	6.3
15.8	**Shrewsbury Peak Trail** to **Shrewsbury Peak** (3720 ft/1135 m), 2.0 mi E; **CCC Road**, 4.0 mi. E	3500/1067	7.9
13.1	**Governor Clement Shelter**	1850/564	10.6
11.7	**Upper Road**	1630/497	12.0
11.0	**Gould Brook** ford	1480/451	12.7
10.2	**Cold River (Lower) Road**	1400/427	13.5
7.8	**Beacon Hill**	1740/530	15.9
7.3	**Clarendon Shelter**, 400 ft E via spur	1350/412	16.4
6.3	**Vt. 103**	860/262	17.4
6.2	**Clarendon Gorge** suspension bridge over Mill River	800/244	17.5
5.5	**Airport Lookout**, 50 ft W via spur	1400/427	18.2
4.2	**Spring Lake Clearing**	1600/488	19.5
3.6	**Minerva Hinchey Shelter**, 200 ft E via woods road	1530/466	20.1
2.7	**Patch Hollow**	1800/549	21.0
1.0	**Domed ledge** vista, 300 ft W via spur	1575/480	22.7
0.0	**Vt. 140**	1300/396	23.7

SOUTH
▼

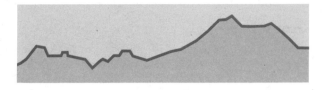

Division 5
Vt. 140 to U.S. 4

Massachusetts: 80.5 miles   **Canada: 192.2 miles**

Tenting near Pico Camp is very limited. Do not plan to camp near the site if the shelter is full.

The Long Trail (LT) and the Appalachian Trail (AT) coincide throughout this division.

The following organization and person have contributed to endow the future maintenance of 2 miles of the LT within this division: Long Trail Brewing Company and Joan Sibley.

Camping and Fires

This division of the LT traverses a mix of state and federally owned AT corridor land, with two campsites on private property. Camping is limited to shelters. Small wood fires, although discouraged, are permitted at the shelters' established fire rings, with the exception of Cooper Lodge, due to its sensitive high-elevation location, and Churchill Scott Shelter, owing to permit guidelines. Camping is prohibited in the vicinity of Clarendon Gorge. Refer to Leave No Trace principles (pages 11 to 12) to minimize your impact.

Group Use

Groups hiking this division of the LT may need an Outfitter-Guide Special Use Permit from the Green Mountain National Forest (GMNF). Groups planning to camp at Cooper Lodge may need a Commercial Use Permit from the Vermont Department of Forests, Parks and Recreation. Group tenting space is available at Minerva Hinchey and Clarendon Shelters and Cooper Lodge. Gifford Woods State Park Campground, east of Sherburne Pass on Vt. 100, is available for base camp hiking. Refer to group use guidelines (pages 13 to 19) to determine whether your group needs a permit.

Winter Use

All suggested hikes in this division make good winter trips, except for the Shrewsbury Peak loop owing to the CCC Road's unmaintained winter condition. The challenging terrain is suitable only for advanced cross-country skiers.

Access to the Long Trail

Vt. 140. Refer to directions on page 87 in Division 4.

Vt. 103. The LT crosses this highway just north of Clarendon Gorge. The road crossing is 2.4 mi. east of U.S. 7, and 6.0 mi. west of East Wallingford and Vt. 155. There is a parking lot on the south side of the highway, just west of the railroad crossing. Long term parking is not recommended.

COLD RIVER (LOWER) ROAD. Take Lincoln Hill Road north from Vt. 103, 0.7 mi. east of the LT crossing. Follow this road 2.5 mi. to Shrewsbury and continue 2.8 mi. more to North Shrewsbury where the Cold River Road turns left opposite an old store. Proceed on Lower Cold River Road (the Upper Road is to the right just beyond the fire station) 2.4 mi. west to the LT. It is another 7.3 mi. west to U.S. 7 in Rutland. There is limited parking on the north side of the road just east of a bridge.

U.S. 4. This trail crossing is 8.6 mi. east of U.S. 7 in Rutland, and 1.0 mi. west of the crest of Sherburne Pass. An unpaved lot on the south side of the highway provides ample parking. The Catamount Trail shares this highway crossing. This parking lot is not always plowed in winter; however another area about 0.3 mi. east is always plowed. *Use extreme caution when crossing the fast traffic of U.S. 4.*

Suggested Day Hikes

Airport Lookout. This hike south on the LT from Vt. 103 crosses Clarendon Gorge over a suspension bridge and climbs to a lookout with views to the west. Round trip, 1.6 mi., 1¾ hr.

Beacon Hill. This hike on the LT north of Vt. 103 passes Clarendon Lookout, then leads to views from an old hilltop pasture. Round trip, 3.0 mi., 2 hr.

Shrewsbury Peak. This hike at the south end of the Coolidge Range combines the Shrewsbury Peak Trail and Black Swamp Trail with a 1.5 mi. walk on the CCC Road for a loop hike over the summit of Shrewsbury Peak, one of the high peaks of the range. Round trip, 5.4 mi., 3½ hr.

Pico Circuit. This trip combines the Sherburne Pass Trail, the former, historic route of the LT, south from U.S. 4 at Sherburne Pass with the LT south of U.S. 4. The full circuit requires a 1-mile road walk alongside the highway where traffic may be heavy. This destination features views from the ski slopes and the summit of Pico (an optional destination). Round trip, 7.9 mi., 5 hr. Add 0.8 mi. and ¾ hr. if summiting via the Pico Link.

Killington Peak. With sweeping views from its rocky summit, this peak is directly accessed by the Bucklin Trail and Killington Spur. Round trip, 7.2 mi., 5¼ hr. A longer hike with an optional climb of Pico Peak follows the Sherburne Pass Trail south from U.S. 4 at Sherburne Pass. Round trip, 11.2 mi., 7 hr.

Long Trail Description

Cross **Vt. 140 (0.0 mi.)**, *Use caution when crossing Vt. 140; traffic moves at high speeds,* climb past boulders to a large asphalt parking lot (0.1 mi.), and then gently ascend a woods road to abandoned hillside pastures separated by stone walls. Turn right, join the abandoned Bear Mtn. Road (0.6 mi.), and follow it 50 ft. east. Turn right to leave the road, pass through an old orchard, and ascend by switchbacks to a **spur (1.0 mi.)** leading 300 ft. west to a **domed ledge vista** of White Rocks Mtn. and Dorset Peak. Continue the steady ascent; near the crest of Bear Mtn.'s ridge, the grade moderates. Pass west of a springtime vernal pool, and reach the trail's height of land (2.1 mi.) on Bear Mtn. Follow switchbacks downhill to a former homesite at **Patch Hollow (2.7 mi.)**, at the north end of a beaver pond. Continue to descend on an abandoned road, which the trail shares with a cross-country ski trail, and then bear north to cross under a power line. Turn left to follow a grassy woods road before turning left to ascend the ridge. Here the **woods road (3.6 mi.)** continues east 200 ft. to **Minerva Hinchey Shelter**.

This frame structure, with bunk space for eight, was constructed by Sandy Stare and members of the GMC Killington Section in 1969 and renovated by Killington Section volunteers led by Gerry Parker in 2006. It is named for Minerva Hinchey in tribute to her twenty-two years of service as GMC corresponding secretary, 1955–1977. Future maintenance of Minerva Hinchey Shelter has been endowed by Scott and Debbie Livingston. Water can be found at a small spring 150 ft. south. **Greenwall Shelter to Minerva Hinchey Shelter, 5.3 mi., 8.5 km., 3¼ hr. (SB 3¼ hr.).**

Climb to the ridge and then descend to **Spring Lake Clearing (4.2 mi.)**, where the forest is reclaiming a highland meadow. Reenter the woods, pass the airport beacon power line (4.3 mi.), and follow a narrow ridge for over a mile before reaching a spur leading west 50 ft. to **Airport Lookout (5.5 mi.)**. Drop off the ridge to the head of picturesque **Clarendon Gorge (6.2 mi.)**. *Refrain from camping here; owing to its proximity to the highway many non-hikers inhabit the area during the* *warmer months*. Cross the **suspension bridge over Mill River**. The bridge was built in 1974 to replace a similar structure swept away in the 1973 flood. It was repaired in 2008 by Eagle Scout Denis Murphy and the Rutland Hard Core Crew. It is dedicated to the memory of Robert Brugmann. Follow the old road uphill to the parking lot on Vt. 103 (6.3 mi.). *Use caution when crossing Vt. 103; traffic moves at high speeds.*

Cross the highway and the Green Mountain Railroad, and then traverse a small pasture, climbing over stiles to negotiate its barbed wire fences. Turn left and follow a woods road uphill to a power line, and then climb up through a boulder-filled ravine. At the top of the ravine, bear right and rise gradually along the ridge to Clarendon Lookout (6.7 mi.) with views to the south and west, and then continue along the ridge before dropping gradually to an abandoned town road. Just beyond that road, a spur descends east 400 ft. to **Clarendon Shelter (7.3 mi.).** This frame building, with bunks for twelve, was constructed by the Killington Section in 1952. A brook 50 ft. east furnishes water. **Minerva Hinchey Shelter to Clarendon Shelter, 3.8 mi., 6.1 km., 2½ hr. (SB 2½ hr.).**

From the spur, continue east to cross a brook, briefly following it before climbing to the partially open summit of **Beacon Hill (7.8 mi.),** where there is a view of the nearby countryside. Turn north to drop down through a sugarbush, traverse a pasture, pass through a gate (please keep the gate closed so the cows don't escape), and cross Lottery Road (8.2 mi.) west of the village of Shrewsbury. Reenter the woods (8.3 mi.) and pass Hermit Spring (8.6 mi.), unreliable in dry seasons. Ascend a ridge, drop through another old pasture, and continue to the gravel Kieffer Road (9.9 mi.). Bear left on Kieffer Road, and then enter a field to the right with views of the Coolidge Range and descend to the west bank of Cold River (10.1 mi.), which you follow downstream to the paved **Cold River (Lower Road) (10.2 mi.),** 2.4 mi. west of North Shrewsbury.

Turn right on the road to cross a bridge over the Cold River, then bear left onto a woods road to pass through a clearing. Reenter the woods and follow the woods road a short distance, then bear right (10.4 mi.) to ascend a ridge high above the brook. Traversing this ridge and passing a vista of the Coolidge

HIKER SAFETY IS HIKER AWARENESS

Although the trail is safer than most places, problems can occur. Hiker awareness is one of your best lines of defense.

HIKING WITH OTHERS IS SAFER. If you encounter a stranger or a situation that makes you feel uncomfortable, move on.

DON'T CAMP NEAR ROAD CROSSINGS, even at established campsites. If tenting away from an established campsite, camp out of sight of the trail.

ELIMINATE OPPORTUNITIES FOR THEFT. Don't leave gear on the trail or in a shelter unattended. Don't leave anything valuable or visible in vehicles parked at trailheads.

USE TRAIL AND SHELTER REGISTERS. Please sign them. Doing so will help locate you in an emergency. Be sure your at-home contact knows your trail name, if you use one.

Range, the trail then drops to the **Gould Brook ford (11.0 mi.)**, which can be challenging in high water. Parallel Gould and Sargent Brooks to the unpaved **Upper Road (11.7 mi.)**, 2.4 mi. west of North Shrewsbury.

Cross the Upper Road and continue paralleling the stream to another road (12.3 mi.). Turn left onto the road to cross a bridge over Sargent Brook and, in 150 ft., turn right into the woods. After ascending a ridge, pass through an overgrown clearing (12.7 mi.), the site of the former Haley Farm. The GMC's 1920 *Guide Book of the Long Trail* described the farm as providing, "good beds and board; telephone." Follow the brook, crossing it on a bridge, and immediately cross a woods road before reaching **Governor Clement Shelter (13.1 mi.)**, located on a dirt road in an overgrown field. This stone structure was built by the family of William H. Field of Mendon in 1929 and is named for Percival W. Clement, governor of Vermont, 1919 to 1921. The sleeping deck and roof were repaired in 2010 by the Killington Section led by Wayne Krevetski. There is bunk space for ten. Abundant water is available at the brook 200 ft. to the east. There have been problems over the years with partying on this spot, and GMC is working with the GMNF to limit inappropriate use. There was a gate installed on the road used to access the shelter by the town of Shrewsbury in 2008 helping to alleviate the problems. However, move on if you encounter problems. **Clarendon Shelter to Governor Clement Shelter, 5.9 mi., 9.5 km., 3½hr. (SB 3 hr.).**

Follow the road behind the shelter to the north, then bear left into the woods (13.4 mi.) and, sometimes following woods roads, climb steadily to two small brook crossings (15.3 mi.). Slab the steep south slope of Little Killington to the north end of the **Shrewsbury Peak Trail (15.8 mi.)**, which leads 2.0 mi. east to Shrewsbury Peak. From the junction, ascend through stunted evergreens to a view of Mendon Peak to the west. From the height of land on Little Killington (16.2 mi.), pass mossy conifers and continue by easy grades along the west flank of Killington Peak to **Killington Spur (17.4 mi.)**, which leads uphill steeply east 0.2 mi. to the summit of **Killington Peak**. Bear left at the spur and proceed downhill 100 ft. to **Cooper Lodge**.

There are tent platforms at the spur junction's clearing, the site of a steel camp that preceded the lodge.

Cooper Lodge, of stone and wood construction with bunks for twelve, was built by the Vermont Forest Service and CCC in 1939. It is located on land given to the state by Mortimer R. Proctor, president of the GMC from 1916 to 1917 and later governor of Vermont, and named in honor of Charles P. Cooper, president of the club from 1917 to 1925, when a considerable portion of the LT was completed. It is the highest shelter (3850 ft.) on the LT. There is a composting privy to the east of the lodge, and a spring 100 ft. west on the LT. A GMC caretaker may be present during the hiking season to assist and educate hikers, help maintain the local trails and campsites, and compost sewage to protect water quality. An overnight fee may be charged. **Governor Clement Shelter to Cooper Lodge, 4.3 mi., 6.9 km., 6¾ hr. (SB 5¼ hr.).**

From the lodge, descend past the spring, passing just above the barely discernible site of the nineteenth-century summit hotel, and then diverge to the right from the abandoned Killington carriage road in a swampy glade. Reach the top of the **Bucklin Trail (17.6 mi.)**, which leads 3.3 mi. downhill east to the Wheelerville Road, and bear right to slab through an area of many seeps and brooklets, before reaching the trail's height of land on Snowden Peak (18.4 mi.). Descend to the east of the Killington-Pico ridge before crossing back to the west side of the ridge (18.8 mi.), and then remain nearly level to Jungle Junction and the south end of the **Sherburne Pass Trail (19.9 mi.)**. The name originated with the LT's former junction with Pico's abandoned West Side Trail where the 1938 hurricane left behind a "jungle" of blowdowns. The Sherburne Pass Trail, the former route of the LT, leads north 0.4 mi. to **Pico Camp** and 3.1 mi. to U.S. 4 at Sherburne Pass. Pico Camp, built by the LTP in 1959, is a frame cabin with bunks for twelve. It has a view of Killington Peak directly south and Mt. Ascutney to the southeast. A small spring is located 100 ft. north of the camp on the Sherburne Pass Trail. A GMC caretaker may be present, and an overnight fee may be charged. **Cooper Lodge to Pico Camp, 2.9 mi., 4.7 km., 1¾ hr. (SB 2 hr.).**

From the Sherburne Pass Trail, bear left to wrap around the

west flank of Pico and descend through conifers and then open white birch forest to **Mendon Lookout (21.5 mi.)**. Follow a series of switchbacks down to a **spur (21.8 mi.)** leading west 0.1 mi. to **Churchill Scott Shelter**. This post-and-beam structure, with space for eight, was built by Erik and Laurel Tobiason, the Killington Section, and other GMC volunteers in 2002. It is named for a longtime leader and trail maintainer for the section and dedicated to the memory of Alice H. Ferrance, an AT long-distance hiker, whose family donated funds for the project. The water source is a spring located 450 ft. south of the shelter. The campsite includes a tent platform and an accessible composting privy. A GMC caretaker may be present during the hiking season to help maintain trails and campsites and compost sewage to protect the water quality of the Rutland City watershed. An overnight fee may be charged. **Cooper Lodge to Churchill Scott Shelter, 4.5 mi., 7.2 km., 2¼ hr. (SB 3¼ hr.).**

From the shelter spur, descend to a brook crossing (21.9 mi.), and continue downhill on easy grades to **U.S. 4 (23.7 mi.)**, 1.0 mi. west of Sherburne Pass and the Inn at Long Trail.

Side Trails

Shrewsbury Peak Trail. This trail links the CCC Road south of the Coolidge Range with the LT near Little Killington. The trail starts at a parking lot on the CCC Road 3.0 mi. east of North Shrewsbury, and 3.5 mi. west of Vt. 100. The CCC Road leaves Vt. 100 10.7 mi. north of the junction of Vt. 100 and Vt. 103 and 3.1 mi. south of the junctions of Vt. 100 and U.S. 4. The CCC Road is not maintained in winter.

From the parking lot (0.0 mi., 2336 ft.), climb Russell Hill (0.2 mi.), then descend into a small ravine (0.5 mi.) before ascending to the summit of Shrewsbury Peak (1.8 mi.), where there are views to the south and east. Descend to a junction with the Black Swamp Trail (1.9 mi.), and continue north to a wooded summit (2.0 mi.). Drop into a swale (3.2 mi.) and climb to the northwest, crossing three brooks before turning south to join the LT (4.0 mi., 3500 ft.) on the south slope of Little Killington. **CCC Road to LT, 4.0 mi., 6.8 km., 3¼ hr. (Rev. 2½ hr.).**

BLACK SWAMP TRAIL. This is an easier route from the CCC Road to Shrewsbury Peak and the LT beyond. It begins at the intersection of the Black Swamp and CCC Roads, 4.5 mi. east of North Shrewsbury, 1.3 mi. east of the Shrewsbury Peak Trail, and 2.0 mi. west of Vt. 100. Because this is a spring feeding area for black bears, the Black Swamp Road is gated until at least mid-July. The CCC Road is not maintained in winter.

From the CCC Road (0.0 mi., 2421 ft.) ascend the gravel Black Swamp Road to its end (0.8 mi.). Follow the blazed trail and climb steadily on more primitive woods roads to Shrewsbury Peak Shelter (1.8 mi.), a log lean-to with space for eight, built by the Civilian Conservation Corps. Continue the ascent to the junction with the Shrewsbury Peak Trail (2.1 mi.), 0.1 mi. north of Shrewsbury Peak and 2.1 mi. south of the LT. **CCC Road to Shrewsbury Peak, 2.2 mi., 3.5 km., 1½ hr. (Rev. 1 hr.).**

KILLINGTON SPUR. This trail scrambles up Killington Peak from the LT near Cooper Lodge. The spur bears east from the LT 100 ft. south of Cooper Lodge (0.0 mi., 3900 ft.), and then climbs steeply to the summit (0.2 mi., 4235 ft.).

Killington Peak (4235 ft.) is the second highest mountain in Vermont; only Mt. Mansfield is higher. It is part of the Coolidge Range, which also includes Pico Peak, Mendon Peak, Little Killington, and Shrewsbury Peak. From the summit, a path descends a short distance east to the facilities of the Killington resort. The summit is on a self-guided Killington Ski Area nature trail that starts near the gondola station.

There are views in all directions from the rocky summit of Killington Peak, including all the prominent Green Mountain peaks from Glastenbury Mtn. to Mt. Mansfield. To the southeast is Mt. Ascutney and to the northeast are the White Mountains. To the west are the Taconics, including Bird Mtn. with its precipitous south face, Lake Champlain, and the Adirondacks. To the east is the village of Plymouth where Calvin Coolidge was born and where he was sworn in as president by his father in 1923. **LT to Killington Peak, 0.2 mi., 0.3 km., ⅓ hr. (Rev. ⅓ hr.).**

BUCKLIN TRAIL. This trail ascends the west slope of Killington Peak from the town of Mendon. The trail begins at Brewers Corners on the unpaved Wheelerville Road, 4.0 mi. south of U.S. 4 and 6.5 mi. east of downtown Rutland. From Sherburne Pass follow U.S. 4 west 4.3 mi. then turn south onto the Wheelerville Road. Follow the road 4.0 mi. to a sharp turn, Brewers Corners, and the beginning of the trail. To reach Brewers Corners from Rutland, turn onto Killington Avenue east from U.S. 7 at Christ the King Church, 0.5 mi. south of the junction of U.S. 7 and U.S. 4 East. Turn right at the end of Killington Avenue onto Notch Road. Beyond the end of the pavement, turn left onto Wheelerville Road and follow it 3.1 mi. to the trail. Do not block woods roads when parking.

From Brewers Corners (0.0 mi., 1786 ft.), follow a level woods road, joining the Catamount Trail, and cross a bridge over Brewers Brook (0.2 mi.). Continue east on the woods road while the Catamount Trail bears left, and follow the north side of the brook except where it ascends to a limited view west. Leave the woods road and descend to the second stream crossing (1.2 mi.), challenging except in times of low water. Rejoin the woods road and follow the south side of the brook until turning right (2.0 mi.) to climb steadily out of the valley to meet the LT (3.3 mi.) about 0.1 mi. north of Cooper Lodge and the Killington Spur. **Brewers Corners to LT, 3.3 mi., 5.3 km., 2¾ hr. (Rev. 1¾ hr.).**

SHERBURNE PASS TRAIL (SOUTH OF SHERBURNE PASS). This trail extends north and south from U.S. 4 and is the former, historic route of the LT. It connects with the AT on both sides of the pass, providing an alternate hiking route across U.S. 4. The Sherburne Pass Trail north of Sherburne Pass is described on page 122.

The trailhead is at Sherburne Pass, 9.3 mi. east of U.S. 7 in Rutland, and 1.4 mi. west of Vt. 100 north near the Killington Access Road. There is a large, unpaved parking lot on the south side of the highway, across from the Inn at Long Trail. *Use caution when crossing U.S. 4; traffic moves at high speeds.*

From the highway (0.0 mi., 2150 ft.), follow an old road south from the back of the parking lot. Note that in the woods just west of the parking lot are the ruins of the former Long Trail Lodge, which was sold by GMC in 1954 and destroyed by fire in 1968. Turn right at a trail register (0.1 mi.), enter the woods, and ascend steadily to Sink Hole Brook (1.1 mi.), a permanent stream that disappears into a sink hole beside the trail. Continue uphill to a ski trail, with a wide view of the Green Mountains to the north. Follow the ski trail uphill 300 ft. before turning left to reenter the woods at Pico Junction (2.1 mi.). The Summit Glades and 49er ski trails lead uphill 0.4 mi. to Pico Peak. Proceed south along the rugged route with little change in elevation to pass a spring and then reach Pico Camp and Pico Link (2.5 mi.), which leads uphill to the summit of Pico. Beyond the camp, follow the contour to cross a pipeline clearing (2.7 mi.), and arrive at the LT (3.1 mi., 3480 ft.) at Jungle Junction, 2.5 mi. north of Cooper Lodge and 3.8 mi. south of U.S. 4. **Sherburne Pass south to LT, 3.1 mi., 4.7 km., 2¼ hr. (Rev. 1½ mi.).**

PICO LINK. This route provides access to the summit of Pico Peak from the Sherburne Pass Trail. Enter the woods on the north side of Pico Camp (0.0 mi., 3520 ft.) and climb steeply to the pipeline clearing, and then continue uphill to the open summit of Pico Peak (0.4 mi., 3957 ft.). Note your route carefully after entering the summit ski trails, because blazes may be hard to see when you return. An alternative descent follows the 49er ski trail down to the Summit Glades ski trail leading to the Sherburne Pass Trail at Pico Junction, 0.4 mi. below the summit. **Sherburne Pass Trail to Pico Peak, 0.4 mi., 0.6 km., ½ hr. (Rev. ¼ hr.).**

Wood sorrel and moss

Division 6
U.S. 4 to Brandon Gap

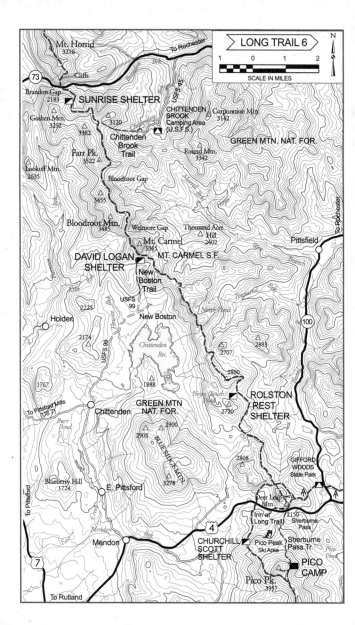

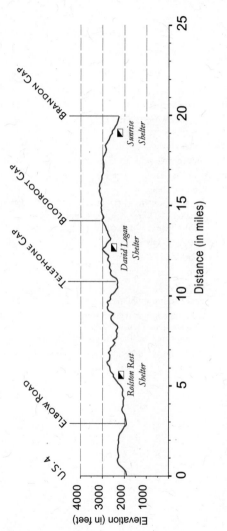

Division 6 Profile

U.S. 4 to Brandon Gap

miles northbound	▲ NORTH	elevation at Long Trail (feet/meters)	miles southbound
19.9	**Vt. 73** at **Brandon Gap**	2183/665	0.0
19.0	**Sunrise Shelter**	2564/782	0.9
17.6	**Chittenden Brook Trail** to **USFS** Road 45, 3.7 mi E	2951/899	2.3
16.2	**Farr Peak**, east ridge	3150/960	3.7
15.7	**Bloodroot Gap**	3110/948	4.2
14.0	**Bloodroot Mtn.**, east ridge	2900/884	5.9
13.2	**Wetmore Gap**	2600/792	6.7
12.7	**New Boston Trail** to **David Logan Shelter** (2620 ft/799 m), 0.2 mi W, to USFS Road 99, 1.2 mi W	2760/841	7.2
10.8	**Telephone Gap**	2300/701	9.1
8.9	**Green Road**	2500/762	11.0
5.0	**Rolston Rest Shelter**	2240/683	14.9
3.3	**Elbow Road**	1951/595	16.6
1.4	**Tucker-Johnson Shelter**	2250/686	18.5
1.0	**Maine Junction** at **Willard Gap**: **Appalachian Trail**; to **U.S. 4** via **Sherburne Pass Trail**, north branch, 1.4 mi	2250/686	18.9
0.0	**U.S. 4** west of Sherburne Pass	1880/573	19.9

SOUTH
▼

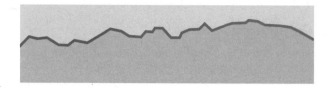

Division 6
U.S. 4 to Brandon Gap

Massachusetts 104.2 miles **Canada 168.5 miles**

Water is scarce between Rolston Rest and David Logan Shelters. Hikers should take advantage of the water sources at these two sites.

South of Wetmore Gap, this division of the Long Trail (LT) passes through some private lands that are managed for timber. Be prepared to encounter logging operations and yield to logging trucks.

The LT and the Appalachian Trail (AT) coincide in Division 6 for 1.0 mile from U.S. 4 to Maine Junction at Willard Gap. Please note that at Willard Gap, three white-blazed trails meet at the junction. The LT north heads north to Canada. The AT north heads *south* and reaches the north end of the Deer Leap Trail in 0.1 mi., and the LT south heads west and descends to U.S. Route 4.

The following people and organizations have contributed to endow the future maintenance of 3 miles of the LT within this division: Ben Rose and Lori Fisher and family, John and Judy Stearns, and the Appalachian Trail Conservancy Biennial Conference 2009.

Note: Tucker Johnson Shelter burned in the spring of 2011. The site shall remain open as a tenting area with plans underway to rebuild the shelter in 2012.

Camping and Fires

This division of the LT crosses federal, state, and private lands. Camping is limited to shelters between Sherburne Pass and Wetmore Gap. Small wood fires, although discouraged, are permitted at the shelters' established fire rings.

From Wetmore Gap to Brandon Gap the trail crosses the Green Mountain National Forest. Primitive off-trail camping with small wood fires is permitted. Refer to Leave No Trace principles (pages 11 to 12) to minimize your impact.

Group Use

Groups hiking this division of the LT may need an Outfitter-Guide Special Use Permit from the Green Mountain National Forest (GMNF). Group tenting space is available at Rolston Rest and David Logan Shelters. Gifford Woods State Park Campground, east of Sherburne Pass on Vt. 100, is available for base camp hiking. GMNF Chittenden Brook Campground, near the trailhead for the Chittenden Brook Trail, is also available for base camp hiking. Refer to group use guidelines (pages 13 to 19) to determine if your group needs a permit.

Suggested Day Hikes

DEER LEAP TRAIL. This circuit hike uses the Sherburne Pass Trail north of U.S. 4, the Deer Leap Trail, and the AT to provide a stunning view of Sherburne Pass and Pico Peak. The side trails are described on pages 122 to 124, and the AT description starts on page 233. Round trip, 3.6 mi., 2½ hr.

CHITTENDEN BROOK TRAIL. This hike alongside a mountain brook leads from USFS Road 45 uphill to the LT. Round trip, 7.4 mi., 4⅓ hr.

Winter Use

This division loses its "green tunnel" aspect after the leaves have fallen. Much of it is suitable for intermediate cross-country skiers. A recommended trip is to follow the LT from Brandon Gap to a suitable halfway point, and then follow your tracks back to Vt. 73. The trailhead parking lot on the south side of Vt. 73 is plowed in winter.

Access to the Long Trail

U.S. 4. Refer to directions on page 102 in Division 5.

Brandon Gap, Vt. 73. The LT crosses this highway 9.2 mi. west of Vt. 100 just south of Rochester and 5.2 mi. east of Forest Dale and 8.2 mi. east of Brandon from U.S. 7. There is a parking lot for thirty cars on the south side of the highway just west of the LT crossing.

Long Trail Description

Cross **U.S. 4 (0.0 mi.)**. *Use caution when crossing U.S. 4; traffic moves at high speeds.* North of the highway, follow the Catamount Trail across a wet area and, after the Catamount Trail diverges west, climb gradually to a view of Pico Peak (0.8 mi.). Continue to **Maine Junction (1.0 mi.) at Willard Gap**. Here the **Appalachian Trail** bears right, toward Gifford Woods State Park and ultimately Katahdin in Maine, while the LT bears left, north, to Canada. A description of the AT from here to the Connecticut River begins on page 242.

From Maine Junction follow an old woods road north on level ground to **Tucker-Johnson Shelter (1.4 mi.)**. This frame shelter, with bunks for eight, was built by the Long Trail Patrol (LTP), Louis Stare, and members of the Killington Section in 1969. It was repaired by the LTP in 2006. It is named for Fred H. Tucker of Boston, a longtime member of the GMC, and for Otto Johnson of Proctor, Vermont, who bequeathed funds for its construction. *Note:* Tucker-Johnson Shelter burned in March 2011 and will be rebuilt. Tenting at the site is allowed. Nearby

Eagle Square Brook furnishes water. **Churchill Scott Shelter to Tucker-Johnson Shelter, 3.4 mi., 5.5 km., 2 hr. (SB 2¼ hr.).**

North from the shelter, cross the brook, and continue, with minor changes in elevation and occasional stretches of rough footing, to the east side of the ridge, reaching the abandoned **Elbow Road (3.3 mi.)** or Chittenden-Pittsfield Road, now an active logging road, at a three-way junction. Follow the middle logging road north, turn right to climb the embankment, and continue without much change in elevation to **Rolston Rest Shelter (5.0 mi.).** This post-and-beam lean-to, with space for eight, is the second shelter at this site and was built by Tom Abbott and GMC volunteers in 2004. The shelter is named for Ben Rolston, a former GMC guidebook editor and trail maintainer. The water source is a small brook that crosses the LT just south of the shelter. **Tucker-Johnson Shelter to Rolston Rest, 3.6 mi., 5.8 km., 2¼ hr. (SB 2¼ hr.).**

Just north of the shelter cross a private road, which descends east to Vt. 100. Climb moderately to the top of a ridge (5.5 mi.), passing west of an unnamed summit (2800 ft.), and continue northwest on or near the ridgeline with occasional views. Leave the crest in a shallow gap (7.2 mi.) to slab the west side of the ridge. In a small rocky gap, cross the abandoned **Green Road (8.9 mi.)** that runs from Chittenden to Pittsfield, which was used as early as 1796 and is now a snowmobile trail. There is a view west of Chittenden Reservoir just north of the road. Slab the west slope and pass about 100 ft. west of an enormous split boulder. Cross to the east side of the ridge, drop to a sag known as **Telephone Gap (10.8 mi.)**, and, swinging back to the

PLAN AHEAD AND PREPARE

Prepare for extreme weather and emergencies;
bring appropriate clothing; carry and know how to use
a map and compass; be able to purify drinking water;
and leave your itinerary with somebody you trust.

northwest, ascend to the west side of the ridge again. Follow a snowmobile trail (11.9 mi.), then ascend the south slope of Mt. Carmel and continue with minor elevation changes along the ridge to the **New Boston Trail (12.7 mi.)**.

This trail descends west 0.2 mi. to David Logan Shelter and 1.2 mi. to USFS Road 99. The shelter is a frame lean-to with bunks for eight. It was built with the help of sixty campers from the Vermont Camping Association under the direction of GMC's George Pearlstein in 1976 and is named in memory of David Logan, an active club member. The shelter was rebuilt by the LTP in 1996 with funds donated by the Logan family. A reliable spring is located 200 ft. north of the shelter along the New Boston Trail. **Rolston Rest Shelter to David Logan Shelter, 7.9 mi., 12.7 km., 5¼ hr. (SB 5¼ hr.).**

Continue north from the trail junction, briefly ascend the west slope of Mt. Carmel, and drop to **Wetmore Gap (13.2 mi.)**. Climb the east ridge of **Bloodroot Mtn. (14.0 mi.)**, and then contour around the east slope of the mountain to **Bloodroot Gap (15.7 mi.)**, another snowmobile trail crossing.

From the gap, slab the east ridge of **Farr Peak (16.2 mi.)**, named for Albert G. Farr of Brandon who supplied the funds to complete the LT between Lincoln and Brandon Gaps. Continue with little change in elevation around the east slope of the peak until reaching the **Chittenden Brook Trail (17.6 mi.)**, which leads 3.7 mi. east to USFS Road 45. Beyond the junction, begin a gradual descent on an old woods road to **Sunrise Shelter (19.0 mi.)**. This frame shelter was built by the LTP in 1964, a gift of Mortimer R. Proctor, governor of Vermont from 1945 to 1947, and former president of the GMC. The shelter has space for eight, and the water source is a brook 200 ft. south on the LT. **David Logan Shelter to Sunrise Shelter, 6.5 mi., 10.5 km., 4 hr. (SB 4 hr.).**

Continue downhill on the old woods road, which is maintained for cross-country skiing south of Brandon Gap. Pass a clearing with a view of the Great Cliff of Mt. Horrid and reach **Brandon Gap at Vt. 73 (19.9 mi.)**. The trailhead parking lot is just west of the LT. *Use caution when crossing Vt. 73; traffic moves at high speeds.* USFS Road 45, which leads to the Chittenden Brook Trail and a Forest Service campground, is 3.7 mi. east.

Side Trails

DEER LEAP TRAIL. This trail leads to the ledge looming over the north side of Sherburne Pass on U.S. 4. The Deer Leap Trail begins and ends on the AT north of its crossing U.S. 4. It is most commonly accessed from the south via the Sherburne Pass Trail, formerly the LT and AT.

From the south, the Deer Leap Trail leaves the AT 220 ft. north of its junction with the Sherburne Pass Trail (0.0 mi., 2290 ft.). Bear west and climb through an attractive birch forest to the Overlook Spur (0.4 mi.). The spur leads 0.2 mi. south to the dramatic rock outcropping visible from the pass below. The outcrop features views of the nearby Coolidge Range and to the west, New York's Adirondacks. Continue north from the spur, drop to a brook (0.5 mi.), climb again to the height of land on Deer Leap Mtn. (0.7 mi.), and then descend gradually to the north junction with the AT (1.3 mi., 2250 ft.), 0.1 mi. south of Willard Gap and 0.8 mi. north of the Sherburne Pass Trail. **Deer Leap Trail from the AT near the Sherburne Pass Trail to the AT near Willard Gap, 1.3 mi., 2.1 km., 1¼ hr. (Rev. 1¼ hr.), to Long Trail at Willard Gap, 1.4 mi. 2.2 km**.

SHERBURNE PASS TRAIL, NORTH OF SHERBURNE PASS. This trail extends north and south from U.S. 4 and is the former, historic route of the LT. It connects with the AT on both sides of the pass, providing an alternate hiking route across U.S. 4. Trailhead directions and a trail description for the Sherburne Pass Trail south of Sherburne Pass are described on page 111.

From U.S. 4 at Sherburne Pass (0.0 mi., 2150 ft.) enter the woods at the east end of the Inn at Long Trail's parking lot and

---

IT'S YOUR DRINKING WATER

Wash dishes and yourself away from the water source. The next person might not like secondhand oatmeal or the taste of detergent.

---

wind uphill to the AT (0.5 mi., 2440 ft.). The south end of the Deer Leap Trail is 220 ft. beyond on the AT. The LT is another 0.9 mi. north at Willard Gap. **Sherburne Pass north to AT, 0.5 mi., 0.8 km., ½ hr. (Rev. ¼ hr.). Sherburne Pass north to LT, 1.4 mi., 2.3 km., 1 hr. (Rev. ¾ hr.).**

APPALACHIAN TRAIL. This trail serves as access to the LT from Vt. 100 near Gifford Woods State Park. It is important to note that the AT is the only white-blazed side trail of the LT. See Kent Pond Fishing Access Trailhead directions on page 233. From the parking lot, carefully cross Vt. 100 (0.0 mi., 1580 ft.) and follow the white blazes through the campground. Enter the woods from the upper campground (0.3) and climb steadily to the spur (1.1 mi.) leading 50 ft. to Ben's Balcony with views of Pico and Killington. Continue west, descending gently to the junction with the Sherburne Pass Trail (1.4 mi.) leading south 0.5 mile to U.S. 4 at Sherburne Pass next to the Inn at Long Trail. Slab the east side of Deer Leap Mountain, passing two junctions with the Deer Leap Trail, and reach the LT at Willard Gap (2.3 mi.). From here the LT coincides with the AT south for approximately 105 miles to Massachusetts, while the LT north leads nearly 170 miles to Canada. **Kent Pond Fishing Access to LT at Willard Gap via AT, 2.3 mi. 3.7 km, 1¾ hr. (Rev. 1¼ hr.).**

NEW BOSTON TRAIL. From the Civil War monument in Chittenden (0.0 mi.) follow the road to Mountain Top Ski Touring Center 1.8 mi. north to a fork in the road just beyond Mountain Top Inn. Continue straight ahead on the right-hand fork on the unpaved town road to a small pullout (2.4 mi.) on the right. Here the road becomes USFS Road 99. Continue past USFS Road 99A to a primitive campsite with a privy at the trailhead (3.7 mi.).

From the trailhead (0.0 mi., 1940 ft.), bear left off the logging road and ascend on a woods road for 0.75 mi. to a fork. Here the Mt. Carmel snowmobile trail follows the wide woods road to the right. Continue straight, uphill, on an old woods road and climb steadily to David Logan Shelter (1.0 mi.). Just above the shelter pass a piped spring to the left, and arrive at the LT (1.2 mi.). **USFS Road 99 to LT, 1.2 mi., 1.9 km., 1¼ hr. (Rev. ¾ hr.).**

CHITTENDEN BROOK TRAIL. Located in the Chittenden Brook Recreation Area (named for Vermont's first governor, Thomas Chittenden), this trail offers a pleasant approach to the LT as well as some good hiking and skiing loops with other trails in the recreation area. From Vt. 100 near Rochester, follow Vt. 73 west 5.5 mi. and turn south onto USFS Road 45. Continue 0.6 mi. on this road to the trailhead parking area. The USFS Chittenden Brook Campground is another 1.7 mi. up the road from the trailhead. USFS Road 45 is not maintained for winter travel.

From the trailhead lot (0.0 mi., 1395 ft.), follow the stream on old woods roads and climb steadily through spruce and fir forest, passing a cross-country trail on the right, and reach the Beaver Pond Spur (1.7 mi.), which leads to a wetland with the chance to see beaver, tree swallows, and the occasional moose. After crossing a major branch of the brook, pass a short spur (1.9 mi., 1763 ft.) leading left to the campground, cut across the last of the cross-country ski loops (2.2 mi.), and then climb steadily to the LT (3.7 mi.). **USFS Road 45 to LT, 3.7 mi., 6.0 km., 2⅓ hr. (Rev. 2 hr.).**

Looking north

Division 7
Brandon Gap to
Cooley Glen

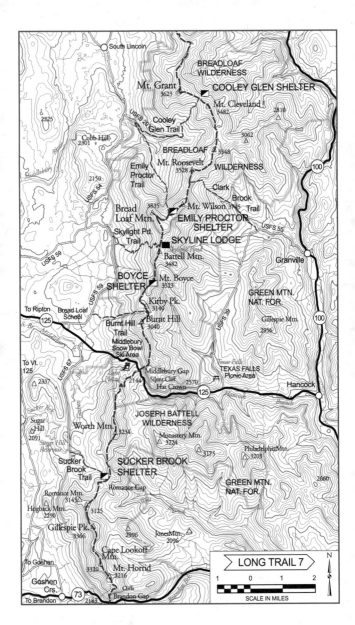

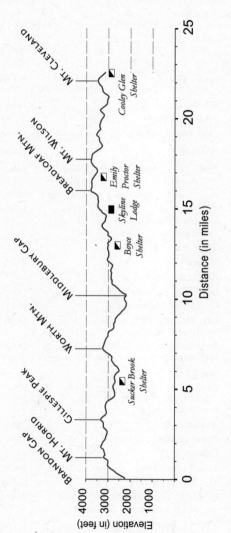

Division 7 Profile

Distance (in miles)

Elevation (in feet)

BRANDON GAP
MT. HORRID
GILLESPIE PEAK
WORTH MTN.
MIDDLEBURY GAP
BREADLOAF MTN.
MT. WILSON
MT. CLEVELAND

Sucker Brook Shelter
Boyce Shelter
Skyline Lodge
Emily Proctor Shelter
Cooley Glen Shelter

Brandon Gap to Cooley Glen

miles north-bound	▲ NORTH	elevation at Long Trail (feet/meters)	miles south-bound
22.5	**Cooley Glen Trail** 3.2 mi W to USFS Road 201, **Cooley Glen Shelter**	3130/954	0.0
22.0	**Mt. Cleveland**	3482/1061	0.5
20.3	**Little Hans Peak**	3348/1020	2.2
18.5	**Clark Brook Trail** to USFS Road 55, 3.0 mi E	3390/1033	4.0
17.7	**Mt. Wilson**	3745/1141	4.8
16.8	**Emily Proctor Shelter; Emily Proctor Trail** to USFS Road 201, 3.5 mi W	3460/1055	5.7
16.2	**Breadloaf Mtn.** to vista, 0.1 mi W via spur	3835/1169	6.3
15.0	**Skylight Pond Trail** to **Skyline Lodge** (3380 ft/1030 m), 0.1 mi E; to USFS Road 59, 2.5 mi W	3420/1042	7.5
13.9	**Mt. Boyce**	3323/1013	8.6
13.0	**Boyce Shelter**	3020/920	9.5
12.4	**Burnt Hill Trail** to USFS Road 59, 2.2 mi W	2950/899	10.1
10.3	**Silent Cliff Trail** to vista, 0.4 mi E	2480/756	12.2
9.9	**Vt. 125** at Middlebury Gap	2144/653	12.6
9.5	**Lake Pleiad** (2128 ft/649 m), 0.1 mi. W via spur	2150/655	13.0
8.9	**Middlebury Snow Bowl; Worth Mtn. Lodge** (2450 ft/747 m), 0.2 mi W via ski slope	2640/805	13.6
7.2	**Worth Mtn.**	3234/986	15.3
5.4	**Sucker Brook Trail** to **Sucker Brook Shelter** (2420 ft/738 m), 0.1 mi W; to USFS Road 67, 1.0 mi W	2440/744	17.1
4.5	**Romance Gap**	2685/818	18.0
4.1	**Romance Mtn.**, east summit	3125/953	18.4
3.3	**Gillespie Peak**	3366/1026	19.2
1.8	**Cape Lookoff Mtn.**	3320/1012	20.7
1.3	**Mt. Horrid**	3216/980	21.2
0.7	**Great Cliff of Mt. Horrid** (2860 ft/872 m), 0.1 mi E via spur	2760/841	21.8
0.0	**Vt. 73** at **Brandon Gap**	2183/665	22.5

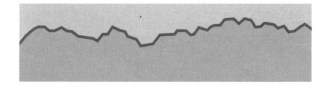

Division 7
Brandon Gap to Cooley Glen

Massachusetts: 124.1 miles   **Canada: 148.6 miles**

This division of the Long Trail (LT) remains on or near the ridgeline. Water is scarce and hikers should take advantage of sources noted in the text.

From Brandon Gap to the top of Middlebury Snow Bowl, the LT traverses the Joseph Battell Wilderness, established by the New England Wilderness Act of 2006; a provision of the act provides for the perpetuation of shelters along the LT.

From Middlebury Gap to Cooley Glen, the LT traverses the Breadloaf Wilderness. Refer to wilderness information on pages 8 to 9. The halfway point of the LT is just south of the Burnt Hill Trail Jct., 12.2 mi. north of Brandon Gap.

The following people and organizations have contributed to endow the future maintenance of 3 miles of the LT within this division: Ed Amidon and Louise McCarren, Eastern Mountain Sports, and Dan and Mary Dempsey and family.

Camping and Fires

This division of the LT crosses the Green Mountain National Forest (GMNF) from Brandon Gap to Worth Mtn. and from Middlebury Gap to Cooley Glen. Primitive off-trail camping with small wood fires is allowed. Refer to Leave No Trace principles (pages 11 to 12) to minimize your impact.

Note: Camping within 500 ft. of Skylight Pond is limited to Skyline Lodge (tenting around the pond is prohibited), and wood fires are prohibited within 500 ft. of Skylight Pond. The designated tenting area for Skyline Lodge is on the LT just south of the Skylight Pond Trail junction. Campers are requested to use the composting privy for the lodge to protect water quality.

Between Worth Mtn. and Middlebury Gap, the LT traverses private Middlebury College property; camping and fires are prohibited along this portion of the trail, and hikers are asked to stay off and away from chairlift equipment and all other buildings. From May 1 to October 31, LT hikers can stay at Middlebury College's Worth Mtn. Lodge, which is 0.2 mi. west of the LT from the upper chairlift station of the Snow Bowl.

Suggested Day Hikes

LAKE PLEIAD. This out-and-back hike follows the LT south from Middlebury Gap and the spur to Lake Pleiad and is especially suitable for children. Round trip, 1.0 mi., 1½ hr.

MT. HORRID'S GREAT CLIFF. This climb on the LT north from Brandon Gap provides a sweeping view south from its precipitous heights. The cliffs may be closed to hikers from March 15 to August 1 because they are a prime peregrine falcon nesting site. In recent years, the falcons have nested far to the east of the hiking trails, and the cliffs have remained open. However, if falcons return to nest near the trails, the spur to the cliff will be closed until August 1. Round trip, 1.4 mi., 1¼ hr.

MT. ROOSEVELT. This trip follows the Clark Brook Trail and LT into the Breadloaf Wilderness to an open ledge just north of the summit. Round trip, 6.8 mi., 4½ hr.

Note: Worth Mtn. Lodge will be closed for repairs for 2011. Look for updates concerning future use of Worth Mtn. Lodge at trailhead bulletin boards and at www.greenmountainclub.org.

Group Use

Groups hiking this division of the LT may need an Outfitter-Guide Special Use Permit from the GMNF. Groups can stay at Worth Mtn. Lodge. (*Note:* Worth Mtn. Lodge will be closed for repairs for 2011. Refer to camping and fires section above.) Tenting at Middlebury College's Snow Bowl is not permitted. Group tenting space is available at Emily Proctor and Cooley Glen Shelters. Primitive campsites are also available at the trailheads for the Sucker Brook, Skylight Pond, Clark Brook, and Cooley Glen Trails. GMNF Chittenden Brook Campground, near the trailhead for the Chittenden Brook Trail east of Brandon Gap, is available for base camp hiking. Refer to pages 13 to 19 for additional group use guidelines.

Winter Use

All suggested hikes in this division are suitable as snowshoe treks. Most of the terrain is too rugged for beginner and intermediate cross-country skiers. Winter trail navigation is challenging in Wilderness Areas due to less-frequent blazing. Map and compass skills are recommended.

Access to the Long Trail

Vt. 73 at Brandon Gap. Refer to directions on page 119 in Division 6.

Vt. 125 at Middlebury Gap. This LT crossing is 2.5 mi. east of Middlebury College's Bread Loaf Campus, 5.6 mi. east of Ripton, and 10.1 mi. east of the junction with U.S. 7, south of Middlebury. It is also 6.2 mi. west of Vt. 100 in Hancock. There is a large area for pull-off parking on the highway's south shoulder.

MUD SEASON

The Green Mountain Club requests that hikers avoid higher elevation trails during the spring mud season (late March through the end of May). Snowmelt creates extremely muddy trails and makes them vulnerable to damage from foot traffic, often compounded when hikers walk beside the trail to avoid the mud.

Spring and Fall Hiking Guidelines

- If a trail is so muddy that you need to walk on the vegetation beside it, turn back and seek an alternative area to hike.
- Hike in the hardwood forest at lower elevations.
- Trails on state lands are closed from April 15 through the Friday of Memorial Day weekend: Coolidge State Forest, Camel's Hump State Park, Mansfield State Forest, Long Trail State Forest, and Jay State Forest.
- Late fall and winter thaws can present similar

Long Trail Description

Cross **Vt. 73 at Brandon Gap (0.0 mi.)**. *Use caution when crossing Vt. 73; traffic moves at high speeds.* Climb up an old road, reenter the woods, and ascend steadily on a trail rebuilt by the Long Trail Patrol (LTP) and Forest Service trail crews in the mid-1990s. At the top of a rock staircase, a **spur (0.7 mi.)** leads east 0.1 mi. to the **Great Cliff of Mt. Horrid**. The cliff top, 600 ft. above the road, provides a view of the gap and the mountains to the south. The spur may be closed between March 15 and August 1 to prevent disturbance of nesting peregrine falcons. Continue west of the ridge to the summit of **Mt. Horrid (1.3 mi.)**, and then along the wooded ridge to **Cape Lookoff Mtn. (1.8 mi.)** and **Gillespie Peak (3.3 mi.)**. There are many vistas along this ridge.

North from Gillespie Peak (formerly White Rocks Mtn.) to Mt. Wilson, the LT traverses forest land bequeathed to Middlebury College in 1915 by Col. Joseph Battell. The college still owns 700 acres at the Snow Bowl ski area, including 1.8 mi. of the LT and Lake Pleiad; the remainder is now part of the GMNF. Battell established the Bread Loaf Inn west of Middlebury Gap, now used as Middlebury College's Bread Loaf Campus. He also cut a trail from Mt. Abraham north to Mt. Ellen in 1901.

From Gillespie Peak, follow the ridge north, passing a spur to a view west just before reaching the east summit of **Romance Mtn. (4.1 mi.)**. Switchback down to **Romance Gap (4.5 mi.)** and continue west of the ridge to a junction with the **Sucker Brook Trail (5.4 mi.)**, which leads west 0.1 mi. to **Sucker Brook Shelter** and 1.0 mi. west to USFS Road 67. This frame shelter, which sleeps eight, was built by the U.S. Forest Service in 1963. Future maintenance of Sucker Brook Shelter has been endowed by Warren and Barry King in honor of Robert S. Schultz and in memory of Jane S. Schultz. The water source is Sucker Brook, 50 ft. farther down the Sucker Brook Trail. **Sunrise Shelter to Sucker Brook Shelter, 6.4 mi., 10.3 km., 4 hr. (SB 4¼ hr.).**

From the Sucker Brook Trail junction, climb gradually up the ridge of Worth Mtn. passing by vistas to the south and west.

7

Continue the moderate ascent, passing two vistas to the east, before reaching the wooded summit of **Worth Mtn. (7.2 mi.)**. From the summit, follow the ridge, passing Eastern Lookout, then descend moderately, passing over a couple of minor summits until reaching the clearing for **Middlebury Snow Bowl's** upper chairlift station **(8.9 mi.)**. There are views to the north and east. **Worth Mtn. Lodge**, 0.2 mi. west of the LT down the ski slope just beyond the chairlift station, is open to the public for camping from May 1 to October 31. (**Note:** Worth Mtn. Lodge will be closed for repairs for 2011.) Refer to camping and fires section on pages 129 to 130. Camping on the ski trails is prohibited. Pass to the west of the chairlift on a ski trail and descend steadily, continuing to follow and cross ski trails several times. Pay close attention to blazes and signs. At the bottom of the descent, cross a small brook at a junction with a **spur (9.5 mi.)** leading west 0.1 mi. to **Lake Pleiad**.

Pass over a low ridge to **Vt. 125 at Middlebury Gap (9.9 mi.)**. The Snow Bowl entrance is 0.7 mi. west and U.S. 7 south of Middlebury is 10.1 mi. west. Vt. 100 in Hancock is 6.4 mi. east.

Cross the highway. *Use caution when crossing Vt. 125; traffic moves at high speeds.* Climb the road embankment and enter the Breadloaf Wilderness at its south boundary. The LT may be more challenging to follow in the Wilderness Area due to minimal brushing and blazing. Climb steadily to a junction with the **Silent Cliff Trail (10.3 mi.)**, which leads east 0.4 mi. to the vista at Silent Cliff. North of the trail junction, ascend to the ridge (10.8 mi.), continue to Burnt Hill, then descend to the west side of the ridge and a junction with the **Burnt Hill Trail (12.4 mi.)**, which descends west 2.2 mi. to USFS Road 59. From the junction, follow the rugged west slope of Kirby Peak (12.6 mi.), before descending to **Boyce Shelter (13.0 mi.)**. This frame shelter, with space for eight, was built by the U.S. Forest Service in 1963. A small, unreliable brook 200 ft. north via the LT supplies water. **Sucker Brook Shelter to Boyce Shelter, 7.7 mi., 12.4 km., 5¼ hr. (SB 5½ hr.)**

Beyond the shelter, climb **Mt. Boyce (13.9 mi.)** and continue along the ridge over Battell Mtn. (14.9 mi.), to reach an established tenting area with a spur leading west to a vista at Sunset Rock. Descend to a junction with the **Skylight Pond**

Trail (**15.0 mi.**), which descends west 2.5 mi. to USFS Road 59 and east 0.1 mi. to **Skyline Lodge** at Skylight Pond.

Skyline Lodge, an enclosed shelter with bunk space for fourteen, was built by the GMC and U.S. Forest Service in 1987. Future maintenance of Skyline Lodge has been endowed by the Olsen family and Peregrine Outfitters. The lodge sits on a steep hillside overlooking shallow Skylight Pond, which is not suitable for fishing or swimming. Water is available from a spring 250 ft. north of the shelter. The area around the pond is vulnerable to resource damage. There is sometimes a caretaker on duty at Skylight Pond. The caretaker composts sewage to protect water quality; a fee is charged for overnight use when a caretaker is present. Tenting is not allowed in the vicinity of the pond, the designated tenting area for Skyline Lodge is on the LT just south of the Skyline Pond Trail junction. Wood fires are not allowed within 500 ft. of the pond to permit the surrounding forest to recover from years of tree and branch cutting by campers. **Boyce Shelter to Skyline Lodge, 2.1 mi., 3.4 km., 1½hr. (SB 1¼ hr.).**

From the junction, follow the ridge north and begin a steep ascent to the top of the ridge on **Breadloaf Mtn. (16.2 mi.).** At a sharp turn to the right, a spur leads west, 0.1 mi. to a western vista just beyond the summit of the mountain. Follow the rugged path downhill to cross a brook just before reaching **Emily Proctor Shelter** and the **Emily Proctor Trail (16.8 mi.),** which descends 3.5 mi. west to USFS Road 201 out of South Lincoln.

Emily Proctor Shelter, a log lean-to with space for five, was built by the LTP in 1960, rebuilt by the U.S. Forest Service in 1983, and rebuilt again by the LTP to replace rotten sill logs in 2002. The brook crossed by the LT just south of the shelter provides water and may be the most reliable water source on the LT in the Breadloaf Wilderness. There are two tent platforms and a privy on spurs north of the shelter. **Skyline Lodge to Emily Proctor Shelter, 1.9 mi., 3.1 km., 1¾ hr. (SB 1¼ hr.).**

Turn sharp right at the north end of the shelter, enter the woods, and ascend steadily to the ridge. Continue along the crest to **Mt. Wilson (17.7 mi.),** where a short spur leads east to a summit vista with views to the south and east. Leave the summit and descend steadily to a sag between Mt. Wilson and Mt. Roosevelt, and then continue to a junction with the **Clark Brook Trail (18.5 mi.)**. This trail leads east downhill 3.0 mi. to USFS Road 55.

From the trail junction, ascend Mt. Roosevelt (18.9 mi.); just beyond is a rock outcrop, Killington View, with sweeping views to the south and east. From here, descend then traverse a series of knobs along the northeast ridge of Mt. Roosevelt before dropping to a sag and crossing a small seep. Reach wooded **Little Hans Peak (20.3 mi.)** before dropping steadily and then climbing to the wooded summit of **Mt. Cleveland (22.0 mi.)**. Descend gradually to a sharp right turn, and then drop steeply to the junction with the **Cooley Glen Trail (22.5 mi.)**, which leads 3.2 mi. west to USFS Road 201, where it shares a trailhead with the Emily Proctor Trail. **Cooley Glen Shelter** is a short distance farther north on the Long Trail.

A frame lean-to with room for eight, Cooley Glen Shelter was built by the U.S. Forest Service in 1965. A spring is located 600 ft. west on the Cooley Glen Trail. **Emily Proctor Shelter to Cooley Glen Shelter, 5.7 mi., 9.2 km., 3¾ hr. (SB 3¾ hr.).**

Side Trails

Sucker Brook Trail. This trailhead is at the end of USFS Road 67 (Brooks Road) 3.8 mi. south of Vt. 125. USFS Road 67 starts 3.5 mi. east of Ripton or 0.5 mi. east of Middlebury College's Bread Loaf Campus, and 8.5 mi. west of Vt. 100 in Hancock or 2.1 mi. west of the LT crossing in Middlebury Gap. The road may be gated near its beginning during spring and fall mud seasons. *Note:* USFS 67 is only maintained about 0.25 mi. in from Vt. 125 in winter. There is parking for several cars at a USFS primitive campsite at the end of the road where the trail begins (0.0 mi., 2020 ft.). Enter the Joseph Battell Wilderness, follow old logging roads west, and ascend gently, then more steadily, to Sucker Brook Shelter (0.9 mi.). Beyond the shelter, climb to the LT junction. **USFS Road 67 to LT, 1.0 mi., 1.6 km., ¾ hr. (Rev. ½ hr.).**

Silent Cliff Trail. This spur leaves the LT 0.4 mi. north of Middlebury Gap and leads east 0.4 mi. to Silent Cave and Silent Cliff. Monastery Gap and the Green Mountains beyond are visible to the south from the cliff. **LT to Silent Cliff, 0.4 mi., 0.6 km., ¼ hr. (Rev. ¼ hr.).**

BURNT HILL TRAIL. This trail begins on the east side of USFS Road 59, 1.1 mi. north of Vt. 125. USFS Road 59 (Steam Mill Road) is 2.7 mi. east of Ripton and 0.2 mi. west of Bread Loaf Campus. There is a small grassy parking lot just off the road at the trailhead (0.0 mi., 1640 ft.). Follow an old woods road where the trail coincides with the Norske Ski Trail. At an intersection (0.7 mi.) at the crest of a rise, turn left and ascend on an old logging road, where the Norske Ski Trail descends straight ahead. Enter the Breadloaf Wilderness (1.0 mi.) and climb steadily to the LT. **USFS Road 59 to LT, 2.2 mi., 3.5 km., 1¾ hr. (Rev. 1 hr.).**

SKYLIGHT POND TRAIL. This trail starts at a primitive campsite on the east side of USFS Road 59 (Steam Mill Road), 3.6 mi. north of Vt. 125. Refer to directions for the Burnt Hill Trail. There is a large gravel parking lot at the trailhead. USFS Road 59 is not plowed north of the Burnt Hill Trail in winter. From the parking lot (0.0 mi., 1960 ft.), which is also a primitive campsite, ascend gently on an old woods road and cross two small streams (the upper crossing over a bridge), before entering Breadloaf Wilderness (0.4 mi.). Continue uphill on long, sweeping switchbacks, ascending moderately to the LT (2.5 mi.), 0.1 mi. west of Skyline Lodge. Continue down the east side of the ridge 0.1 mi. to Skyline Lodge at Skylight Pond. **USFS Road 59 to Skylight Pond, 2.6 mi., 4.2 km., 2 hr. (Rev. 1¾ hr.).**

EMILY PROCTOR TRAIL. This trailhead, shared with the Cooley Glen Trail, is reached via USFS Roads 54 and 201. From the north, follow USFS Road 54 (South Lincoln Road) south off Lincoln Gap Road, 1.2 mi. east of Lincoln, and 3.5 mi. west of the LT crossing in Lincoln Gap. Continue through South Lincoln, then bear left onto USFS Road 201, 4.2 mi. from Lincoln Gap Road. Follow USFS Road 201 east 0.3 mi. to the trailhead and a USFS primitive campsite, where there is parking at a turn-around. From the south, follow USFS Road 59 north either from Ripton or near Middlebury College's Breadloaf Campus (refer to directions for the Burnt Hill Trail). From USFS Road

7

59 take USFS Road 54 north to USFS Road 201. USFS Road 201 is not maintained in winter. The Emily Proctor Trail and the Cooley Glen Trail share this trailhead.

From the trailhead (0.0 mi., 1520 ft.), turn right and ascend on a logging road, cross the edge of a clear-cut, and follow an older woods road, entering Breadloaf Wilderness (0.6 mi.). Leave the old road (1.4 mi.), and stay on the west side of the New Haven River, before crossing it on some large rocks. After crossing two small streams, make a steady, rocky ascent to the clearing in front of Emily Proctor Shelter (3.5 mi.) at the LT. **USFS Road 201 to LT, 3.5 mi., 5.6 km., 2¾ hr. (Rev. 1¾ hr.).**

CLARK BROOK TRAIL. From Vt. 100 at the north end of Granville take USFS Road 55 (West Hill Road) west. At a gated road (0.5 mi.), bear left and continue on USFS Road 55. Follow this road 1.3 mi., ignoring three right-hand turns, before reaching the trailhead shortly after a sharp left turn over a bridge above Clark Brook. There is roadside parking adjacent to a USFS primitive campsite. USFS Road 55 is not plowed in winter. Leave the road (0.0 mi., 1331 ft.) and ascend gently along Clark Brook, crossing it twice, and then enter Breadloaf Wilderness (1.1 mi.). After a brook crossing (2.5 mi.), the ascent becomes steeper and rockier before reaching the LT (3.0 mi.). **USFS 55 to LT, 3.0 mi., 4.8 km., 2¾ hr. (Rev. 1½ hr.).**

COOLEY GLEN TRAIL. This trail shares a trailhead with the Emily Proctor Trail. Refer to directions for the Emily Proctor Trail. From the turn-around (0.0 mi., 1520 ft.), follow the extension of USFS Road 201 to a bridge crossing of the New Haven River (0.4 mi.). Pass through a clearing, and then stay on the north bank of the river. Enter the Breadloaf Wilderness (1.6 mi.) shortly after a brook crossing. Ascend the west flank of Mt. Cleveland and, after passing a spring (3.1 mi.) that provides water for Cooley Glen Shelter, reach the LT (3.2 mi.) in Cooley Glen just south of the shelter. **USFS Road 201 to LT, 3.2 mi., 5.1 km., 2½ hr. (Rev. 1¾ hr.).**

Birch Glen Camp

Division 8
Cooley Glen to Birch Glen

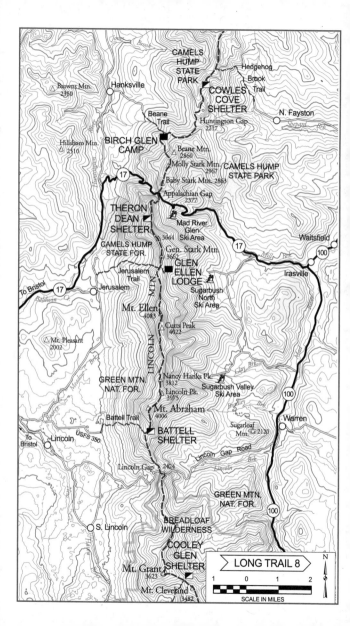

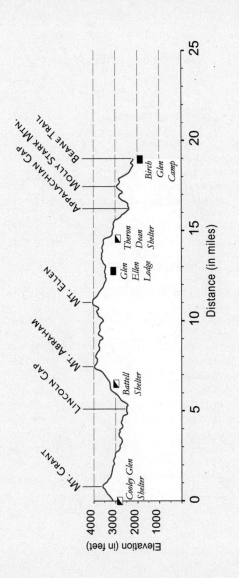

Division 8 Profile

Cooley Glen to Birch Glen

miles north-bound	▲ NORTH	elevation at Long Trail (feet/meters)	miles south-bound
18.9	**Beane Trail** to **Birch Glen Camp** 100 ft W, to Carse Road, 1.5 mi W	2020/616	0.0
17.6	**Molly Stark's Balcony**	2900/884	1.3
16.7	**Baby Stark Mtn.**, east slope	2807/856	2.2
16.3	**Vt. 17** at **Appalachian Gap**	2377/725	2.6
14.5	**Theron Dean Shelter**; 25 ft W via spur	3320/1012	4.4
13.8	**Stark's Nest**, Mad River Glen single chairlift station	3644/1111	5.1
13.2	**General Stark Mtn.**, highest summit	3662/1117	5.7
12.9	**Barton Trail** to **Glen Ellen Lodge** (3250 ft/991 m) 0.3 mi E	3430/1046	6.0
12.8	**Jerusalem Trail** to Jim Dwire Road, 2.4 mi W	3430/1046	6.1
11.4	**Green Mountain National Forest** north boundary	3800/1159	7.5
11.0	**Mt. Ellen**, Sugarbush Mt. Ellen upper chairlift	4083/1245	7.9
9.4	**Castlerock chairlift**	3750/1144	9.5
8.1	**Lincoln Peak**	3975/1212	10.8
7.3	**Mt. Abraham**	4006/1222	11.6
6.5	**Battell Shelter**	3240/988	12.4
6.4	**Battell Trail** to USFS Road 350, 2.0 mi W	3220/982	12.5
4.7	**Lincoln Gap Road** at **Lincoln Gap**	2424/739	14.2
3.6	**Sunset Ledge**	2811/857	15.3
0.8	**Mt. Grant**	3623/1105	18.1
0.0	**Cooley Glen Trail** 3.2 mi W to **USFS** Road 201, **Cooley Glen Shelter**	3130/954	18.9

SOUTH
▼

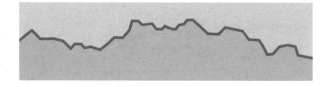

Division 8
Cooley Glen to Birch Glen

Massachusetts: 146.6 miles   **Canada: 126.1 miles**

This division of the Long Trail (LT) remains on or near the ridgeline. Water is scarce and hikers should take advantage of sources noted in the text. It also crosses Mt. Abraham, one of three summits along the route with alpine plants. Please take care to do the "rock walk" and tread only on the rocks, not the plants.

From Cooley Glen to Lincoln Gap, the LT traverses the Breadloaf Wilderness. Refer to wilderness information on pages 8 to 9.

The LT from Lincoln Gap north to the Winooski River is called the Monroe Skyline in honor of Prof. Will S. Monroe who led the building of this section of the trail.

Mad River Glen Ski Area generously allows hikers to use Stark's Nest, their ski patrol warming hut; this use depends on respect for the facility, and its status is subject to change.

The following people and organizations have contributed to endow the future maintenance of 8.5 miles of the LT within this division: Cecilia Elwert, Geordie Hall, Terry Edelstein in memory of Debby Edelstein, Winifred Vogt in memory of Roy S. Vogt, Stark Mountain Foundation, and gifts in memory of Billy Greene.

8

Camping and Fires

This division of the LT is in the Green Mountain National Forest (GMNF) from Cooley Glen to the forest boundary north of Mt. Ellen. Primitive off-trail camping with small wood fires is allowed. Refer to Leave No Trace principles (pages 11 to 12) to minimize your impact.

Note: Wood fires are prohibited within 500 ft. of Battell Shelter to protect high-elevation spruce-fir forest. Camping and wood fires are prohibited on the summit of Mt. Abraham to protect the alpine plant community.

North of Mt. Ellen, the LT crosses state and private land. Camping is limited to shelters. Wood fires are prohibited at Glen Ellen Lodge and Theron Dean Shelter due to their sensitive, high-elevation settings. Small wood fires, although discouraged, are permitted at Birch Glen Camp.

Group Use

Groups hiking this division's LT south of Mt. Ellen may need an Outfitter-Guide Special Use Permit from the GMNF. Groups hiking this division's Long Trail north of Stark's Nest may need

Suggested Day Hikes

MOLLY STARK'S BALCONY. This hike follows the LT north from Appalachian Gap to a lookout with views to the north. Round trip, 2.6 mi., 2 hr.

MT. ELLEN. South on the LT from Appalachian Gap, this wooded summit features views from its upper slopes. Round trip, 10.6 mi., 6½ hr. A shorter trip to Mt. Ellen uses the Jerusalem Trail and the LT south. Round trip, 8.4 mi., 5½ hr.

a Commercial Use Permit from the Vermont Department of Forests, Parks and Recreation. Groups can stay at Stark's Nest if available. Group tenting space is available at Cooley Glen Shelter and Birch Glen Camp. Primitive campsites are also available at the trailhead for the Cooley Glen Trail. Refer to group use guidelines (pages 13 to 19) to determine whether your group needs a permit.

Winter Use

The suggested hikes for the north end of this division make challenging snowshoe treks. The summit of Mt. Abraham is more readily accessible from the Battell Trail to the west than the LT because the upper portions of the Lincoln Gap Road leading to the LT are not plowed in winter. Although the LT crosses the Catamount Trail at Lincoln Gap, the rugged terrain the LT traverses is not suitable for beginner or intermediate cross-country skiers. See Catamount Trail information on page 27.

Access to the Long Trail

LINCOLN GAP ROAD AT LINCOLN GAP. The LT crosses this steep, winding road at Lincoln Gap, 4.7 mi. east of Lincoln and 8.1 mi. east of its junction with Vt. 17 and Vt. 116 in Bristol. The crossing is also 4.7 mi. west of Vt. 100 in Warren. There is roadside parking at the crossing and a large secondary parking lot just east of the trail on the road's south side. This trailhead is heavily used during the hiking season; however, long-term parking is not recommended. The road through Lincoln Gap is closed during winter.

VT. 17 AT APPALACHIAN GAP. The LT intersects this highway at Appalachian Gap, 1.4 mi. west of Mad River Glen Ski Area, 6.0 mi. west of Vt. 100 in Irasville, and 9.5 mi. east of Vt. 116. There is a large parking lot on the north side of the road just west of the LT. Vt. 17 is open year-round, subject to winter weather conditions.

Long Trail Description

From **Cooley Glen Shelter (0.0 mi.)** to Lincoln Gap, the LT traverses the Breadloaf Wilderness, where it may be more challenging to follow due to minimal brushing and blazing. Ascend northwest to the summit of **Mt. Grant (0.8 mi.)**, where there is a broad view south into the heart of the Breadloaf Wilderness. From the summit, descend steadily along the ridge through a hardwood forest before following a series of switchbacks downhill to a sag (2.9 mi.). Climb out of the sag, cross some open areas and ledges with views to the south and east, then traverse a short ridge and drop down to another sag. After ascending to a smaller open area with views to the south, arrive at **Sunset Ledge (3.6 mi.)**, which has an expansive western vista. Continue along the ridge, then drop steeply to the north boundary of the Breadloaf Wilderness and cross Lincoln Gap Road at **Lincoln Gap (4.7 mi.)**.

Climb north out of Lincoln Gap, bear to the west of a knoll, and begin a steady ascent, passing en route the Carpenters (5.9 mi.), two huge boulders named after a pair of trail workers. Soon after crossing a brook, reach a junction where the **Battell Trail (6.4 mi.)** descends west 2.0 mi. to USFS Road 350. Turn right and climb to **Battell Shelter (6.5 mi.)**. This shelter, a frame structure built by Farm and Wilderness Camp volunteers in 1967, sleeps eight. Joe and Cathy Frank have endowed the future maintenance of Battell Shelter, where they first met each other. Water is from a small spring 100 ft. to the east. A caretaker may be in seasonal residence during the hiking season to help protect the alpine plants on Mt. Abraham, assist and educate hikers, help maintain trails and campsites, and compost sewage to protect water quality. A fee is charged for overnight use. Wood fires are not allowed within 500 ft. of the shelter. Tenting near Battell Shelter is very limited. **Cooley Glen Shelter to Battell Shelter, 6.5 mi., 10.5 km., 4¼ hr. (SB 4¼ hr.).**

Bear north from the shelter and follow an old road for the initially gradual, then steep, ascent of Mt. Abraham. Scramble up bare ledge in places; extra care should be used in wet weather. The alpine summit of **Mt. Abraham (7.3 mi.)** offers one of the best panoramas on the entire LT, ranging from nearby valley farms to New Hampshire's White Mountains, 80 miles east. Due west is Mt. Marcy and its Adirondack neighbors. To the south the Green Mountains may be visible as far south as Killington Peak. To the north, though partly hidden by nearby higher peaks, the Greens may be visible as far as Belvidere Mtn.

The summit of Mt. Abe is above treeline and supports a small community of alpine vegetation, one of only three such communities along the LT. The fragile alpine plants do not tolerate foot traffic. They are damaged when hikers stray from the trail. Above treeline, take care to walk only on the rocks. Please leash dogs. Camping and wood fires are prohibited on the summit of Mt. Abraham.

Enter the woods, cross a sag, and ascend Little Abe (8.0 mi.), a minor summit, just beyond which is **Lincoln Peak (8.1 mi.)**. A spur leads east to an observation platform just off the trail. Built by Sugarbush Valley Resort and the U.S. Forest Service, it offers wide views.

Enter a ski trail clearing and bear left to reenter the woods and head north, following the wooded ridge of Lincoln Mtn. After passing over Nancy Hanks Peak (8.7 mi.), continue along the ridge to the upper station of the **Castlerock chairlift (9.4 mi.)**. Turn left and pass behind the lift station, following a ski trail to Holt Hollow (9.5 mi.), where water may be found on a spur leading 200 ft. west.

Follow the skyline and gradually ascend to Cutts Peak (10.6 mi.), where there are views. From this point, it is easy going to the wooded summit of **Mt. Ellen (11.0 mi.)**, which is tied with Camel's Hump at 4083 ft. as Vermont's third-highest peak. Leave the summit and enter a clearing at the upper station of the Sugarbush North summit chairlift. Follow a ski trail downhill for 150 ft. before turning left to reenter the woods. Descend, steeply at first and then more moderately, to the **north boundary of the GMNF (11.4 mi.)**. Wind back and forth across the ridge, passing several limited lookouts, before reaching a junction with the **Jerusalem Trail (12.8 mi.)**, which descends 2.4 mi. west to Jim Dwire Road.

8

Just beyond the junction pass a spur leading west 50 ft. to Orvis Lookout, and then reach the **Barton Trail (12.9 mi.)**, which leads east 0.3 mi. downhill to **Glen Ellen Lodge**. The current lodge, built by the Long Trail Patrol (LTP) in 1933, is of log construction with bunks for eight. Water sources for the lodge include an unreliable spring located to the west of the LT near the junction of the Barton Trail. A second intermittent water source is a brook that may be found by following the contour south beyond the lodge's composting outhouse. Wood fires are prohibited at the lodge. There are views to the east from Glen Ellen Lodge. Beyond the Mad River Valley are the Northfield Mountains, the Granite Mountains, and, on the horizon, several ridges of the White Mountains. **Battell Shelter to Glen Ellen Lodge, 6.7 mi., 10.8 km., 4 hr. (SB 4 hr.).**

The small clearing to the west of the trail junction is the site of the original Glen Ellen Lodge. From the Barton Trail junction, climb steadily to the ridge of General Stark Mtn. After passing **General Stark's highest summit (13.2 mi.)**, continue along the ridge and then join a ski trail, following it for 600 ft. to the north peak and **Stark's Nest (13.8 mi.)**, Mad River Glen Ski Area's summit warming hut and single chairlift station. Camping may be allowed here. *Wood fires are prohibited.* There are views to the east and limited views of Lake Champlain and the Adirondacks to the west.

Pass to the west of the summit building and enter Camel's Hump State Forest, following a ski trail, then reenter the woods to the left. Rejoin the ski trail, and then cut back into the woods again, before continuing along the ridge and then descending very steeply, using a ladder at one point (14.3 mi.), to a **spur** leading west 25 ft. to **Theron Dean Shelter (14.5 mi.)**.

This small log shelter, with space for five, was originally built by the LTP in 1966 and renovated by the LTP led by Tony Stoltzfus in 2009. It is named for Theron Dean, an energetic promoter of the GMC in its early years and a close friend of Will Monroe. Future maintenance of Theron Dean Shelter has been endowed by Geordie Hall in memory of his daughter Elisha Hall. The sole water source is a small, unreliable spring to the west of the shelter. Wood fires are prohibited at Theron

Dean Shelter. **Glen Ellen Lodge to Theron Dean Shelter, 1.9 mi., 3.1 km., 1¾ hr. (SB 1¼ hr.).**

From the shelter, the spur leads back to the LT, while an alternate route leads straight ahead to Dean Panorama where there is a view north. This trail then drops and switchbacks to the right, passing through Dean Cave, before rejoining the LT 150 ft. north of the shelter.

Continue the steep descent, passing the upper station of another chairlift (14.7 mi.), and then leveling out along the ridge. Drop sharply once again, pass a vista to the north, cross over a knoll, and then descend to cross **Vt. 17 at Appalachian Gap (16.3 mi.).** *Use caution when crossing Vt. 17; traffic moves at high speeds.* There is a parking lot west of the LT at the summit of the highway with a fine western vista. At Appalachian Gap, the LT enters Camel's Hump State Park and passes in and out of it until entering it on Mts. Ira and Ethan Allen for the remainder of the route north over Camel's Hump to Duxbury Road.

At the gap, turn right and follow the highway east for 100 ft. Climb the north embankment of the road into the woods, pass a spur (16.4 mi.) to the Mad River Glen Lookout, and reach the trail's height of land on the **east slope of Baby Stark Mtn. (16.7 mi.).** Drop to a brook (16.9 mi.), and then ascend to the ridgeline. Pass over Molly Stark Mtn, (17.3 mi.) and continue to **Molly Stark's Balcony (17.6 mi.)** where there is a view of Camel's Hump, with the Worcester Range standing out to the northeast. Follow a circuitous route around the cliff below the Balcony, and descend moderately, passing west of Beane Mtn. to the **Beane Trail (18.9 mi.),** which leads west 100 ft. to **Birch Glen Camp** and 1.5 mi. to Carse Road. This log structure was built by GMC volunteers in 1930. A renovation by the LTP in 1999 was dedicated in memory of Marc von Trapp. Future maintenance of Birch Glen Camp has been endowed in memory of Mark W. McLendon. It has an open front "living room" and semi-enclosed sleeping quarters with bunk space for twelve. The water source is the brook 100 ft. south. **Theron Dean Shelter to Birch Glen Camp, 4.4 mi., 7.1 km., 2¾ hr. (SB 3¼ hr.).**

8

Side Trails

BATTELL TRAIL. From Lincoln turn north off Lincoln Gap Road onto Quaker Street by the general store. At 0.7 mi. turn right onto USFS Road 350 (Elder Hill Rd.). Follow this road (with signs to the trail) 1.9 mi. to a left turn, which continues 0.1 mi. to the Battell Trail and a small parking lot. The final 0.1 mi. is not maintained in the winter.

From the road (0.0 mi., 1473 ft.), climb steadily through a sugarbush for almost a mile. After crossing two small streams and an old woods road (1.0 mi.), and then another woods road (1.2 mi.), arrive at the LT (2.0 mi.) just south of Battell Shelter. **USFS Road 350 to LT, 2.0 mi., 3.2 km., 2 hr. (Rev. 1 hr.).**

JERUSALEM TRAIL. Take the east branch of Jerusalem Road south from Vt. 17, 6.0 mi. west of the LT at Appalachian Gap and 3.5 mi. east of Vt. 116. Follow this road 1.2 mi. south and turn left onto Jim Dwire Road and follow it 0.5 mi. to the trailhead on the right. Roadside parking space is limited; please park considerately.

From the road (0.0 mi., 1628 ft.), ascend easily through open hardwoods on old woods roads, cross a logging road, and then climb steeply to the LT (2.4 mi.), south of the Barton Trail. The Jerusalem Trail is on private timberland, thanks to the generosity of the owner. **Jim Dwire Road to LT, 2.4 mi., 3.9 km., 2¼ hr. (Rev. 1¼ hr.).**

BEANE TRAIL. Take Gore Road north from Vt. 17, 2.7 mi. west of the LT at Appalachian Gap and 7.0 mi. east of Vt. 116. Follow this road 2.9 mi. and then take Carse Road east across a bridge; at 0.5 mi., bear right and then immediately left. At 1.1 mi. there is parking on the north side of the road at a large bend before the farmhouse of the old Beane Farm.

From the gate (0.0 mi., 1361 ft.), follow a grassy road before turning right (0.4 mi.) to leave the road and climb into the woods. Continue uphill and cross two brooks before reaching Birch Glen Camp (1.5 mi.), 100 ft. from the LT junction. **Carse Road to LT, 1.5 mi., 2.4 km., 1¼ hr. (Rev. ¾ hr.).**

Krumholtz at Harrington's View, 2585 ft.

Division 9
Birch Glen to
Bolton Mountain

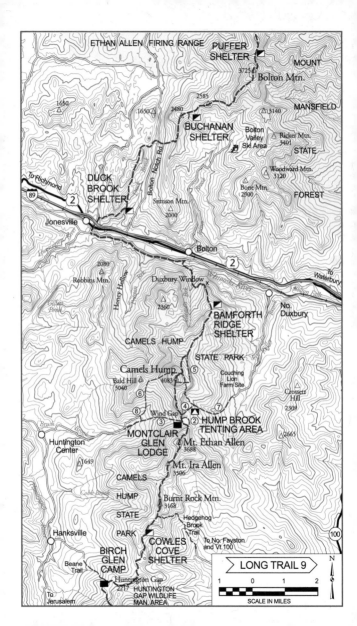

ETHAN ALLEN FIRING RANGE

PUFFER SHELTER

MOUNT

3725
Bolton Mtn.

2585

1650

1650

3480

BUCHANAN SHELTER

MANSFIELD

3140

Bolton Valley Ski Area

Ricker Mtn. 3491

Woodward Mtn. 3120

STATE

To Richmond

DUCK BROOK SHELTER

89 2

Bolton Notch Rd.

Stimson Mtn. 2000

Bone Mtn. 2900

FOREST

Jonesville

Bolton

2

To Waterbury

Winooski River

Robbins Mtn. 2080

Duxbury Window

No. Duxbury

Bolton Falls

Honey Hollow

2360

BAMFORTH RIDGE SHELTER

Gillett Brook

CAMELS HUMP

STATE PARK

Crossett Hill 2309

Camels Hump 4083

Couching Lion Farm Site

5

Bald Hill 3040

6

7

8

Wind Gap

3

4

2

HUMP BROOK TENTING AREA

Huntington Center

1649

MONTCLAIR GLEN LODGE

Mt. Ethan Allen 3688

2665

Cobb Brook

CAMELS

Mt. Ira Allen 3506

HUMP

Burnt Rock Mtn. 3168

STATE

Hedgehog Brook Trail

Hanksville

PARK

To No. Fayston and Vt.100

COWLES COVE SHELTER

100

Beane Trail

BIRCH GLEN CAMP

To Jerusalem

Huntington Gap 2217

HUNTINGTON GAP WILDLIFE MAN. AREA

LONG TRAIL 9

1   0   1   2

SCALE IN MILES

N

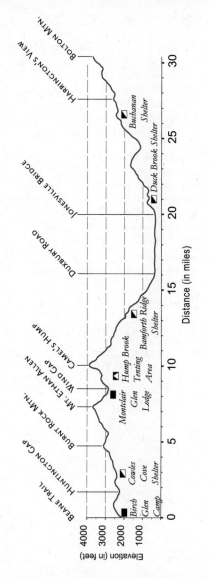

Division 9 Profile

Birch Glen to Bolton Mountain

miles north-bound	▲ NORTH	elevation at Long Trail (feet/meters)	miles south-bound
30.3	**Bolton Mtn.**	3725/1136	0.0
27.6	**Harrington's View**, 150 ft E via spur	2585/788	2.7
26.6	**Buchanan Shelter**, (2180 ft/664 m), 0.3 mi E via spur	2310/704	3.7
24.3	**Bolton Notch Road**	1120/341	6.0
21.0	**Duck Brook Shelter**	670/204	9.3
19.3	**Winooski River bridge**; U.S. 2 in Jonesville	326/99	11.0
16.1	**Duxbury Road**	400/122	14.2
15.5	**Gleason Brook bridge**	580/177	14.8
13.4	**Bamforth Ridge Shelter**, 0.2 mi E via spur	1900/579	16.9
11.0	**Alpine Trail** (5) north end	2930/893	19.3
10.6	**Gorham Spring**	3400/1037	19.7
10.2	**Camel's Hump Hut Clearing; Burrows Trail** (6) to Camel's Hump Road, 2.1 mi W; **Monroe Trail** (7) to Couching Lion parking lot, 3.1 mi E	3800/1159	20.1
9.9	**Camel's Hump**	4083/1245	20.4
9.7	**Alpine Trail** (5), south end to **Long Trail** north of summit, 1.7 mi E	3800/1159	20.6
8.2	**Wind Gap; Allis Trail** (2) north end; Deane Trail (4) to **Hump Brook Tenting Area** (2420 ft/738 m), 0.8 mi E; to Couching Lion parking lot via **Monroe Trail** (7), 2.3 mi E	2800/853	22.1
8.0	**Forest City Trail** (3) to Camel's Hump Road, 2.2 mi W	2660/811	22.3
8.0	**Montclair Glen Lodge**	2670/814	22.3
7.8	**Allis Trail** (2), south end to **Long Trail** at Wind Gap, 0.3 mi N	2890/881	22.5
7.0	**Mt. Ethan Allen**, north peak	3680/1122	23.3
4.4	**Burnt Rock Mtn.**	3168/966	25.9
3.8	**Hedgehog Brook Trail** (1) to Big Basin Road, 2.0 mi E	2800/853	26.5
2.9	**Cowles Cove Shelter**	2520/768	27.4
1.5	**Huntington Gap**	2217/676	28.8
0.0	**Beane Trail** to Birch Glen Camp, 100 ft W; to Carse Road, 1.5 mi W	2020/616	30.3

SOUTH

▼

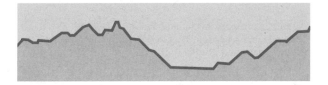

Division 9
Birch Glen to Bolton Mountain

Massachusetts: 165.5 miles   **Canada: 107.2 miles**

This division of the Long Trail (LT) crosses Camel's Hump, the state's highest undeveloped mountain. It is one of three summits on the LT with alpine vegetation. Please take care to do the "rock walk" and tread only on the rocks, not the plants. See pages 159 to 160 for information about Camel's Hump.

Backpacking groups camping on Camel's Hump should use Hump Brook Tenting Area to reduce impact at the mountain's heavily used shelter sites.

From Lincoln Gap to the Winooski River, the LT is called the Monroe Skyline in honor of prof. Will S. Monroe, who led the effort to build this section of the trail. Side trails in the division are numbered to correspond with both the division map (page 152) and Camel's Hump map (page 157).

The Green Mountain Club (GMC) continues to seek a footbridge across the Winooski River. As this goal comes closer to a reality, it will result in a rerouting of the LT to minimize the road walk for hikers. Please be aware of this ongoing effort and contact the GMC at (802) 244-7037 with any questions.

The following people have contributed to endow the future maintenance of 6 miles of the LT within this division: the Dickson family, Andrew and Reidun Nuquist, Steve Titcomb and Maureen

Delaney in memory of Sumner Williams, Doris E. Washburn, Charles L. and Mary Ann Wolf in honor of Karen Sharpwolf and Stephen Sharp, and Priscilla Page.

Camping and Fires

This division of the LT south of the Winooski River primarily traverses Camel's Hump State Park. Primitive off-trail camping with small wood fires below 2500 ft. is allowed.

Tenting at Cowles Cove and Montclair Glen is permitted only if the shelter is filled to capacity. Small wood fires, although discouraged, are permitted in established fire rings at Birch Glen and at Hump Brook Tenting Area.

North of the Winooski River the trail crosses both state land and private property. Camping is allowed only at shelters. Small wood fires, although discouraged, are permitted at the shelters' established fire rings.

Suggested Day Hikes

MT. ETHAN ALLEN. This moderate ascent from Huntington reaches the north peak of Mt. Ethan Allen via the Forest City Trail and the LT. It offers a less crowded summit with views. Round trip, 6.4 mi., 4¼ hr.

DUXBURY WINDOW. This steady climb out of the Winooski River valley provides a vista of the south face of Bolton Mountain. Round trip from Duxbury Road, 3.2 mi., 2½ hr.

HARRINGTON'S VIEW. This ascent north on the LT from Bolton Notch Road leads to a blocky ledge with views of Bolton Mtn. Round trip, 6.6 mi., 3¾ hr.

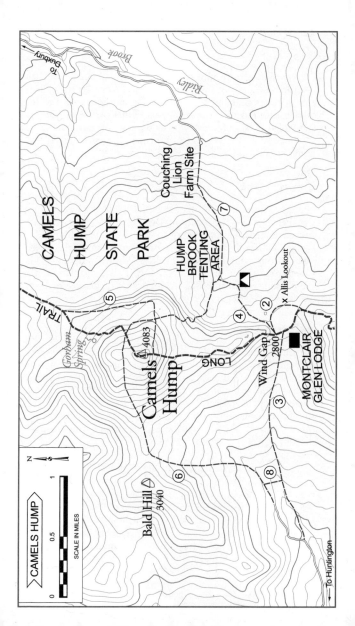

CAMELS HUMP

CAMELS HUMP STATE PARK

To Duxbury

Ridley Brook

Couching Lion Farm Site

HUMP BROOK TENTING AREA

⑦

x Allis Lookout

⑤

Gorham Spring

TRAIL

LONG

Camels Hump 4083

Wind Gap 2800

②

④

MONTCLAIR GLEN LODGE

③

Bald Hill 3040

⑥

⑧

To Huntington

N

0   0.5   1

SCALE IN MILES

Note: Fires are prohibited at Cowles Cove Shelter, Montclair Glen Lodge, and Bamforth Ridge Shelter to protect the vulnerable vegetation at these sites. Camping and wood fires at the hut clearing and above timberline on Camel's Hump are illegal, and violators are subject to fine by the state of Vermont.

Refer to Leave No Trace principles (pages 11 to 12) to minimize your impact.

Group Use

Groups hiking this division of the LT may need a Commercial Use Permit from the Vermont Department of Forests, Parks and Recreation. Group tenting space is available at Birch Glen Camp; Hump Brook Tenting Area; and Bamforth Ridge, Duck Brook, and Buchanan Shelters. Little River State Park Campground, east of the LT off U.S. 2, is available for base camp hiking. Refer to group use guidelines (pages 13 to 19) to determine whether your group needs a permit.

Winter Use

Camel's Hump is a challenging winter ascent. Its lower slopes, particularly on the east side with open hardwood forest, are popular with skilled backcountry skiers. Both skiers and winter hikers should maintain a comfortable distance from each other: skiers should recognize the trails exist for hikers, and hikers should recognize that backcountry skiers may be descending the mountain. The LT crosses the Catamount Trail at Huntington Gap.

Access to the Long Trail

U.S. 2. The LT crosses this highway in Jonesville next to the post office opposite the bridge over the Winooski River, 3.5 mi. east of Richmond and 9.5 mi. west of Vt. 100 in Waterbury. There is limited parking opposite the post office by the railroad tracks. The LT north from here follows Stage Road uphill. The LT south crosses the Winooski and follows Duxbury Road eastward.

Duxbury Road. *Western approach:* From Jonesville, follow Cochran Road south from U.S. 2 and cross the bridge over the Winooski River (0.0 mi.). Turn left onto Duxbury Road and proceed east, passing the Honey Hollow parking lot (formerly the LT lot from 1986 to 1995) across from a field at 2.1 mi., to the LT parking lot (3.2 mi.) in the woods on the south side of the road.

Eastern approach: From the junction of U.S. 2 and Vt. 100 in Waterbury, follow U.S. 2 east, take the first right on Winooski Street, cross the bridge over the river (0.0 mi.), and turn right to follow River Road, which becomes Duxbury Road in Bolton, west to the LT parking lot (6.5 mi.).

Bolton Notch Road. From Jonesville, follow U.S. 2 east 1.0 mi. and turn north (left) on Bolton Notch Road. The LT crossing is 2.7 mi. north of U.S. 2. From the road, the trail can be difficult to find; on the east side of Bolton Notch Road it coincides with an abandoned road that splits off from the start of a driveway. There is limited parking on the east side of the road.

Camel's Hump Area

The summit profile of Camel's Hump makes it one of the most distinctive peaks in the Green Mountains. It is tied with Mt. Ellen (4083 ft.) as Vermont's third highest mountain.

The Waubawakee called Camel's Hump the Tawabodi-e-wadso, meaning "the mountain that is like a seat," and Samuel de Champlain's explorers named it *le lion couchant*, translated "the couching lion" or, in more contemporary language, "the sleeping lion." Either name is more descriptive of the mountain's profile seen from the east or west than is Camel's Hump, a name amended by Zadock Thompson in 1830 from the less genteel Camel's Rump listed on Ira Allen's 1798 map.

Camel's Hump is the only undeveloped peak over 4000 ft. elevation in Vermont. State land acquisition began in 1911 with a gift of 1,000 acres, including the summit, from Col. Joseph Battell of Middlebury, Vermont. The present size of Camel's Hump State Park is nearly 24,000 acres. In 1965 the summit area was designated a State Natural Area; in 1968 it was designated a

9

National Natural Landmark; and in 1969 the Vermont General Assembly expanded this protected zone, making the mountain itself the focal point of Camel's Hump Forest Reserve.

Camel's Hump is one of three high summits that supports communities of rare alpine vegetation along the LT. Several of the flowers and grasses growing above treeline are listed on Vermont's endangered plant list. Although these plants are hardy to the weather, they are extremely fragile to foot traffic. Please take care to walk only on the rocks, not the plants. Above treeline, walk only on marked trails. Camping is not permitted in any of Vermont's alpine zones.

Camel's Hump is one of the most popular peaks in the Northeast. Each year roughly 22,000 people and hundreds of dogs visit the summit. Please leash your dog on the summit out of consideration for other visitors and to reduce impact to the alpine vegetation. GMC posts a summit caretaker at or near the summit.

PROTECT CAMEL'S HUMP'S ALPINE PLANTS.
DO THE ROCK WALK!

Walk only on the rocks, not the plants.
Leash your dogs and keep them off the plants.

Long Trail Description

Proceed north from the **Beane Trail junction (0.0 mi.)**, 100 ft. east of Birch Glen Camp, and contour around the north side of Beane Mtn., crossing two woods roads before reaching **Huntington Gap (1.5 mi.)**. Both a snowmobile trail and the Catamount Trail follow an abandoned road across the gap.

Climb northwest to the west side of the ridge, and then cross over **(2.0 mi.)** to slab the east slope through mature woods to **Cowles Cove Shelter (2.9 mi.)**. This log lean-to, with space for eight, is named for Judge Clarence Cowles of Burlington, Vermont, a charter member of the GMC who helped build trails on

Mt. Mansfield and the Monroe Skyline section of the LT. The shelter was built by the New York Section under the direction of Prof. Roy O. Buchanan in 1956. The brook 100 ft. south on the LT is a dependable water source. Wood fires are prohibited at Cowles Cove Shelter. The clearing near the brook was the site of the original Cowles Cove Shelter built in 1920. **Birch Glen Camp to Cowles Cove Shelter, 2.9 mi., 4.7 km., 1¾ hr. (SB 1½ hr.).**

From the shelter ascend gradually and, after gaining the crest of the ridge, reach the **Hedgehog Brook Trail (1) (3.8 mi.)**, which descends 2.0 mi. east to Big Basin Road. Beyond the junction, the LT becomes increasingly rugged. Continue to a spur (4.0 mi.) that leads west a short distance to a small glacial pothole, one of the highest of its kind in New England. Beyond the spur, emerge from the woods and begin an up-and-down scramble over bare rocks and cobbles to the summit of **Burnt Rock Mtn. (4.4 mi.).** The summit provides views in nearly every direction. To the north are Mts. Ira and Ethan Allen and Camel's Hump, to the west lies Lake Champlain, to the east are the Northfield Mountains and Granite Mountains, and to the south stands Lincoln Mtn. Several other knobs lie north of the main summit.

Descend a ladder to drop into Ladder Ravine (4.8 mi.), and then commence a steady ascent along the Paris Skidway, an old skid road (5.5 mi.). After some rough going reach a height of land on the east slope of Mt. Ira Allen (5.9 mi.) about 100 ft. below the summit, which is at the top of the cliff west of the LT. Contour along the sidehill and slowly descend, passing Rock Refuge, a shallow cave in the rocks to the west of the LT, one of many features named by Will Monroe.

After more rough but relatively level scrambling, climb to the south peak of Mt. Ethan Allen (6.9 mi.) and, after a small dip, reach the **north peak of Mt. Ethan Allen (7.0 mi.)**, with a lookout facing east. Descend to a small rocky area (7.2 mi.) and drop through a birch glade to the south end of the **Allis Trail (2) (7.8 mi.).**

At the junction, turn left, continuing downhill through more birch woods to **Montclair Glen Lodge (8.0 mi.)**, a log cabin with bunks for ten, built by the Long Trail Patrol (LTP) for

9

the New York Section in 1948 and renovated by the LTP led by Matt Wels in 2009. Future maintenance of Montclair Glen Lodge has been endowed by Carol Hignite. The water source is a brook 80 ft. north along the LT. A GMC caretaker is in residence during the hiking season. A fee is charged for overnight use. Wood fires are prohibited at Montclair Glen Lodge. **Cowles Cove Shelter to Montclair Glen Lodge, 5.1 mi., 8.2 km., 3¼ hr. (SB 3¼ hr.).**

From the lodge, proceed north to the site of the original Montclair Glen Shelter, built in 1917, where the **Forest City Trail (3)** descends west 2.2 mi. to Huntington Center's Camel's Hump Road. Ascend north to **Wind Gap (8.2 mi.)**, where the north end of the **Allis Trail (2)** ascends to the east and, just beyond, the **Dean Trail (4)** descends east 0.8 mi. to **Hump Brook Tenting Area** and 2.3 mi. east to North Duxbury's Couching Lion parking lot via the Monroe Trail.

At Wind Gap, the craggy cliffs of the mountain's south ridge loom above the trail. Turn west, then east, to steeply ascend the ridge. Break into the open and follow the east slope, with views of the beaver ponds alongside the Dean Trail below. Clamber over rocks and through thickets of spruce and balsam scrub, and reenter the woods.

Cross to the west side of the ridge and skirt two minor knobs with intermittent views. Climb steadily and steeply to the south end of the yellow-blazed **Alpine Trail (5) (9.7 mi.)** near treeline. This trail leads east 1.7 mi. to circle the mountain and rejoin the LT north of the summit cone and is a safer way around Camel's Hump in inclement weather. Above the Alpine Trail junction, bear west around the forbidding south wall of the summit cone, climb the exposed west face, and arrive at the summit of **Camel's Hump (9.9 mi.)** from the southwest.

The views from the summit are extensive and remarkable. To the south, the Green Mountains are visible to Killington Peak. To the north, Bamforth Ridge leads to the Winooski Valley. Beyond the valley Mt. Mansfield stands out, with the Sterling Range and the Worcester Range to its right. Mt. Washington is a little south of east, dominating the White Mountains' Presidential Range. Mt. Marcy is somewhat south of west, surrounded by a contingent of Adirondack peaks, while

Whiteface Mtn. stands alone to the north. Lake Champlain is visible for much of its length.

Descend north from the summit, skirting the exposed north-west slope before dropping down to the **Camel's Hump Hut Clearing (10.2 mi.)**. This was the site of a nineteenth-century rustic hotel (Green Mountain House), which failed financially and burned in 1875. The clearing was also the location for three metal huts managed by the Camel's Hump Club of Waterbury for hikers from 1912 until the early 1950s. Camping and wood fires are prohibited at the Hut Clearing. From the clearing, the **Burrows Trail (6)** descends west 2.1 mi. to Huntington Center's Camel's Hump Road, and the **Monroe Trail (7)** leads east 3.1 mi. to North Duxbury's Couching Lion parking area.

Reenter the woods at the north end of the clearing and descend steadily to a spur leading west a short distance to **Gorham Spring (10.6 mi.)** near the site of Gorham Lodge, which was removed in 2001. Camping and wood fires are not permitted here because the site is recovering from fifty years of intensive use. Continue a gradual but rugged descent along Bamforth Ridge following the original LT route developed by Will Monroe. The ridge is named in memory of dedicated trail maintainer and guidebook editor Eugene Bamforth.

North of the spring, drop to the first rocky opening along the ridge and reach the north end of the yellow-blazed **Alpine Trail (5) (11.0 mi.)**. This side trail leads 1.7 mi. to the LT south of the summit cone. Descend steeply over rocks and continue along the ridge, in and out of the woods with frequent views. Pass over several prominent knobs until reaching a **spur (13.4 mi.)** leading east 0.2 mi. to **Bamforth Ridge Shelter**. This cedar log lean-to was built by the Montpelier Section and other GMC volunteers in 2002 and has space for nine. The shelter is dedicated to the memory of section members David Morse and Harlan Farnsworth. There are tent platforms for group use and for campers who prefer to tent. There is a composting privy to protect water quality. Wood fires are prohibited at this site. The water source is the brook, which is, reached by a spur north from the shelter and may fail during droughts. **Montclair Glen Lodge to Bamforth Ridge Shelter, 5.6 mi., 9.0 km., 4 hr. (SB 4½ hr.).**

Follow the ridge north, passing an open ledge with a view south of Camel's Hump at the top of Spruce Knob (13.9 mi.). Drop steeply over "banister ledge," passing under some prominent ledges, to Duxbury Window (14.5 mi.) with its tree-framed view of the Winooski Valley. There is a bench here dedicated in memory of John Notte, whose family and friends funded trail scouting on Bamforth Ridge. From the window, steadily descend until reaching the former site of Buchanan Lodge (15.2 mi.), destroyed by fire in 1978, where the trail turns right to follow abandoned logging roads until descending to cross the **Gleason Brook Bridge (15.5 mi.)**, built by the On Top School in 1994. Cross over a low ridge and descend to **Duxbury Road (16.1 mi.)**, where there is a large parking lot. Turn left and follow the paved road along the Winooski River, then turn right (19.2 mi.) onto Cochran Road and cross the **Winooski River Bridge (19.3)**, which was replaced in 2002. To the left, Cochran Road leads 4.0 mi. west to Richmond. Cross the New England Central Railway and U.S. 2, and enter Jonesville (19.3 mi.). *Use caution when crossing U.S. 2; traffic moves at high speeds.*

Jonesville (326 ft.) is at the lowest elevation on the LT. The Jonesville post office is located just west of the LT on U.S. 2. Mail may be sent here in care of general delivery, marked "Hold for Long Trail Hiker." See page 21 for more information.

From Jonesville, go north on the gravel-surfaced Stage Road. After passing beneath Interstate 89, climb toward an electric utility crossing. Just before the power lines, turn right off the road (19.8 mi.), cross under the power line where you may encounter poison ivy, and ascend the north edge of the utility

---

KEEP YOUR DRINKING WATER CLEAN

Proper disposal of human and pet waste prevents the spread of giardiasis and other diseases. If an outhouse is not available, bury waste in a six- to eight-inch deep hole 200 feet from water and 50 feet from trails.

line. At a height of land, bear north from the clearing, ascending and descending a series of ledges, which will require care to negotiate, before reaching a short spur leading south to **Duck Brook Shelter (21.0 mi.)**. This open-front frame shelter, with space for twelve, was built by the LTP for the Burlington Section in 1966. Duck Brook, in a deep ravine below the shelter, is the water supply. **Bamforth Ridge Shelter to Duck Brook Shelter, 7.8 mi., 12.6 km., 4¼ hr. (SB 4¾ hr.).**

From the shelter, follow an old woods road a short distance, cross a brook, and then turn sharp left, leaving the woods road. Hikers should follow the blazes carefully through this area. Proceed north and climb steadily, passing three lookouts and then descend first gradually, then steeply, before ascending to the top of a bedrock ridge. From the ridge, begin a gradual descent to a logging road (23.5 mi.), cross Duck Brook (24.0 mi.), and continue to the unpaved **Bolton Notch Road (24.3 mi.)**.

Cross the road and begin to ascend along a series of woods roads. Cross several unreliable small brooks, before reaching the top of Oxbow Ridge (25.2 mi.). Follow the ridge north, pass several lookouts to the east, then one to the west (25.5 mi.) that offers a view of Lake Champlain and the Adirondacks, and then yet another lookout (25.9 mi.) with views of Camel's Hump and the Adirondacks. From the lookout, reach the height of land along the ridge and, bearing east, arrive at a spur (26.0 mi.) that leads east 120 ft. to a lookout over Bolton Valley. Bear left, descend to cross a brook (26.5 mi.), and reach a spur **(26.6 mi.)**, which descends east 0.3 mi. to **Buchanan Shelter**. This frame structure, built by the Burlington Section led by Basil Goodrich and Jack Lance in 1984, is named for Prof. Roy O. Buchanan, longtime leader of the LTP. It has an open-front porch and enclosed bunkroom with space for sixteen. Water is located 100 ft. to the north. **Duck Brook Shelter to Buchanan Shelter 5.9 mi., 9.5 km., 4 hr. (SB 3½ hr.).**

The steady ascent from Buchanan Shelter to Bolton Mtn. is characterized by numerous ups and downs. From the shelter spur, continue with minor changes in elevation to reach another **spur (27.6 mi.)** leading east 150 ft. to **Harrington's View**, discovered by Jack Harrington of the Burlington Section. It offers views of Mt. Mansfield, Bolton Mtn., Bolton

9

Valley, and Ricker Mtn. After a short descent, continue east, cross a small brook (28.2 mi.), and make a zigzag ascent to a wooded, unnamed summit (29.0 mi., 3236 ft.) with a view south to Camel's Hump. Descend gradually to a saddle (29.7 mi.), then climb to the wooded summit of **Bolton Mtn. (30.3 mi.).**

Side Trails

Refer to the Camel's Hump map (page 157) or the division map (page 152) for the location of numbered trails. All of Camel's Hump's side trails are marked with blue blazes, except for the yellow-blazed Alpine Trail.

1. Hedgehog Brook Trail. This trail is located entirely on private land. Hikers are allowed to use the trail thanks to the generosity of the landowners. Please stay on the trail and away from buildings. Inconsiderate hiker behavior could lead to trail closure. The North Fayston Road leads west from Vt. 100, 4.5 mi. north of Vt. 17 in Waitsfield and 8.0 mi. south of U.S. 2 in Waterbury. Follow the North Fayston Road; at 2.5 mi. this road turns to dirt; at 4.0 mi. stay straight at a four-way offset intersection, continuing on Big Basin Road to the trailhead (5.0 mi.) at a heavy metal gate, near a parking lot that can accommodate ten cars.

The trail descends from the parking lot (0.0 mi., 1160 ft.) to cross Hedgehog Brook over stepping-stones. The trail then climbs the slope and contours north to a woods road (0.5 mi.). Turn left and follow the woods road uphill. Climb west steadily to the ridge and the LT (2.0 mi.). **Big Basin Road to LT, 2.0 mi., 3.2 km., 1¼ hr. (Rev. 1 hr.).**

2. Allis Trail. This loop trail by-passes Montclair Glen Lodge, following the ridgeline between Mt. Ethan Allen and Wind Gap, and its south end begins on the LT 0.2 mi. south of the lodge. From the junction ascend east to a view south of Mt. Ethan Allen. At the top of the initial climb, reach Allis Lookout (0.1 mi.) with the David Morse Memorial Bench and a striking view of Camel's Hump. The bench was built by the Montpelier Section led by Bob Lindemann in 2000 and honors the memory of a longtime Montpelier Section volunteer and trail maintainer. Descend south and west to the LT at Wind Gap, 0.2 mi. north of Montclair Glen Lodge. **LT south of Montclair Glen to LT at Wind Gap, 0.3 mi., 0.5 km., ¼ hr. (Rev ¼ hr.).**

3. FOREST CITY TRAIL. Follow the Huntington Road to Camel's Hump Road in Huntington Center, 6.1 mi. north of Vt. 17 and 2.5 mi. south of the Huntington post office. Follow Camel's Hump Road east 2.8 mi. to the trailhead, where there is limited parking. The road continues 0.7 mi. uphill to a larger parking lot and the beginning of the Burrows Trail. The Forest City–Burrows Connector (8) links these two trails.

From the road (0.0 mi., 1600 ft.), follow an old logging road, cross Brush Brook, and reach Forest City (0.3 mi.), the site of a former 1930's CCC camp. Continue on the logging road, re-cross Brush Brook, reach the junction with the Forest City–Burrows Connector (8) (0.8 mi.), and then bear right, leaving the logging road. Climb gradually, with several brook crossings, to the LT (2.2 mi.) 200 ft. north of Montclair Glen Lodge at the site of the original Montclair Glen Shelter, built in 1917. The LT leads north 1.9 mi. to Camel's Hump and 1.0 mi. south to Mt. Ethan Allen. **Camel's Hump Road to LT, 2.2 mi., 3.2 km., 1¾ hr. (Rev. 1¼ hr.); Camel's Hump Road to Camel's Hump, 4.1 mi., 6.3 km., 3½ hr. (Rev. 2¼ hr.).**

4. DEAN TRAIL. This trail diverges west from the Monroe Trail (7), 1.3 mi. from the Couching Lion parking lot, and makes a popular day hike loop over Camel's Hump with that trail and the LT. From the Monroe Trail (0.0 mi., 2460 ft.), descend west to cross the Hump Brook bridge (0.2 mi.), built by the Vermont Youth Conservation Corps, and reach a spur (0.3 mi.) leading south 0.1 mi. to Hump Brook Tenting Area, with tent platforms and campsites. A GMC caretaker is in residence during the hiking season. A fee is charged for overnight use.

From the spur, climb steadily to a beaver pond (0.7 mi.) with views of Camel's Hump. Ascend more gently to Wind Gap (1.0 mi.) and the junction with both the LT and the north end of the Allis Trail (2). The LT leads south 0.2 mi. to the

9

Forest City Trail and then Montclair Glen Lodge and north 1.7 mi. to Camel's Hump. **Couching Lion parking lot to Montclair Glen Lodge, 2.5 mi., 4.0 km., 2 hr. (Rev. 1¼ hr.); Couching Lion parking lot to Camel's Hump via Monroe, Dean, and Long Trails, 4.0 mi., 6.4 km., 3½ hr. (Rev. 2 hr.).**

5. ALPINE TRAIL. Named by Will S. Monroe for one of his St. Bernard dogs, the yellow-blazed Alpine Trail skirts the east side of the Camel's Hump summit cone and is rarely in deep woods. Although this trail can provide a safer route around Camel's Hump in bad weather, its elevation and exposure make it a poor choice in a thunderstorm, when you should seek shelter or descend immediately.

From the LT (0.0 mi., 3800 ft.) at treeline, 0.2 mi. south of Camel's Hump, descend east moderately, to the Monroe Trail (7) (0.5 mi., 3320 ft.). Continue north and proceed, mostly along ledges featuring views toward the summit and with little change in elevation, before dropping to a brook crossing (1.0 mi.). Continue north over Basque Ledges, and then descend to the north junction with the LT (1.7 mi., 2930 ft.), 1.1 mi. north of the summit of Camel's Hump. **LT south of Camel's Hump to LT north of Camel's Hump, 1.7 mi., 2.7 km., 1 hr. (Rev. 1½ hr.).**

6. BURROWS TRAIL. Refer to directions to the Forest City Trail (3). From the Forest City trailhead continue up the Camel's Hump Road 0.7 mi. to the large gravel parking lot at the end of the road, 3.5 mi. east of Huntington Center. The Forest City–Burrows Connecter (8) descends south from the trailhead to the Forest City Trail.

Enter the woods (0.0 mi., 1800 ft.) in an internationally recognized site for research on acid deposition, soils, insects, and other forest health issues. Cross a brook, ascend moderately to a ridge between Camel's Hump and Bald Hill (1.7 mi.), and follow the ridge to the LT and the Monroe Trail (7) at the Camel's Hump Hut Clearing (2.1 mi.). The LT ascends south 0.3 mi. to the summit. **Camel's Hump Road to LT, 2.1 mi., 3.4 km., 2¼ hr. (Rev. 1 hr.); Camel's Hump Road to Camel's Hump summit, 2.4 mi., 3.9 km., 2½ hr. (Rev. 1¼ hr.).**

7. MONROE TRAIL. This trail begins at the end of North Duxbury's Couching Lion parking lot.

Eastern approach via Waterbury's Winooski Street bridge: From the junction of U.S. 2 and Vt. 100 (0.0 mi.) just off Interstate 89's exit 10, drive south on Vt. 100 and pass under a railroad trestle. Turn right on Winooski Street (0.1 mi.) and cross the Winooski Street bridge (0.4 mi.). Turn right onto River Road and proceed west to Camel's Hump Road (5.0 mi.). Turn left (south) and ascend, passing several side roads off the Hump Road; be sure to stay on the main road. At 6.4 mi. bear left at a fork and cross the bridge. Continue across another bridge and pass a sign that says "Welcome to Camel's Hump State Park." A side road to the left leads to the Camel's Hump View Trail and the winter parking area. Bear right and continue to climb over rough road to two large parking areas (8.7 mi.). The Monroe Trail begins at the far end of the upper parking lot.

Emergency vehicles and local residents require access to both the trailhead and the gated woods road near the parking area; please avoid blocking the gated road and do not park on the shoulder of this narrow road. *Note:* If the upper parking lots are full, please use the winter parking area.

Western approach via the Jonesville bridge: Camel's Hump Road is 6.0 mi. west of the Jonesville bridge on Duxbury Road (it becomes River Road in Duxbury). Turn right onto Camel's Hump Road and follow the previous directions to the trailhead.

The estate of Prof. Will S. Monroe left Couching Lion Farm to the state of Vermont. Monroe sponsored the planting of many of the trees surrounding the parking lot, including the Norway spruce from which the caretaker cabin was built in 1973 by the Department of Forests, Parks and Recreation, as well as the spruce and larch harvested in 1999 to rebuild Butler Lodge. Will Monroe, his sister Katherine, and his beloved dogs are buried in a small cemetery 100 ft. north of the parking lot.

From the parking lot (0.0 mi., 1500 ft.), enter the woods, pass a trailhead bulletin board and trail register, and begin a steady ascent. Shortly after leaving the registration box, cross the first of three footbridges. Cross the third footbridge at 0.8

mi. and ascend to the Dean Trail (4) (1.3 mi.). Resume climbing to a crossing of Hump Brook (2.1 mi.).

Recross the brook, turn north, and ascend steadily. Cross the Alpine Trail (5) (2.5 mi.), and continue uphill to the LT (3.1 mi.) at the Camel's Hump Hut Clearing. The LT ascends 0.3 mi. south to Camel's Hump. **Couching Lion parking lot to LT, 3.1 mi., 5.0 km., 2¾ hr. (Rev. 1½ hr.); Couching Lion parking lot to Camel's Hump summit, 3.4 mi., 5.5 km., 3 hr. (Rev. 1¾ hr.).**

8. BURROWS–FOREST CITY CONNECTOR. This trail starts at the Burrows Trail (6) trailhead and connects with the Forest City Trail to eliminate a road walk in the Burrows–Forest City circuit over Camel's Hump. Bear right off the Burrows Trail just beyond the parking lot and proceed south, crossing a small brook on a wooden bridge. Cross a large bridge built by the On Top School over the impressive gorge of Brush Brook and descend to the Forest City Trail. **Burrows Trail to Forest City Trail, 0.1 mi.**

Mt. Mansfield from Puffer Shelter, 3200 ft.

Division 10
Bolton Mountain to Lamoille River

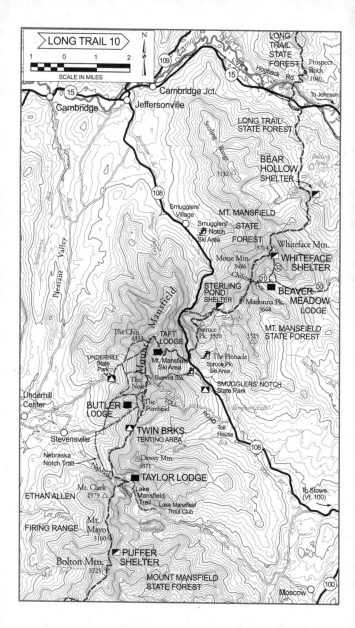

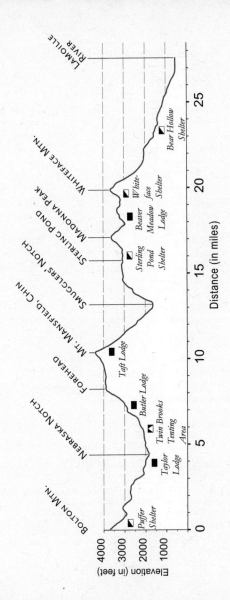

Division 10 Profile

Bolton Mountain to Lamoille River

miles north-bound	▲ NORTH	elevation at Long Trail (feet/meters)	miles south-bound
27.6	**Suspension bridge** across Lamoille River	500/152	0.0
27.2	**Vt. 15** at cemetery	500/152	0.4
26.6	**Lamoille Valley Rail Trail** at West Settlement Road	500/152	1.0
23.3	**Bear Hollow Shelter**, E via spur	1380/421	4.3
20.2	**Whiteface Mtn.**	3714/1132	7.4
19.7	**Whiteface Shelter; Whiteface Trail** (32) to **Beaver Meadow Lodge** (2214 ft/675 m), 1.0 mi S	3156/962	7.9
18.9	**Morse Mtn.**, east slope	3380/1030	8.7
18.6	**Hagerman Overlook**	3190/972	9.0
18.2	**Chilcoot Pass; Chilcoot Trail** (31) to **Beaver Meadow Lodge** (2214 ft/675 m), 0.8 mi E	2950/899	9.4
17.4	**Madonna Peak**, chairlift	3668/1119	10.2
16.2	**Sterling Pond Shelter; Elephant's Head Trail** (28)	3030/924	11.4
16.0	**Sterling Pond** outlet	3000/915	11.6
15.9	**Sterling Pond Trail** (29) to Vt. 108, 1.1 mi W	3040/927	11.7
15.6	**Snuffy's Ski Trail; Elephant's Head Trail** (28) to **Sterling Pond Shelter**, 0.7 mi E	3080/939	12.0
14.9	**Elephant's Head Cliff** (2800 ft/853 m), 0.1 mi W via spur	3020/920	12.7
12.6	**Smugglers Notch Picnic Area; Vt. 108** at Long Trail north	1600/488	15.0
12.4	**Vt. 108** at Long Trail south	1600/488	15.2
10.7	**Profanity Trail** (24); **Taft Lodge**, 200 ft S via spur, **Hell Brook Cutoff** (27)	3650/1113	16.9
10.4	**Eagle Pass; Adam's Apple Trail** (25) to **Adam's Apple** (4060 ft/1250 m), 0.2 mi N; **Hell Brook Trail** (26) to Vt. 108, 1.5 mi E	3990/1217	17.2
10.1	**Chin**, Mt. Mansfield's highest peak	4393/1340	17.5
9.9	**Sunset Ridge Trail** (21) to **Laura Cowles Trail** (23), 250 ft W; to Underhill State Park, 3.1 mi W; **Profanity Trail** (24) to **Taft Lodge**, 0.5 mi E	4260/1299	17.7

Bolton Mountain to Lamoille River

continued

9.7	**Cliff Trail** (15) to Cliff House (3600 ft/1098 m), 0.4 mi E	4020/1226	17.9
9.6	Lower Lip	4030/1229	18.0
9.4	Upper Lip	3964/1209	18.2
9.2	Drift Rock; **Amherst Trail** (14) to TV Road, 0.3 mi S	3940/1202	18.4
8.9	**Halfway House Trail** (20) to Underhill State Park, 2.3 mi W	3880/1183	18.7
8.7	**Mt. Mansfield Visitor Center**: Toll Road to **South Link** (11) and **Haselton Trail** (13), 0.5 mi E	3849/1173	18.9
8.4	Forehead By-Pass, north end; **TV Road**	3900/1190	19.2
8.1	Forehead; **Wampahoofus Trail** (10) to **Butler Lodge**, 0.8 mi S; to Underhill State Park via **Maple Ridge Trail** (9), 3.6 mi W	3940/1202	19.5
7.4	Needle's Eye; **Forehead By-Pass** (8) to **Long Trail** north of Forehead, 1.2 mi N	3080/939	20.2
7.2	**Wallace Cutoff** (4) to **Butler Lodge** (3030 ft/924 m), 0.1 mi W; to Stevensville parking lot via **Butler Lodge Trail** (5), 1.9 mi W	3100/945	20.4
6.0	**Twin Brooks Tenting Area**, 100 ft W via spur	2300/701	21.6
4.6	**Nebraska Notch Trail** (3) to Stevensville parking lot, 1.5 mi W	1780/543	23.0
4.3	**Clara Bow Trail** (2) to **Taylor Lodge**, 0.4 mi E	1860/567	23.3
3.9	**Lake Mansfield Trail** (1) to **Taylor Lodge** and **Clara Bow Trail** (2), 0.1 mi E; to Nebraska Valley Road, 1.6 mi E	1850/564	23.7
2.8	**Mt. Clark**, east slope	2800/853	24.8
1.4	**Mt. Mayo**	3160/964	26.2
0.5	**Puffer Shelter**	3200/975	27.1
0.0	**Bolton Mtn.**	3725/1136	27.6

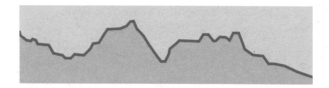

Division 10

Bolton Mountain to
Lamoille River

Massachusetts: 195.8 miles **Canada: 76.9 miles**

This division of the Long Trail (LT) travels mostly above treeline on Mt. Mansfield for 2.3 mi. from the Forehead to the Adams's Apple and is exposed to strong winds and sudden storms. The portions of the LT south from the Forehead and north from the Chin can be treacherous in poor weather. Hikers should be familiar with the side trails that can be used to avoid or escape the exposed summit ridge; particularly the Forehead By-Pass (8) and the Profanity Trail (24).

Mt. Mansfield, Vermont's highest summit, is one of three sites along the LT with alpine vegetation. Take care to walk only on the rocks, not the plants. For more information on Mt. Mansfield, see pages 182 to 183.

Backpacking groups camping on Mt. Mansfield should stay at Twin Brooks Tenting Area rather than the mountain's heavily used shelter sites.

Due to radio frequency radiation from broadcast facilities that exceeds federal exposure standards, the Nose remains temporarily closed to hikers. Reopening of the Triangle Trail is anticipated following the completion of a realignment of tower facilities on the Nose. For trail updates, check trailhead bulletin boards or visit www.greenmountainclub.org.

The LT relocation through the Lamoille Valley was completed in 2005. This effort included building a suspension bridge across the river and eliminated a dangerous road walk along Vt. 15 and Hogback Road in Johnson.

The following people and organizations have contributed to endow the future maintenance of 11 miles of the LT within this division: Faith Bieler, Ted and Jill Haas, Phil Hazen, Linda Scott in memory of Rebecca Camp Skillin, John and Sue Sharp, Tony Smith, an anonymous Burlington Section member, the Burlington Section, Yellow Jacket, Short Circuit, Caveman, and gifts in memory of Dorothy Stewart Stein and in honor of Benjamin C. Stein.

Side trails in this division, blazed blue unless otherwise noted in the descriptions, are numbered to correspond with the division map on page 172 and Mt. Mansfield maps on pages 178 and 179.

Camping and Fires

This division of the LT south of Smugglers' Notch crosses state, Stowe Mountain Resort, and University of Vermont land. North of the notch it crosses mostly state land and some private property. Camping above 2500 ft. is allowed only at shelters (tenting is allowed only if a shelter is filled to capacity) and designated tenting areas. Primitive off-trail camping with small wood fires is allowed below 2500 ft.

Wood fires are prohibited in Division 10 at all shelters south of Whiteface Mtn. to protect vulnerable vegetation. Small wood fires, although discouraged, are permitted in established fire rings at Twin Brooks Tenting Area, Bear Hollow Shelter, and Beaver Meadow Lodge.

10

Refer to Leave No Trace principles (pages 11 to 12) to minimize your impact.

Note: Camping and wood fires above timberline on Mt. Mansfield are illegal and may be subject to a fine.

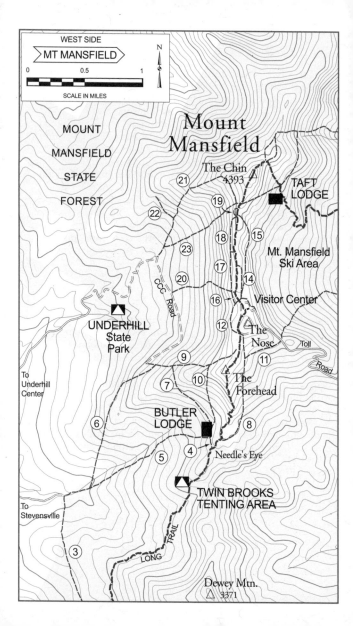

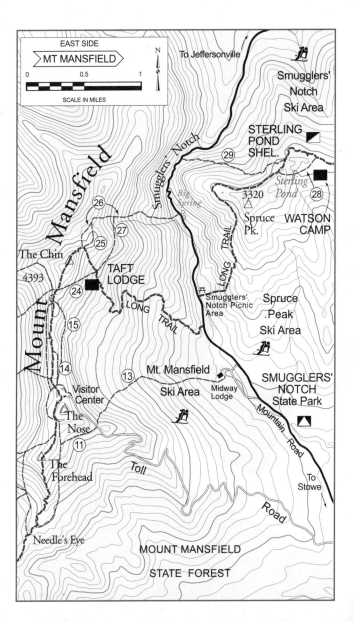

Suggested Day Hikes

STERLING POND. This popular destination features a subalpine pond with
striking views of Mt. Mansfield across
Smugglers' Notch. Follow the Sterling
Pond Trail, the former route of the LT, north from
the height of land on Vt. 108 at Smugglers' Notch.
Round trip from Vt. 108, 2.4 mi., 2 hr.

NEBRASKA NOTCH. This climb on the Lake Mansfield
Trail to the rugged notch features a glacial cirque
with views of the north wall of the notch, a large
beaver meadow, and a fine view of the rugged ridges
of Bolton Mtn. from Taylor Lodge. Continue on the
Clara Bow trail through the boulders on the floor
of the notch and return to Taylor via the LT south.
Return by reversing your direction on the Lake
Mansfield Trail. Round trip, 4.0 mi., 2¾ hr.

BUTLER LODGE LOOP. This hike, with views of the
Forehead from the LT and of Lake Champlain and
the Adirondacks from Butler Lodge, follows the
Nebraska Notch, Long, Wallace Cutoff, and Butler
Lodge Trails from the Stevensville Road parking lot.
Round trip, 6.0 mi., 4 hr.

MANSFIELD TRAVERSE. Ascending through the picturesque
forest of the Haselton Trail under Mt. Mansfield's
Nose, this route features a 2.0 mi. alpine ridge walk
along the LT north to the Chin, Vermont's highest
point (4393 ft.). The descent on the LT passes Taft
Lodge and returns to Vt. 108, less than a mile north
of the ski area. Round trip from the gondola parking
lot, 6.5 mi. 4¾ hr.

BEAVER MEADOW. Featuring a subalpine ridge with
views along the Sterling Range, this rugged trip uses

the Beaver Meadow, Chilcoot, Long, and Whiteface Trails. This circuit passes Beaver Meadow Lodge and Whiteface Shelter and makes a fine backpack. Traveling uphill on the Chilcoot Trail is recommended. Round trip from Mud City, 8.7 mi., 6 hr. A climb of Whiteface Mtn. via the LT north lengthens this trip to 9.7 mi., 7 hr.

Group Use

Groups hiking this division of the LT need a Commercial Use Permit from the Vermont Department of Forests, Parks and Recreation. Group tenting space is available at Twin Brooks Tenting Area, Taylor and Beaver Meadow Lodges, and Sterling Pond and Bear Hollow Shelters. Groups can stay at Taft Lodge, where tenting is not permitted. Underhill State Park Campground, on the west side of Mt. Mansfield, and Smugglers' Notch State Park Campground, on the east side, are available for base camp hiking. Elmore State Park, east of the LT off Vt. 15 and Vt. 12 south, is also available for base camp hiking. Refer to pages 13 to 19 for additional group use guidelines.

Winter Use

10

All suggested hikes listed for this division, except for the Beaver Meadow trip, make good snowshoe trips, although some may be longer than indicated owing to unplowed approach roads. Much of the terrain in this division is too difficult for beginner and intermediate cross-country skiers. Vt. 108 through Smugglers' Notch (closed to vehicles in winter) and the Nebraska Notch Trail out of Stevensville make challenging trips for intermediate skiers. The approach trail to Beaver Meadow offers easier terrain for skiing.

Access to the Long Trail

VT. 108. There are two LT trailheads on this road. The south trailhead, leading to the Chin of Mt. Mansfield, is 8.2 mi. north of Vt. 100 in Stowe and 9.6 mi. south of Vt. 15 in Jeffersonville. A pull-off on the west side of the road is just north of the trailhead. The north trailhead, leading to Elephant's Head, is the state picnic area 0.2 mi. north of the south trailhead. Vt. 108 through Smugglers' Notch is designated a Scenic Highway by the state of Vermont.

During the winter, a 3.5-mi. stretch of Vt. 108 through Smugglers' Notch between the Mt. Mansfield Ski Area maintenance entrance (0.3 mi. south of the LT) and the Smugglers' Notch Ski Area upper parking lot (1.3 mi. north of the notch height-of-land) is not plowed.

VT. 15. There is parking at two locations at the north end of this division. Follow Vt. 15 west out of Johnson, cross the Lamoille River just beyond the Long Trail Tavern, and continue 0.6 mi. west of the river to West Settlement Road. Turn and follow this road south 0.4 mi., and bear left at a fork for another 0.3 mi. to an iron gate where limited parking is available. Be sure to park without blocking the road or the gate. West Settlement Road is also 6.7 mi. east of Vt. 108 in Jeffersonville. There is also parking at the LT parking lot on the north side of Vt. 15, 0.5 mile west of West Settlement Road across from the cemetery.

Mt. Mansfield Area

Vermont's highest mountain, Mt. Mansfield (4393 ft.), is known for its distinctive ridgeline, which resembles the profile of a human face, especially when viewed from the east. From south to north, the names of its more prominent features reflect this: Forehead, Nose, Upper and Lower Lips, Chin, and Adam's Apple. The Abenaki called the mountain Mose-o-de-be-Wadso (mountain with the head of a moose), and it received its present name from the town of Mansfield, disestablished and divided among adjacent towns over a century ago.

The Mansfield summit ridge supports the largest community of alpine tundra found in Vermont. This unique and delicate plant life is a remnant of the era when ice sheets covered northern New England. Few species are able to survive the extreme conditions of the summit ridge; those that do grow very slowly and hang in a delicate balance. Although these plants are hardy to the weather, they are extremely fragile to foot traffic. Please take special care to walk only on the rocks, not the plants. Above treeline, walk only on marked trails. Camping is not permitted in any of Vermont's alpine zones.

Mt. Mansfield is the most frequently visited mountain in Vermont with over 40,000 visitors and thousands of dogs annually. This use threatens the fragile alpine ecosystem. Please leash your dog on the summit ridgeline out of consideration for other visitors and to reduce impact to the alpine vegetation. GMC summit caretakers are stationed on the summit ridge during the warm months. The summit ridge of Mt. Mansfield, owned and managed by the University of Vermont as a Natural Area, has been declared a State Natural Area and National Natural Landmark.

Although most people hike the mountain via the LT from Vt. 108 and the Sunset Ridge Trail from Underhill State Park, there are many other challenging and exciting trails on the mountain. Hikers using these side trails should be in good physical condition and have sturdy boots. Backpackers may encounter difficulty on some of these trails due to ladders, steep exposed pitches, and tight squeezes through crevices and ledges.

Base camping in the area can be found at Smugglers' Notch and Underhill State Parks. Overnight facilities can also be found at hotels and other tourist lodgings in the surrounding area.

Groups are encouraged to use Twin Brooks Tenting Area or the group camping area at Underhill State Park. Information is available from the Vermont Department of Forests, Parks and Recreation, Essex Junction Regional Office, 111 West Street, Essex Junction, Vermont 05452; (802) 879-6565.

10

KNOW WHAT TIME THE SUN SETS!
DON'T GET CAUGHT IN THE DARK.

Long Trail Description

Descend east from the summit of **Bolton Mtn. (0.0 mi.)**, then turn north and continue downhill on rugged trail to **Puffer Shelter (0.5 mi.)**. This shelter was built by the Burlington Section in 1975, with the help of over 100 volunteers who carried the materials over Bolton Mtn. to the site. It replaced a log cabin that burned in 1974 and is named in honor of long-time GMC volunteer Louis B. Puffer. There is space for six. A small brook to the west is an unreliable water source. Wood fires are prohibited at Puffer Shelter. **Buchanan Shelter to Puffer Shelter, 4.5 mi., 7.2 km., 3 hr. (SB 2½ hr.).**

Drop to a sag in the ridge, and then climb to the wooded summit of **Mt. Mayo (1.4 mi.)**. Descend to pass several views of Mt. Mansfield and, after reaching the Mayo-Clark col (2.0 mi.), climb to the south ridge of **Mt. Clark**. Follow the contour around the ridge to pass east of the summit **(2.8 mi.)** and reach a lookout (3.0 mi.) with Lake Mansfield below and the Worcester Range beyond. Proceed east and drop steeply over rugged terrain, using a ladder at one point, to a beaver pond. Cross the dam and descend through challenging ledges to the **Lake Mansfield Trail (1) (3.9 mi.)**. This trail leads east 300 ft. to **Taylor Lodge** and descends 1.6 mi. east to Lake Mansfield and Stowe's Nebraska Valley Road. The east end of the **Clara Bow Trail (2)**, which passes through the boulders on the floor of Nebraska Notch, leaves the Lake Mansfield Trail behind Taylor Lodge.

Taylor Lodge, named for James P. Taylor, founder of the GMC, was built by the Burlington Section in 1978. The lodge, with an open front porch, has an enclosed bunkroom with space for fifteen and one tent platform for overflow camping. Future maintenance of Taylor Lodge has been endowed in memory of Debo Leplante. Water runs from a reliable spring 0.2 mi. down the Lake Mansfield Trail. Because two GMC lodges have already burned at this site, wood fires are prohibited at Taylor Lodge. **Puffer Shelter to Taylor Lodge, 3.4 mi., 5.5 km., 2 hr. (SB 2¾ hr.).**

Turn left at the Lake Mansfield Trail junction to climb over a low ridge, by-passing rugged Nebraska Notch. Descend to pass the west end of the **Clara Bow Trail (2) (4.3 mi.)**. Continue west to a large, shallow beaver pond, then climb north back to the ridge and the **Nebraska Notch Trail (3) (4.6 mi.)**, which descends west 1.5 mi. to Stevensville Road in Underhill Center.

Proceed north in a gentle ascent while circling around the west slope of Mt. Dewey, crossing two brooks. Beyond the second brook is a **spur (6.0 mi.)**, which descends west 100 ft. to the **Twin Brooks Tenting Area**, rebuilt in 1997 by Burlington Section volunteers in memory of Roland Boucher, a dedicated trail maintainer. Tent platforms are provided, and small wood fires are permitted in the established fire ring near the group site. The water supply is the brook 0.2 mi. south on the LT.

Continue north from the junction, cross another brook (6.2 mi.), and then cross the Overland cross-country ski trail (6.3 mi.), which can be followed east to a rock feature called the Devil's Dishpan near the ridgeline. Climb through a glade to the ridge (6.8 mi.). Proceed along the ridge to the **Wallace Cut-off (4) (7.2 mi.)**, which descends west about 0.1 mi. to **Butler Lodge**. This trail is the shortest (and from this ridge, the only) route to the lodge from the LT. In good weather, the Wallace Cutoff and Wampahoofus Trail is the best route for backpackers to follow to the Forehead.

Butler Lodge, of log construction, was originally built by the Long Trail Patrol (LTP) in 1933 and reconstructed by Burlington Section volunteers led by Leo Leach in 2000. It is named for Mabel Taylor Butler, who was a member of the Burlington Section and loved the Green Mountains. The reconstructed lodge was dedicated in celebration of James C. Taylor, a LT end-to-end hiker. There are bunks and loft space for fourteen. Future maintenance of Butler Lodge has been endowed by the Burlington Section. Water, though unreliable in late summer, is available at a small brook 75 ft. to the east of the lodge. A GMC caretaker is in residence during the hiking season to assist and educate hikers, help maintain the lodge and local trails, and compost sewage to protect water quality. A fee is charged for overnight use. Wood fires are prohibited at Butler Lodge. **Taylor Lodge to Butler Lodge, 3.4 mi., 5.5 km., 2½ hr. (SB 2 hr.).**

From the lodge there are views of the Champlain Valley and Adirondacks to the west and the south escarpment of the Forehead of Mt. Mansfield to the north. The **Butler Lodge Trail (5)** descends west 1.8 mi. to the Stevensville Road park-

10

ing lot. The Rock Garden Trail (7) follows along the foot of the Forehead cliffs north to the Maple Ridge Trail (9). The Wampahoofus Trail (10) climbs steeply north 0.8 mi. to the LT at the Forehead.

From the Wallace Cutoff, continue north to pass through the **Needle's Eye**, an opening created by two large boulders, to the south end of the **Forehead By-Pass (8) (7.4 mi.)**. It is the less-exposed route to the summit in bad weather. It is also a better route for people with a fear of heights and for pets.

Bear left and begin a steep and rough climb over rocks and ledges, using ladders in some places. Emerge from the ledges and continue to ascend in the open to the highest point of the **Forehead (8.1 mi.)**, Mt. Mansfield's southmost peak, and the junction of the **Wampahoofus Trail (10)**. This trail descends west and south 0.2 mi. to the **Maple Ridge Trail (9)** and 0.8 mi. to Butler Lodge.

Proceed north from the Forehead, enter the woods, and arrive at the north end of the **Forehead By-Pass (8)**, an alternate route in stormy weather. Just beyond is the **TV Road (8.4 mi.)**, which leads south to the north slope of the Nose, and its television station buildings.

Turn left to follow the TV Road north and in 150 ft. pass the south end of the Lakeview Trail (12) on the left. Turn right and reenter the woods (8.6 mi.), then reach the Summit Station and **Mt. Mansfield Visitor Center (8.7 mi.)**. The toll road parking lot is just below the Summit Station to the east. The Visitor Center occupies part of the Summit Station and contains displays on the mountain's natural history, research efforts, and the ridge's alpine ecosystem. It is open from Memorial Day to Columbus Day.

The Summit Station is built on the site of the old Summit House. One of the last of the famous mountain hotels, the Mt. Mansfield Summit House was razed and burned in 1964 after more than 100 years of operation. The **Mt. Mansfield Toll Road** is open during summer and foliage seasons and provides automobile access to the LT from Vt. 108. From the Summit Station, the Toll Road descends east 0.3 mi. to the Runny Nose spring and 0.5 mi. to a road leading left to the Octagon and the upper station of the Mt. Mansfield quad chairlift. At this road junction, the **Haselton Trail (13)** bears northeast down the Nose Dive ski trail. At the parking lot across from the junction, the **South Link (11)** leads west to the Forehead By-Pass (8). The toll road continues east downhill another 4.0 mi. to Vt. 108.

Continue north past the Summit Station where the coinciding Lakeview (12) and Canyon (16) Trails lead west to parallel the ridge. Cross the TV Road (8.8 mi.), which leads east 200 ft. to the Amherst Trail (14). Beyond the TV Road, emerge from the stunted spruce and fir trees on the rocky ridge of the mountain. From this point north over the Chin, hikers must take special care to not trample the alpine tundra by walking only on the marked trail. Pass the **Halfway House Trail (20) (8.9 mi.)**, which descends west 2.3 mi. to Underhill State Park, and then climb to Frenchman's Pile, a cairn marking the spot where a traveler was killed by lightning many years ago. Electrical storms on the exposed ridge of Mt. Mansfield are sudden and severe. Hikers are strongly urged to take shelter on any side trail leading off the ridge during thunderstorms (they are usually brief). To the east, use the Profanity, Cliff, or Amherst Trails; to the west, the Laura Cowles or Halfway House Trails. Fissures and overhanging rocks along the open ridge do not provide adequate shelter from lightning strikes.

Proceed north from Frenchman's Pile to **Drift Rock (9.2 mi.)**, a large glacial erratic, and the north end of the **Amherst Trail (14)**, which provides a sheltered route south to the TV Road on the east side of the ridge. Ascend the **Upper Lip (9.4 mi.)**, then pass just west of the **Lower Lip (9.6 mi.)** with its Rock of Terror (a prominent boulder that appears ready to topple down the east side of the ridge), and reach a junction **(9.7 mi.)** where the **Cliff Trail (15)** descends very steeply east 0.4 mi. to the Cave of the Winds and the Cliff House. To the west at this junction are the Canyon North Extension (18) and the Subway (19).

Follow the ridge north, pass the north end of the Subway and reach another junction **(9.9 mi.)** in a sedge meadow where the **Sunset Ridge Trail (21)** descends west 250 ft. to the more sheltered **Laura Cowles Trail (23)** and 3.1 mi. to Underhill State Park. The **Profanity Trail (24)** drops steeply east 0.5 mi. to Taft Lodge and is the recommended bad weather route

10

off the Chin. Straight ahead, ascend the **Chin (10.1 mi.)**, Mt. Mansfield's highest summit.

The view from the Chin is dramatic. East of north lie the Sterling Range and Jay Peak. Under very favorable conditions, Montreal's Mt. Royal in Canada is visible to the northwest. To the east is the Worcester Range. Mt. Washington in New Hampshire is south of east. Right of Mt. Washington lie the Franconia Range and Mt. Moosilauke. To the south, the Green Mountains are visible to Killington Peak. To the west beyond Lake Champlain is lofty pointed Whiteface, which lies north of the dense cluster of Adirondack peaks surrounding Mt. Marcy.

From the Chin's highest point, continue north to an escarpment where there is a view of the Adam's Apple, the Lake of the Clouds, and the cliffs of Smugglers' Notch. Drop steeply from the Chin on precipitous ledges to **Eagle Pass (10.4 mi.)**, where the **Hell Brook Trail (26)** bears north to the Lake of the Clouds before plunging 1.5 mi. to Vt. 108 in Smugglers' Notch. Descending the Hell Brook Trail is not recommended. The **Adam's Apple Trail (25)** leads 0.2 mi. over the **Adam's Apple** to the Lake of the Clouds.

Bear right and descend through scrub to a junction with the lower end of the **Profanity Trail (24)**. Just beyond is a **spur (10.7)**, opposite a composting privy, leading south 200 feet to **Taft Lodge**, perched on a shelf below the Chin. This log structure, largest shelter on the LT, sleeps twenty-four. Originally built by the Burlington Section in 1920, it was a gift of Judge Elihu B. Taft of Burlington. A large corps of volunteers, led by the Burlington Section and Dana Baron and Fred Gilbert, reconstructed the lodge in 1996. Daan Zwick, Taft caretaker from 1938 to 1940, generously funded the project. Future maintenance of Taft Lodge has been endowed by Ray and Nomi Unsworth in memory of Julia E. Unsworth. Water is found in a reliable brook 300 ft. south of the lodge. A GMC caretaker is in residence during the hiking season. A fee is charged for overnight use. Wood fires are prohibited at Taft Lodge. **Butler Lodge to Taft Lodge, 3.6 mi., 5.8 km., 2¾ hr. (SB 2¼ hr.).**

Just north of the spur is the **Hell Brook Cutoff (27)**, which follows the contours of the Adam's Apple north 0.7 mi. to the

Hell Brook Trail (26). Descend steadily on ledges, level out briefly, and bear left near the Chin Clip ski trail (11.3 mi.). Descend to a stream crossing (11.6 mi.) and continue to drop to **Vt. 108** south of Smugglers' Notch (**12.4 mi.**). Vt. 108 leads south downhill 0.3 mi. to the Mt. Mansfield Ski Area, 0.5 mi. to the Spruce Peak Ski Area, 0.6 mi. to Smugglers' Notch State Park Campground, and 8.2 mi. to Vt. 100 in Stowe. *Use caution when crossing Vt. 108; traffic moves at high speeds.*

Turn left alongside Vt. 108 and follow the highway north to the **Smugglers' Notch Picnic Area (12.6 mi.)**. Turn right to cross the highway (with caution) and bear right to follow the path at the south end of the picnic area. Here the LT follows the former Elephant's Head Trail out of the notch. From the picnic area, descend to and cross Notch Brook, which can be a challenging ford in high-water conditions. Start a steady ascent on switchbacks to the ridge south of Spruce Peak, crossing and recrossing a slide with views of Mt. Mansfield. Continue to ascend at a more moderate grade along the steep sidehill before descending to a **spur (14.9 mi.)**, which drops sharply 0.1 mile west to the top of **Elephant's Head Cliff** with its commanding view over the notch. When peregrine falcons nest on the east wall of the notch, the spur is closed during the nesting season (generally mid-March to mid-August, posted by the state of Vermont) to keep from disturbing the birds.

Beyond the spur, bear east and climb steadily to **Snuffy's ski trail (15.6 mi.)**, a service road that leads south 0.2 mi. to the top of Spruce Peak chairlift. The **Elephant's Head Trail (28)** continues across the ski trail and rejoins the LT at the east end of Sterling Pond. Turn left and follow Snuffy's ski trail past the **Sterling Pond Trail (29) (15.9 mi.)**, which leads west downhill 1.1 mi. to Vt. 108 at the height of land in Smugglers' Notch. Descend to the **Sterling Pond outlet (16.0 mi.)**. Cross the outlet and ascend to a chairlift (16.1 mi.) just above a ski area warming hut. Follow the ridge east to **Sterling Pond Shelter (16.2 mi.)** and the **Elephant's Head Trail (28)**.

Sterling Pond Shelter is a pavilion-style lean-to built by the Montpelier Section led by Eric Seidel, Bill Clark, and Duncan Wilkie in 2005 and has space for at least twelve campers. Future maintenance of Sterling Pond Shelter has been endowed by Amy

10

Golodetz and Greg Leech in honor of the Sterling College community. There is a small, unreliable spring 300 ft. south of the shelter on the Elephant's Head Trail. A GMC caretaker is on duty during the hiking season, and a fee is charged for overnight use. Wood fires are prohibited at Sterling Pond Shelter. **Taft Lodge to Sterling Pond Shelter, 5.5 mi., 8.9 km., 3½ hr. (SB 3¾ hr.).**

From Sterling Pond Shelter, climb over a knob, the Sawtooth, and ascend steadily to the ridge of the Sterling Range, which includes Spruce and Madonna Peaks and Morse and Whiteface Mtns. and is named for the now-defunct town of Sterling. Cross the Drifter ski trail, climb to rejoin the ski trail, and follow it uphill to the summit of **Madonna Peak (17.4 mi.)**, where open areas at the chairlift upper station afford views in all directions. Descend east down the Chilcoot ski trail. Bear north into the woods near the Catwalk ski trail and drop steeply to **Chilcoot Pass** and, just north of the ski area, the **Chilcoot Trail (31) (18.2 mi.).** This trail descends steeply south 0.8 mi. to **Beaver Meadow Lodge** and the Beaver Meadow Trail (30). Beaver Meadow Lodge, a log cabin built by the Sterling Section, was completed in 1947. It was renovated by Sterling Section volunteers led by Mike McCole and Bob Lindemann in 2005. It has space for fifteen. Water is found in several adjacent brooks. Beaver Meadow Lodge, while a convenient base camp for hiking the Sterling Range, is well below the ridgeline and isn't usually a destination for long-distance backpackers. **Sterling Pond Shelter to Beaver Meadow Lodge, 2.8 mi., 4.5 km., 1¾ hr. (SB 2½ hr.).**

Follow the ridge north and climb gradually to **Hagerman Overlook (18.6 mi.)**, named in memory of Robert L. Hagerman, an active member of the Sterling Section, author of a detailed history of Mt. Mansfield, and former editor of the *Long Trail News.* The overlook offers a unique view of Mt. Mansfield. Ascend to pass just east of the summit of **Morse Mtn. (18.9 mi.)** and reach an eastern vista of Beaver Meadow below. Bear east and descend gradually to **Whiteface Shelter (19.7 mi.)** Here the **Whiteface Trail (32)** drops 1.0 mi. south to **Beaver Meadow Lodge**.

Whiteface Shelter, a log lean-to with space for five, was built by the LTP in 1958. The water source is a brook 150 ft. east on the Whiteface Trail. From the shelter, Madonna Peak is visible above the Beaver Meadow Basin. To its right, Mt. Mansfield can be seen above Chilcoot Pass. Wood fires are prohibited at Whiteface Shelter. **Sterling Pond Shelter to Whiteface Shelter, 3.5 mi., 5.6 km., 2¼ hr. (SB 2¾ hr.).**

From the shelter, climb steadily north to the wooded summit of **Whiteface Mtn. (20.2 mi.).** A spur leads straight ahead to several openings, which permit views in almost every direction, including vistas of Mt. Mansfield and the west wall of Smugglers' Notch. Descend moderately following the summit ridge and reach a shelf with views of the Lamoille River Valley below. Descend steeply along trail eroded to bedrock and then descend to cross Waterman Brook at an overhanging rock. Follow the brook downstream to a scenic cascade, then leave the brook to enter open hardwood forest and cross a major logging road. After several minor brook crossings, bear right onto an old woods road and descend to a **spur (23.3 mi.)** leading east to **Bear Hollow Shelter**, perched on a rocky knoll above the trail. Built by Bob Lindemann and the Sterling Section in 1991, this open-faced frame shelter sleeps twelve. The water supply is a brook just south of the shelter along the LT. **Whiteface Shelter to Bear Hollow Shelter, 3.6 mi., 5.8 km., 2¼ hr. (SB 3 hr.).**

Beyond the shelter, cross French Hill Brook (23.7 mi.), enter a logged area, and follow old logging roads north. After crossing Smith Brook, enter a clearing, turn right, and follow a gravel road. Pass an iron gate (25.9 mi.), where parking is available in dry seasons, and continue to an intersection with West Settlement Road (26.2 mi.), where there is limited parking. Follow this road north to the **Rail Trail (26.6 mi.).** Turn left and follow the multiple-use Rail Trail west for roughly a quarter mile. Bear right and descend the embankment to cross a field. Ascend a longer embankment and follow the fence line of a cemetery to reach **Vt. 15 (27.2)** 2.3 mi. west of the village of Johnson. Cross Vt. 15 to a parking lot. *Use caution when crossing Vt. 15; traffic moves at high speeds.* Leave the west end of the parking lot, cross an open field, and enter the woods. The trail ascends a knoll, then drops down and runs along the base of the hill to the river. Descending a stepladder, the trail crosses the secondary channel of the Lamoille River, usually dry but

10

subject to flooding during high water, reaching the base of the **suspension bridge (27.6 mi.).**

Note: Do not attempt to cross the secondary channel during times of high water. Use the high water route by following Vt. 15 east (1.1 mi.) to Hogback Road. Turn left on Hogback Road ascending steadily to the junction of the LT (2.0 mi) *Use caution on Vt. 15 and Hogback Road; traffic moves at high speeds.*

Side Trails

Refer to the division map on page 172 and the Mt. Mansfield maps on pages 178 and 179 for the location of numbered trails. Many of the side trails are steep and rough. Wearing rugged footwear and allotting extra time are recommended.

1. LAKE MANSFIELD TRAIL. This trail begins on the private land of the Lake Mansfield Trout Club. Please be considerate of club guests, stay on the trail, and respect the land and all buildings while in this area. Take the Moscow Road west from Vt. 100, 2.5 mi. south of Stowe. Follow the paved road, which becomes the Nebraska Valley Road. Continue beyond the end of the pavement on the gravel-surfaced road, past an open gate to the Trout Club, 6.7 mi. west from Vt. 100. Hiking season day-use parking is available at a large lot to the north of the main building. Winter parking is available next to the gate, just before the Trout Club. The land around the lake and for approximately 0.25 mi. beyond is private property.

From the parking lot (0.0 mi., 1140 ft.), follow the path into the woods and parallel the woods road that follows the north shore of the lake. Descend to join the road briefly, reenter the woods, and cross a bridge. Near the west end of the lake (0.5 mi.), descend to the road again and follow it away from the lake. Cross a small brook and steadily ascend on an old logging road. Bear right near the top of the rise and continue uphill to the alternate winter route (1.1 mi.), which bears left to cross the brook, and ascend 0.4 mi. directly north to Taylor Lodge. The main trail continues at a steeper grade to the entrance of the gorge. This route may not be passable in icy weather. Pass a piped spring (1.4 mi.), which is the water source for Taylor Lodge, and gently climb to a beaver meadow with views of the north wall of Nebraska Notch. Cross the brook, climb to Taylor Lodge (1.6 mi.) and the junction with the east end of the Clara Bow Trail (2), and continue to the LT. **Trout Club to LT, 1.6 mi., 2.6 km., 1¼ hr. (Rev. 1 hr.).**

2. CLARA BOW TRAIL. This trail provides a challenging alternate route through the floor of Nebraska Notch just north of Taylor Lodge. Starting behind the lodge (0.0 mi.), travel north to the entrance of the notch and climb over and under enormous boulders through the notch, using a ladder to negotiate a vertical drop. Rejoin the LT 0.4 mi. north of Taylor Lodge. **Taylor Lodge to LT, 0.4 mi., 0.6 km., ⅓ hr. (Rev. ⅓ hr.).**

3. NEBRASKA NOTCH TRAIL. From Underhill Center take the Pleasant Valley Road north 0.2 mi. and turn east onto the Stevensville Road. Pass Maple Leaf Farm at 1.1 mi. and reach the parking lot at the end of the road at 2.8 mi. This parking area is maintained by the state year-round, although the road can be challenging to negotiate in winter.

From the parking lot (0.0 mi., 1400 ft.), bear right at the trailhead bulletin board and pass the Overland cross-country ski trail (not suitable for hiking use due to wetlands). Climb at an easy grade to an area of beaver activity (1.4 mi.) and bear left to ascend to the LT (1.5 mi.) at the west end of Nebraska Notch. The LT leads south 0.7 mi. to Taylor Lodge. **Stevensville Road to LT, 1.5 mi., 2.4 km., 1¾ hr. (Rev. 1 hr.).**

4. WALLACE CUTOFF. This trail is the shortest route from the LT to Butler Lodge. From the LT, 1.2 mi. north of Twin Brooks Tenting Area and 0.2 mi. south of the Needle's Eye, descend steeply west to the Butler Lodge Trail 100 ft. below Butler Lodge. The lodge is to the right. **LT to Butler Lodge, 0.1 mi.**

5. BUTLER LODGE TRAIL. Refer to directions to the Nebraska Notch Trail (3). From the Stevensville parking lot, this trail follows a logging road east from the trailhead bulletin board (0.0 mi., 1400 ft.). After passing a gate, the Butler Lodge Trail and Frost Trail (6) leave the road to the left at 0.2 mi.

10

From the logging road (0.2 mi.), bear right from the Frost Trail and begin a steady ascent, passing the Wallace Cutoff (4) (1.8 mi.) 100 ft. before Butler Lodge. Owing to unstable terrain and erosion, the former Butler Lodge Trail above the lodge to the LT has been closed. Use Wallace Cutoff. **Stevensville Road to Butler Lodge, 1.8 mi., 2.9 km., 1¾ hr. (Rev. 1 hr.).**

6. FROST TRAIL. See Butler Lodge Trail (5) for initial 0.2 mi. of Frost Trail. From the logging road (0.2 mi.), bear left from the Butler Lodge Trail and cross Stevensville Brook. Climb steadily to the southmost knob of Maple Ridge (0.9 mi.), then ascend the ridge through spruce-balsam scrub to the Maple Ridge Trail (9)

DOG ETIQUETTE

The American Dog Owners Association makes the following recommendations regarding hiking with your pet:

- Leashes protect dogs from becoming lost and from backcountry hazards like porcupines and bears and sick, injured, or rabid animals.

- Unleashed dogs intimidate other hikers and their dogs, depriving them of the peace the backcountry provides.

- A leashed dog's keen senses can enhance your awareness of nearby wildlife and other backcountry visitors.

- Unleashed dogs harass, injure, and sometimes kill wildlife.

(1.4 mi.). The Maple Ridge Trail climbs very steeply 1.1 mi. to the Forehead via the Wampahoofus Trail (10). **Stevensville Road to Maple Ridge Trail, 1.4 mi., 2.3 km., 1½ hr. (Rev. 1 hr.); Stevensville Road to Forehead, 2.5 mi., 4.0 km., 2½ hr. (Rev. 1½ hr.).**

7. ROCK GARDEN TRAIL. This trail connects the Maple Ridge Trail (9) with the Wampahoofus Trail (10) across the base of the Forehead's south face. Its north end starts at the Maple Ridge Trail 0.8 mi. from the old CCC Road and 2.9 mi. from Underhill State Park. From the junction on the ridge (0.0 mi.), follow the south side of the ridge, mostly in the woods among the boulders at the base of the cliff, to the Wampahoofus Trail (0.6 mi.), 0.1 mi. from Butler Lodge. **Underhill State Park to Butler Lodge, 3.6 mi., 5.8 km., 2¼ hr. (Rev. 1¾ hr.).**

8. FOREHEAD BY-PASS. This white-blazed trail offers a less exposed ascent of the Forehead; although recommended in severe weather conditions, it too is rough and slippery when wet. From the LT (0.0 mi.) just north of the Needle's Eye, bear right and steadily ascend the east slope of the Forehead. After the South Link (11) diverges right (0.9 mi.) to the Octagon, the By-Pass climbs to the ridge and joins the LT (1.2 mi.) just south of the TV Road. **Needle's Eye to TV Road, 1.2 mi., 1.9 km., 1 hr. (Rev. ¾ hr.).**

9. MAPLE RIDGE TRAIL. From Underhill Center, take the Pleasant Valley Road 1.0 mi. north and turn east onto the Mountain Road (Town Highway 2). Follow the road 2.7 mi. to its end at Underhill State Park. There is a fee for parking when the park is in season. The Mountain Road is 3.8 mi. east of Vt. 15 in Underhill Flats. The upper 1.5 mi. of the Mountain Road to the state park is not plowed in winter.

10

From the parking lot (0.0 mi., 1800 ft.), follow the old gravel CCC Road uphill past the locked gate, passing the group camping area and continuing to a sharp right turn (1.0 mi.) where the Sunset Ridge Trail (21) leads north to the Laura Cowles Trail (23) and Sunset Ridge. Much of this road walk can be by-passed by the Eagle's Cut Trail, which rejoins the road just below the Sunset Ridge Trail. A gentle ascent on the road leads to the Halfway House Trail (20) (1.2 mi.). Follow the narrowing road to the Maple Ridge Trail (2.1 mi.).

From the old CCC Road, climb steeply over a rough footpath and emerge on the open ridgeline (2.4 mi.) and climb to the Frost Trail (6) (2.5 mi.), which descends south to the Stevensville parking lot. Continue uphill to the Rock Garden Trail (7) (2.9 mi.), a sheltered route to Butler Lodge. Climb very steeply over open ledges to the Wampahoofus Trail (10) (3.4 mi.), 0.2 mi. below the Forehead. *Use caution in wet weather, especially if descending.* **Underhill State Park to Forehead, 3.6 mi., 5.8 km., 3 hr. (Rev. 2 hr.).**

10. WAMPAHOOFUS TRAIL. This rugged trail provides another alternate route up the Forehead from the south and is the easiest route for backpackers in good weather. Proceed north from Butler Lodge (0.0 mi.) and pass the Rock Garden Trail (7) (0.1 mi.), which leads northwest to Maple Ridge. Climb steeply, squeezing through crevices and caves, to a large rock overhanging the trail (0.6 mi.). The LTP thought this rock resembled the open jaws of the mythical "Sidehill Wampahoofus." Just beyond the rock, the Maple Ridge Trail (9) descends west to the old CCC Road. Bear right and follow the open ridge uphill to the LT (0.8 mi.) at the Forehead. **Butler Lodge to Forehead, 0.8 mi., 1.3 km., 1 hr. (Rev. ¾ hr.).**

11. SOUTH LINK. This trail connects the Toll Road near the Octagon with the Forehead By-Pass (8). From a parking area on the Toll Road opposite the spur to the Octagon, follow a rugged, rocky path through the woods to the Forehead By-Pass, 0.3 mi. south of the TV Road. **Toll Road to Forehead By-Pass, 0.6 mi., 1.0 km.**

12. LAKEVIEW TRAIL. Leave the TV Road just north of the LT from the Forehead and emerge on an open shelf. Descend over and between large boulders using an underpass, several switchbacks, and a ladder. Follow a shoulder of the mountain, with views of the Champlain Valley and Adirondacks. Reenter the woods, join the Canyon Trail (16), and, crossing the TV Road, rejoin the LT at the Summit Station. **TV Road to Summit Station, 0.8 mi., 1.3 km.**

13. HASELTON TRAIL. This trail, named after Judge Seneca Haselton of Burlington, the first vice president of the GMC, was part of the original route of the LT between Mt. Mansfield and the Sterling Range. It begins at the far end of the Mt. Mansfield Ski Area Gondola Base Lodge parking lot (the upper lot), 0.6 mi. south of the LT on Vt. 108. From the parking lot adjacent to the gondola station, pass under the gondola, then follow a ski service road uphill to the left (south) of the Midway Lodge. The trail begins on the left about 150 ft. from where the road enters the woods.

Enter the woods (0.0 mi., 1600 ft.) and climb steadily. After following a hogback separating two brooks (0.6 mi.), cross the south brook (0.7 mi.), then cross a ski trail and ascend steeply through glades to join the Nose Dive Ski Trail (1.3 mi.). Climb steeply on the uppermost switchbacks of the ski trail to the Toll Road (1.6 mi.) near the Octagon. The Toll Road leads uphill 0.5 mi. to the Summit Station and the LT. **Midway Lodge to LT, 2.1 mi., 3.4 km., 2¼ hr. (Rev. 1¼ hr.).**

14. AMHERST TRAIL. This trail provides a sheltered route between Drift Rock and the Summit Station, by-passing Frenchman's Pile. From the LT just north of the Summit Station, follow the TV Road east for 200 ft. and turn left into the woods. Pass the Cliff Trail (15), which bears off to the right. Continue north, passing between two ledges and following an open shelf before ducking back into the shelter of the trees and joining the LT at Drift Rock. **TV Road to Drift Rock, 0.3 mi., 0.5 km.**

15. CLIFF TRAIL. This rugged trail is not recommended for backpackers. From the Amherst Trail (14) (0.0 mi.), proceed north and begin a series of ascents and descents on the east side of the summit ridge, some involving ladders and cables. After passing through two "caves" and "Wall Street" (0.7 mi.) a spur (0.8 mi.) leads downhill 0.1 mi. to the Cliff House (i.e., the top of Stowe Mountain Resort's gondola). Continue straight, passing over and under rocks to another obscure spur (1.0 mi.), leading left to the Cave of the Winds where there may be snow as late as July or August. Inside the "cave," there is a 60-ft. descent that should only be attempted by experienced parties with ropes.

10

Beyond the spur, climb steeply to join the LT (1.1 mi.), just north of the Lower Lip. **Amherst Trail to LT, 1.1 mi., 1¼ hr. (Rev. 1¼ hr.).**

From the gondola station, follow the ski trail south a short distance to the spur trail leading to the Cliff Trail (0.0 mi.). Ascend directly on rugged terrain to the Cliff Trail (0.1 mi.). The left fork goes to the Amherst Trail and Toll Road junction (1.0 mi.). The right fork is the direct route to the ridge over steep ledges (0.4 mi. to the LT and 0.8 mi. total to the Chin.)

16. CANYON TRAIL. This trail passes through the Canyon, a large joint in the mountain's west wall. From the LT at the Summit Station (0.0 mi.), proceed west, cross the TV Road to enter the woods, and coincide with the Lake View Trail (12) for a short way. Bear north and emerge from the woods to follow an open shelf with views to the west. After squeezing through narrow passages too tight for a backpack, enter the Canyon, a large chamber overhung by the mountain wall. After climbing ladders and passing through a second chamber, reach the Halfway House Trail (20) (0.6 mi.), 0.1 mi. west of the LT. **Summit Station to Halfway House Trail, 0.6 mi., 1.0 km.**

17. CANYON NORTH TRAIL. This north extension of the Canyon Trail (16) begins on the Halfway House Trail (20) a few feet west (downhill) of the Canyon Trail junction. Cross an open shelf with views to the west before squeezing through a series of caves and crevices. Regain the shelf, reaching the Canyon North Extension (18), then bear right and climb to the LT just south of the Upper Lip. **Halfway House Trail to LT, 0.6 mi., 1.0 km.**

18. CANYON NORTH EXTENSION. This continuation of the Canyon North Trail (17) leaves that trail near the LT just south of the Upper Lip. Climb steadily with fine views to the west, then pass through a crevice and emerge on a narrow ledge, with outstanding views of Sunset Ridge. After another crevice, bear right, passing the Subway (19), and end on the LT opposite the north end of the Cliff Trail (15). **LT south of Upper Lip to Cliff Trail, 0.6 mi., 1.0 km.**

19. THE SUBWAY. This trail is not recommended in unfavorable weather. From the LT across from the Cliff Trail (15) junction, join the Canyon North Extension (18) for a short way, then bear right to a ladder and drop steeply into a maze of crevices, boulders, and caves, which require agile maneuvering. After leaving the boulders, follow a steep, winding climb in the open and return to the LT a few hundred feet north of the Cliff Trail. **Cliff Trail to ridge, 0.3 mi., 0.5 km.**

20. HALFWAY HOUSE TRAIL. This trail once served as a bridle path from the old Halfway House to the ridge. Refer to access directions for the Maple Ridge Trail (9) to get to Underhill State Park. Proceed east from the old CCC Road (0.0 mi., 2600 ft.), 1.2 mi. from the parking lot. Enter the woods and begin a winding course along switchbacks. Climb steeply over ledges to the Canyon North Trail (17) (0.9 mi.) to the left, then the Canyon Trail (16) to the right. Continue straight up on ledges to the LT (1.1 mi.) at the ridge just south of Frenchman's Pile. The LT leads south 0.2 mi. to the Summit Station, and north out in the open 1.2 mi. to the Chin. **Underhill State Park to Summit Station, 2.5 mi., 4.0 km., 2¼ hr. (Rev. 1½ hr.).**

21. SUNSET RIDGE TRAIL. Refer to access directions for the Maple Ridge Trail (9) to get to Underhill State Park. Proceed north from the old CCC Road (0.0 mi., 2340 ft.), at the sharp right turn in the road 1.0 mi. from the parking lot. Pass the Laura Cowles Trail (23) (0.1 mi.), continue uphill past the Cantilever Rock Trail (22) (0.7 mi.), then bear east and climb to the open ridge. Follow cairns (rock pile trail markers) in addition to blue blazes above treeline. Pass the upper end of the Laura Cowles Trail (2.1 mi.) and, 250 ft. beyond, reach the LT on the ridge opposite the Profanity Trail (24), 0.2 mi. south of the Chin. **Underhill State Park to Chin, 3.3 mi., 5.3 km., 3 hr. (Rev. 1¾ hr.).**

22. CANTILEVER ROCK TRAIL. Cantilever Rock, discovered in 1960 by Clyde F. and Clyde H. Smith, is a horizontal blade of rock 60 ft. above the ground wedged into the vertical face of a 100-ft. cliff. It is 40 ft. long, with 31 ft. extending beyond the cliff. Proceed north from the Sunset Ridge Trail (21), 0.7 mi. above the CCC Road, for 0.2 mi. to see this striking phenomenon.

10

23. LAURA COWLES TRAIL. This trail provides a steep but sheltered route on the west side of the mountain. It was named for the first woman president of the Burlington Section and was built by her husband, Judge C.P. Cowles, a charter member of the GMC. Refer to directions to the Maple Ridge Trail (9). Proceed west from the Sunset Ridge Trail (21) (0.0 mi., 2360 ft.), 1.1 mi. from the Underhill State Park, and follow a brook upstream. Cross a bridge built by Boy Scout Troop 627 and ascend steeply in the hollow to the south of Sunset Ridge. After passing a small ledge (0.9 mi.), continue uphill to the Sunset Ridge Trail (1.4 mi.), 250 ft. west of the LT. **Underhill State Park to Chin, 2.7 mi., 4.3 km., 2¾ hr. (Rev. 1½ hr.).**

24. PROFANITY TRAIL. This trail connects the ridge south of the Chin with Taft Lodge and provides a fairly sheltered route around the Chin in unfavorable conditions. It is not as exposed as the LT north of the Chin. Summer thunderstorms blowing in from the west are not visible from this trail. Dogs should be leashed on the lower part of the trail to protect the Taft Lodge water supply. From the LT, just above the Taft Lodge spur, bear left and climb steeply through the scrub under the west face of the Chin. Emerge into the open and gently ascend to the LT opposite the Sunset Ridge Trail (21), 0.2 mi. south of the Chin. **Taft Lodge to LT, 0.5 mi., 0.8 km., ½ hr. (Rev. ⅓ hr.).**

25. ADAM'S APPLE TRAIL. From the junction of the LT and Hell Brook Trail (26) in Eagle Pass, ascend north 0.1 mi. to the open summit of the Adam's Apple, with views of the Chin, the east wall of the notch, and the Lake of the Clouds. Descend north 0.1 mi. to rejoin Hell Brook Trail near Lake of the Clouds. **Eagle Pass to Lake of the Clouds, 0.2 mi., 0.3 km.**

26. HELL BROOK TRAIL. This trail starts on the west side of Vt. 108 in Smugglers' Notch, 9.1 mi. north of Vt. 100 in Stowe and 8.7 mi. south of Vt. 15 in Jeffersonville. It leaves Vt. 108 just 150 ft. north of the Big Spring pullout, which provides limited parking for hikers. Descending this trail is not recommended.

From the highway (0.0 mi., 1803 ft.), climb steeply to the ridge, frequently on precipitous ledges, through woods with several views of the cliffs on the east side of the notch. Pass the Hell Brook Cutoff (27) (0.9 mi.) leading 0.7 mi. south to Taft Lodge, and continue uphill to the Adam's Apple Trail (25) (1.3 mi.) near Lake of the Clouds. Follow the west side of the Adam's Apple to the LT (1.5 mi.) in Eagle Pass. **Vt. 108 to LT, 1.5 mi., 2.4 km., 2 hr. (Rev. 1 hr.).**

27. HELL BROOK CUTOFF. From the Hell Brook Trail (26), 0.9 mi. above Vt. 108, follow the contour of the steep east slope of the Adam's Apple south 0.7 mi. to the LT near Taft Lodge. **Hell Brook Trail to Taft Lodge, 0.7 mi., 1.1 km., ½ hr. (Rev 1½ hr.).**

28. ELEPHANT'S HEAD TRAIL. This trail links the north end of Sterling Pond with the LT at Snuffy's ski trail above Elephant's Head Cliff. From the LT (0.0 mi.) at Sterling Pond Shelter, descend to the spring that feeds the pond, pass Watson Camp (0.1 mi.), and follow the rocky shoreline of Sterling Pond. Climb over a low knoll and descend to Snuffy's ski trail and the LT (0.7 mi.). The LT south crosses the ski trail and descends 0.7 mi. to the spur leading west to Elephant's Head Cliff; the LT north turns right and follows the ski trail to Sterling Pond. **Sterling Pond Shelter to LT at Snuffy's ski trail, 0.7 mi., 1.1 km., ½ hr. (Rev. ½ hr.); Sterling Pond Shelter to Elephant's Head Cliff, 1.5 mi., 2.4 km., 1 hr. (Rev. 1¼ hr.).**

29. STERLING POND TRAIL. This trail begins on Vt. 108 at the top of Smugglers' Notch, 9.8 mi. north of Vt. 100 in Stowe and 8.0 mi. south of Vt. 15 in Jeffersonville. Formerly the LT out of Smugglers' Notch, this route was originally called Mould's Trail, in honor of Fred Mould, an active volunteer in the early days of GMC's Sterling Section.

10

From the east side of the highway (0.0 mi., 2160 ft.) opposite the parking area and information booth, climb a rock staircase built by the LTP. Continue the steady ascent on the rough path that was once a woods road. Reach the LT (1.1 mi.) at Snuffy's ski trail, a service road linking Spruce Peak and Smugglers' Notch ski areas. Turn left to descend on the LT north along Snuffy's ski trail 0.1 mi. to Sterling Pond, or turn right to follow the LT south 0.3 mi. to the Elephant's Head Trail leading around Sterling Pond, and 3.3 mi. to the Smugglers' Notch Picnic Area on Vt. 108, 1.3 mi. south of the

Sterling Pond trailhead. **Smugglers' Notch to Sterling Pond, 1.2 mi., 1.9 km., 1¼ hr. (Rev. ¾ hr.).**

30. BEAVER MEADOW TRAIL. This trail provides access from the east to Beaver Meadow in a bowl 1500 ft. below the LT and the summits of the Sterling Range. From Vt. 100, 1.0 mi. south of Morrisville (0.0 mi., 2160 ft.), follow Morristown Corners Road west, then immediately bear left to Morristown Corners. At the four-way stop sign (0.7 mi.), continue straight on Walton Road. Pass Cote Hill Road by bearing left on Walton Road, and then pass Cole Hill Road on the left before taking the next left on Mud City Loop Road (1.7 mi.). Turn left at the junction with Bryan Road (3.5 mi.) to continue on Mud City Loop Road, and follow it to a fork (4.4 mi.). At a farm, bear right onto Beaver Meadow Road and follow it to a large winter parking lot (5.4 mi.) to the right, or continue on an unimproved road to a small clearing on the right opposite an iron gate where the trail begins (6.0 mi.).

Pass the iron gate (0.0 mi., 1550 ft.) and ascend gradually on old logging roads to an intersection with the Beaver Meadow Cutoff Trail (1.8 mi.). Turn left, leaving the logging road, and cross Beaver Meadow Brook (1.9 mi.). Pass near a beaver pond and, after crossing a stream, reach Beaver Meadow Lodge (2.3 mi.) and the Chilcoot Trail (31). The Beaver Meadow Cutoff Trail bears right to circle the meadow. From the Beaver Meadow Trail, continue straight ahead on the woods road, passing the Whiteface Trail (32) (0.3) mi.), and reach Beaver Meadow Lodge (0.5 mi.). **Iron gate to Beaver Meadow Lodge, 2.3 mi., 3.7 km., 1½ hr. (Rev. 1¼ hr.).**

31. CHILCOOT TRAIL. This trail links Beaver Meadow Lodge with the LT north of Madonna Peak. Follow the path behind the lodge (0.0 mi., 2150 ft.) and initially ascend gently, then steeply to the LT (0.8 mi.) at Chilcoot Pass. **Beaver Meadow Lodge to LT, 0.8 mi., 1.3 km., 1 hr. (Rev. ¾ hr.).**

32. WHITEFACE TRAIL. From Beaver Meadow Cutoff Trail (0.0 mi., 2165 ft.), 0.2 mi. east of Beaver Meadow Lodge, steadily climb to the LT (1.0 mi.) at Whiteface Shelter. **Beaver Meadow Lodge to Whiteface Shelter, 1.0 mi., 1.6 km., 1 hr. (Rev. ½ hr.).**

Lamoille River from Prospect Rock

Division 11
Lamoille River to Tillotson Camp

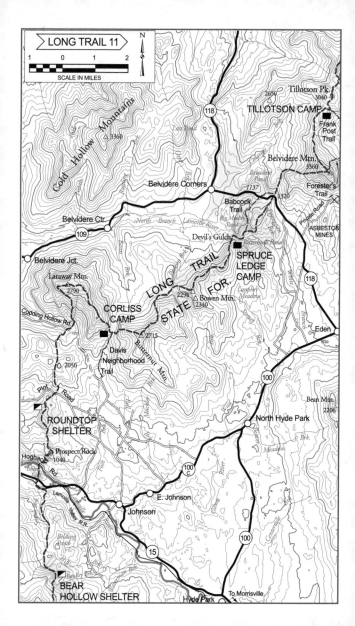

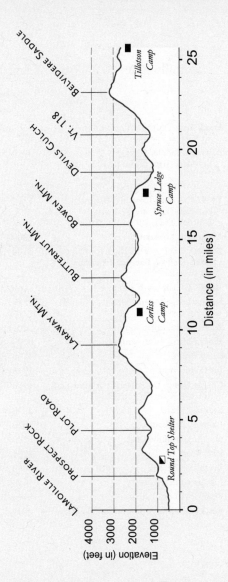

Division 11 Profile

Lamoille River to Tillotson Camp

miles north-bound	▲ NORTH	elevation at Long Trail (feet/meters)	miles south-bound
26.0	Frank Post Trail to **Tillotson Camp**, 50 ft E; to Tillotson Road, 2.0 mi E	2560/780	0.0
23.2	**Belvidere Saddle; Forester's Trail** to **Belvidere Mtn.** (3360 ft/1024 m), 0.2 mi SE; to Tillotson Road via **Frank Post Trail**, 2.7 mi NE	3200/975	2.8
20.6	**Vt. 118 at Eden Crossing; Babcock Extension** to **Long Trail** via **Babcock Trail**, 1.8 mi W	1320/402	5.4
18.9	**Ritterbush Lookout**	1300/396	7.1
18.6	**Babcock Trail** to **Vt. 118**, 1.4 mi N; to **Long Trail** via **Babcock Extension**, 1.8 mi NE	1100/335	7.4
18.0	**Devil's Gulch**, south entrance	1260/384	8.0
17.6	**Spruce Ledge Camp** (1565 ft/477 m), 830 ft E via spur	1515/469	8.4
16.7	**Bowen Mtn.**, north summit	2200/671	9.3
15.2	**Bowen Mtn.**, south summit	2290/698	10.8
14.0	**Basin Brook**	1890/576	12.0
12.2	**Butternut Mtn.**	2715/828	13.8
11.0	**Corliss Camp; Davis Neighborhood Trail** to Cross Road, 1.5 mi S	1900/579	15.0
8.3	**Laraway Mtn.**	2790/850	17.7
8.0	**Laraway Lookout**	2620/799	18.0
6.2	**Codding Hollow Road**	1230/375	19.8
3.8	**Plot Road**	1254/382	22.2
2.9	**Roundtop Shelter**	1650/503	23.1
1.3	**Prospect Rock Road**	960/293	24.7
1.0	**Prospect Rock**	1040/317	25.0
0.0	**Suspension bridge across Lamoille River**	500/152	26.0

SOUTH
▼

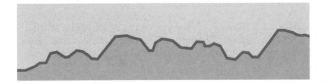

Division 11

Lamoille River to Tillotson Camp

Massachusetts 223.4 miles   **Canada 49.3 miles**

From the Lamoille River to Belvidere Mtn., the Long Trail (LT) is named for Marjorie Hulburd whose father, the Honorable R. W. Hulburd, funded the original trail construction.

The following people have contributed to endow the future maintenance of 2 miles of the LT within this division: Walter Pomroy and a gift in honor of Susan Shea.

Camping and Fires

This division of the LT crosses private and state land. Camping is allowed only at shelters. Small wood fires are permitted at the shelters' established fire rings. Refer to Leave No Trace principles (pages 11 to 12) to minimize your impact.

Note: Wood fires are not permitted at Spruce Ledge Camp to protect surrounding vegetation.

Group Use

Groups hiking this division's LT may need a Commercial Use Permit from the Vermont Department of Forests, Parks and Recreation. Group tenting space is available at Corliss, Spruce

Ledge, and Tillotson Camps. Elmore State Park, east of the LT off Vt. 15 and Vt. 12 south, is available for base camp hiking. Refer to pages 13 to 19 for additional group use guidelines.

Winter Use

This division's suggested day hikes make good snowshoe trips. The Davis Neighborhood Trail is suitable for intermediate cross-country skiing.

Access to the Long Trail

VT. 15. Recommended parking for the Lamoille River bridge is at the parking lot on the north side of Vt. 15 west of Johnson, across from the cemetery a half mile west of West Settlement Road.

Suggested Day Hikes

LARAWAY LOOKOUT. This hike north on the LT from Codding Hollow passes impressive cliffs and features a splendid view. Round trip, 3.6 mi., 2½ hr.

RITTERBUSH/BIG MUDDY POND LOOP. This loop, which passes two backcountry ponds, uses the LT south from Vt. 118, the Babcock Trail, and Babcock Trail Extension to return to the trailhead. Round trip, 3.9 mi., 2½ hr.

BELVIDERE MTN. This challenging hike features sweeping views from the summit fire tower. One route uses the LT north from Vt. 118 and follows the Forester's Trail to the summit. Round trip, 5.6 mi., 3¾ hr. A second option is a loop hike from Tillotson Road that follows the Frank Post, Long, and Forester's Trails past Tillotson Camp and the summit of Belvidere Mtn. This trip is suitable for backpacking. Total loop, 7.9 mi., 5 hr.

PLOT ROAD. The LT crosses this road west of Johnson and north of Vt. 15. From Johnson at the junction of Vt. 15 and Vt. 100C (0.0 mi.), take Vt. 15 west to Foote Brook Road (1.2 mi.). Turn right and follow Foote Brook Road north to an offset intersection (2.7 mi.). Turn left onto Plot Road and continue west to the LT (4.6 mi.). From Waterville, Plot Road leaves Vt. 109 0.3 mi. south of town and leads 3.1 mi. east to the trailhead. There is limited parking along the road. A parking lot is planned for the south side of the road near the trail crossing.

CODDING HOLLOW ROAD. From Waterville (0.0 mi.), follow Vt. 109 north to Codding Hollow Road (1.8 mi.). Turn right and proceed east on this road, crossing a covered bridge over the North Branch of the Lamoille River, and continue, bearing left at the only fork, to the last farm where the road becomes a narrow, unimproved country lane. Pass a winter parking lot on the right at 2.2 mi. The road continues, and at 2.5 mi. the LT enters the road from the south to follow it briefly east before turning left into a former log landing where there is parking. Please make sure to park beyond the last house in the designated parking lot; do not block private access. To the east, it is 1.9 mi. by unimproved road, impassable to vehicles, to Davis Neighborhood.

VT. 118 AT EDEN CROSSING. The LT crosses this road 4.8 mi. west of Vt. 100 in Eden, and 2.0 mi. east of Vt. 109 at Belvidere Corners. There is an off-road parking lot on the north side of the highway, accessed by a short road 300 ft. west of the LT crossing.

Long Trail Description

At the **Lamoille River (0.0 mi.)**, cross the suspension bridge, built by the Long Trail Patrol (LTP) in 2004–2005 and dedicated to Aldie and Bob Gannett, and ascend a framed staircase to Hogback Road. There is no hiker parking here; hikers should park at the LT parking lot on Vt. 15, 0.4 mi. south. *Use caution when crossing Hogback Road; traffic moves at high speeds.* Follow the LT uphill through a hemlock and hardwood forest and then leveling off and turning left onto an old woods road. Follow the road past the base of a cliff, and climb steeply up its west side to **Prospect Rock (1.0 mi.)**, with a commanding view of the pastoral Lamoille River Valley below the Sterling Range.

Continue north on an old road and descend to the **Prospect Rock Road (1.3 mi.)**. Turn left and follow it a short distance before turning right (1.4 mi.) to reenter the woods. Ascend gradually to the broad summit of Roundtop before dropping down to **Roundtop Shelter (2.9 mi.)**. This unique log shelter, with space for ten, was built by Todd and Wendy Jenner with the Laraway Section and other GMC volunteers in 1994. It is dedicated to Todd's brother Jeff. The logs were cut on Roundtop and skidded to the site by hand the previous winter. The water source is a hand pump found at the end of a 450-ft. spur trail, which leaves the LT a short distance north of the shelter. Pump water, like all water along the Long Trail System, should be treated. This source can run dry in drought conditions. In case of pump failure, water might be found in a seep just beyond the pump. **Bear Hollow Shelter to Roundtop Shelter, 7.2 mi,11.6 km, 4½ hr. (SB 4¼ hr.).**

From the shelter follow the ridge north before descending to **Plot Road (3.8 mi.)**. Cross the road and ascend to a shallow saddle (4.8 mi.), before descending into Codding Hollow. Turn right, cross over a stonewall, and continue to the unpaved **Codding Hollow Road (6.2 mi.)**. To the left, this road leads 0.3 mi. west to the winter parking lot.

Turn right and follow the road east about 200 ft., then turn left over a brook into an old log landing where there is additional parking. Enter the woods at the north end of the landing, and ascend on old logging roads, crossing several small brooks and then a large stream (6.4 mi.). Leave the logging road, bear left, and reach some impressive cliffs. Follow along the base of the cliffs before climbing to **Laraway Lookout (8.0 mi.)**. This vista affords a sweeping view from southeast to northwest, featuring Mt. Mansfield from a unique angle. Continue north, then east, along the boggy ridge to the summit of **Laraway Mtn. (8.3 mi.)** with a limited view.

Follow the ridge east and descend at a moderate grade, before making a steeper descent (10.6 mi.) to an old woods road. Follow it downhill to **Corliss Camp and the Davis Neighborhood Trail (11.0 mi.)**, which leads 1.5 mi. south to Cross Road. Corliss Camp, a frame cabin, was built by Peter Hayden and the Laraway Section in 1989 and is named for Robert Corliss of St. Albans, who was an active section volunteer. It has sleeping space for fourteen. Water is found at a small brook about 350 ft. from the camp at the end of a spur to the left off the Davis Neighborhood Trail. **Roundtop Shelter to Corliss Camp, 8.1 mi., 13.1 km, 5½ hr. (SB 5¼ hr.).**

From Corliss Camp proceed east and climb steadily to the highest peak of **Butternut Mtn. (12.2 mi.)** where there is a limited view. Descend moderately to cross the main branch of **Basin Brook (14.0 mi.)**. Cross the brook, follow several woods roads, and then cross a gravel road. Pass through a low wet area, descend a rock stairway to another gravel road. Follow this road for 0.1 mi. before turning right to reenter the woods and climb to the lower of two south summits of **Bowen Mtn. (15.2 mi.)**. Illegal access by all-terrain vehicles is a chronic problem in this area. Pay attention to the blazes.

Continue along a ridge with easy grades to a north summit of **Bowen Mtn. (16.7 mi.)**. Descend to a stream crossing and a **spur (17.6 mi.)** leading 830 ft. east uphill to **Spruce Ledge Camp**. This frame camp with space for eight was built by Gil Patnoe and Cheryl Vreeland, the Laraway Section, and other GMC volunteers in 1998. The camp is dedicated to Don Hill, long an inspiring trail maintainer in northern Vermont. Future maintenance of Spruce Ledge Camp has been endowed by John Brown and Deborah Brown. Water sources are the small stream crossed at the beginning of the spur and a spring 250 ft. behind the camp. Devil's Perch Outlook, just beyond the camp, affords a view of Ritterbush Pond and Belvidere Mtn. **Corliss Camp to Spruce Ledge Camp, 6.8 mi., 10.9 km., 4 hr. (SB 4 hr.).**

From the spur, descend to enter **Devil's Gulch (18.0 mi.)**. Follow the challenging route along the floor of the gulch among jumbled boulders and then descend to a junction with the **Babcock Trail (18.6 mi.)** just west of Ritterbush Pond. This trail leads 1.4 mi. north to Vt. 118. Cross a brook, and then climb steeply on a series of stone stairs to **Ritterbush**

11

Lookout (18.9 mi.) on a cliff overlooking Ritterbush Pond. Continue to the top of a low ridge (19.5 mi.), descend, and then pass under a power line. Reenter the woods and follow the east side of the ridge downhill to **Vt. 118 at Eden Crossing (20.6 mi.).**

Cross the highway and descend to a parking lot. *Use caution when crossing Vt. 118; traffic moves at high speeds.* From the parking area, the **Babcock Trail Extension** bears west 0.4 mi. to the Babcock Trail at Vt. 118. Continue north around a gate to cross Frying Pan Brook (20.8 mi.) and then climb steadily with some steep grades over ledges to **Belvidere Saddle (23.2 mi.)** and a trail junction between the two summits of Belvidere Mtn. To the right, the **Forester's Trail** leads 0.2 mi. uphill to the main summit of Belvidere Mtn. and its fire tower with outstanding views of the northern Green Mountains, and straight ahead it descends east 2.7 mi. to Tillotson Road.

Turn left at Belvidere Saddle and proceed north to follow the ridge through spruce-fir forest devastated by Hurricane Floyd in 1999, leading to a sag at Lockwood Pond. Bear right to skirt the south shore of the pond past some beaver activity and reach the **Frank Post Trail (26.0 mi.)** leading 50 ft. east to **Tillotson Camp** and then 2.0 mi. downhill to Tillotson Road. This classic "Buchanan era" frame camp, with bunks for eight, was built in 1939, replacing the original shelter built by Red Tillotson in 1930. The shelter was renovated in 2007 by the LTP led by Matt Wels. Future maintenance of Tillotson Camp has been endowed in memory of Wayne Taft. Brook water, draining beaver ponds, is 100 ft. to the north on the LT. From the front of the camp there is a limited view of the Lowell Range to the east. **Spruce Ledge Camp to Tillotson Camp, 8.6 mi., 13.8 km., 6 hr. (SB 5 hr.).**

THANK YOU, LANDOWNERS!

The Green Mountain Club thanks the private landowners who allow portions of the Long Trail and side trails to cross their properties.

Side Trails

DAVIS NEIGHBORHOOD TRAIL. This trail uses a class 4 town road and an old logging road in the so-called Davis Neighborhood, north of Johnson. Take Foote Brook Road north from Vt. 15, 1.2 mi. west of Johnson and 0.4 mi. east of the Lamoille River. Drive north on Foote Brook Road for 2.2 mi., crossing Plot Road at an offset intersection. At 2.2 mi., turn right and then immediately left onto Codding Hollow Road, passing Cemetery Road at the intersection. On Codding Hollow Road, pass Swamp Road and turn right onto Cross Road at 3.6 mi. The trailhead, with limited roadside parking, is on the left at 3.7 mi. from Vt. 15.

From Cross Road (0.0 mi., 1200 ft.), follow Davis Neighborhood Trail north on a logging road and ascend moderately past a camp to the LT State Forest boundary. Continue on the now-abandoned road uphill past the site of the former Parker Camp (1.2 mi.) to the LT (1.5 mi.) just east of Corliss Camp. **Cross Road to LT, 1.5 mi., 2.4 km., 1 hr. (Rev. ¾ hr.).**

BABCOCK TRAIL. This trail provides an alternate route to Ritterbush Pond and Devil's Gulch from Vt. 118. Leave Vt. 118 across the highway from the Babcock Trail Extension (0.0 mi., 1200 ft.), and ascend gently on old woods roads south to Big Muddy Pond (0.5 mi.). Climb over a low knoll at the north end of the pond and then continue south above the west shore of the pond. Cross a height of land (1.1 mi.) at the south end of the pond, then descend steadily on old woods roads to the LT (1.4 mi.) just above Ritterbush Pond. **Vt. 118 to LT, 1.4 mi., 2.3 km., 1 hr. (Rev. 1 hr.).**

BABCOCK TRAIL EXTENSION. This trail starts at the LT parking lot at Eden Crossing on Vt. 118. From the LT, bear left and travel west, downhill, to cross a small brook, and then reach a dirt road. Turn left and follow the road 0.1 mi. before reentering the woods to the left and climbing to Vt. 118 directly across from the north end of the Babcock Trail. **LT to Babcock Trail on Vt. 118, 0.4 mi., 0.6 km., ¼ hr. (Rev. ¼ hr.).**

FRANK POST TRAIL. This trail is named for a former Boy Scout leader and Burlington Section member. From Vt. 100 in Eden

11

Mills, follow North Road (which becomes Mines Road at the county line) 5.2 mi. north and turn left on Tillotson Road, a gravel public road. Follow Tillotson Road to the trailhead (5.8 mi.). Tillotson Road is also 3.1 mi. south of Vt. 58 in Lowell via Mines Road. Enter the woods at the parking area (0.0 mi., 1380 ft.) and follow a logging road to the Forester's Trail (0.6 mi.), which leads 2.1 mi. to the LT near the summit of Belvidere Mtn. Continue west, cross a brook and follow old woods roads steadily uphill. At a right turn (1.6 mi.), begin a steep ascent to Tillotson Camp (2.0 mi.), and 50 ft. beyond, the LT. **Tillotson Road to Long Trail, 2.0 mi., 3.2 km., 1¾ hr. (Rev. 1 hr.).**

FORESTER'S TRAIL. This trail begins at the Frank Post Trail, 0.6 mi. west of the trailhead on Tillotson Road. From the Frank Post Trail (0.0 mi., 1480 ft.), ascend gradually at first, crossing a small brook and then the larger Lockwood Brook. Cross several more small brooks and old woods roads, and then climb, following some switchbacks, to Belvidere Saddle (2.1 mi.) and the LT. Turn left and continue uphill to the summit of Belvidere Mtn. (2.3 mi.).

The summit of Belvidere Mtn. features a fire tower maintained by the GMC. From the tower, the Green Mountains are visible south to Camel's Hump. Big Jay and Jay Peak are prominent to the north; to their right stands Owl's Head and other mountains in Quebec near Lake Memphremagog. On a clear day, the White Mountains are visible to the east. An inactive asbestos mine, once a mainstay of northern Vermont's economy, lies at the eastern base of the mountain, with another inactive mine on the south slope. **Tillotson Road to Belvidere Mtn., 2.9 mi., 4.7 km., 2½ hr. (Rev. 1½ hr.).**

Big Jay and Jay Peak from Hazen's Notch Camp

Division 12
Tillotson Camp to
Canadian Border

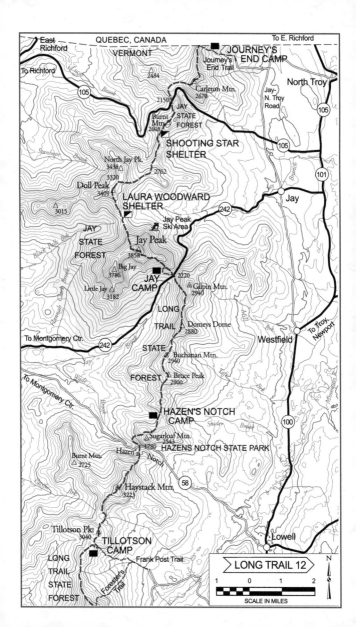

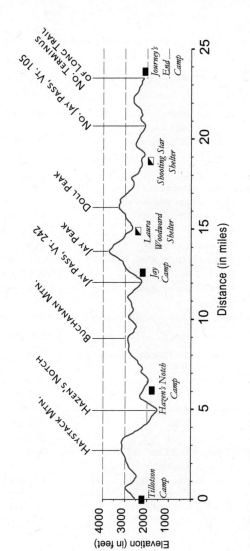

Division 12 Profile

Tillotson Camp to the Canadian Border

miles north-bound	▲ NORTH	elevation at Trail (feet/meters)	miles south-bound
	JOURNEY'S END TRAIL		
1.3	**Northern terminus** of **Long Trail**	2100/640	0.0
0.8	**Journey's End Camp**	1720/472	0.5
0.0	**Journey's End Trail** parking	1350/411	1.3
	LONG TRAIL		
23.3	**U.S.–Canadian Border, Line Post 592, northern terminus of Long Trail**	2100/640	0.0
21.9	**Carleton Mtn.**, lookout	2670/814	1.4
20.7	**Vt. 105** at **North Jay Pass**	2150/655	2.6
19.5	**Burnt Mtn.**	2608/795	3.8
18.9	**Shooting Star Shelter**	2260/689	4.4
16.0	**Unnamed peak** of **North Jay Massif**	3320/1012	7.3
15.5	**Doll Peak**	3409/1039	7.8
14.6	**Laura Woodward Shelter**	2800/853	8.7
13.1	**Jay Peak**	3858/1176	10.2
11.7	**Jay Loop**, north end to **Jay Camp**, 0.2 mi W	2460/756	11.6
11.5	**Jay Loop**, south end to **Jay Camp**, 0.2 mi W	2238/682	11.8
11.4	**Vt. 242** at **Jay Pass; Atlas Valley Shelter** (no camping)	2220/677	11.9
10.6	**Gilpin Mtn.**, south summit	2920/890	12.7
9.6	**Domey's Dome**	2880/878	13.7
8.6	**Chet's Lookout**	2900/884	14.7
8.4	**Buchanan Mtn.**	2940/896	14.9
7.5	**Bruce Peak**	2900/884	15.8
6.1	**Hazen's Notch Camp**, 0.1 mi W via spur	2040/622	17.2
4.6	**Vt. 58** at **Hazen's Notch**	1780/543	18.7
2.7	**Haystack Mtn.**, east slope; summit (3223 ft/982 m), 0.2 mi W via spur	3180/969	20.6
0.6	**Tillotson Peak**, east slope	2980/908	22.7
0.0	**Frank Post Trail** to **Tillotson Camp**, 50 ft E; to **Tillotson Road**, 2.0 mi E	2560/780	23.3

SOUTH
▼

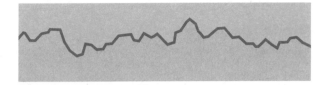

Division 12
Tillotson Camp to Canadian Border

Massachusetts 249.4 miles **Canada 23.3 miles**

Much of the Long Trail (LT) runs on or near the ridge-line in this division. Water is scarce and hikers should take advantage of sources noted in the text.

The north terminus of the LT is in the woods at the Canadian border west of North Troy. The Journey's End Trail, which leads to the border from the east, is the only approach trail to the north terminus. It is described on pages 225 to 226 and included in the division summary on page 218.

The following people have contributed to endow the future maintenance of 1 mile of the LT within this division: Paul and Sybil Moffat.

Camping and Fires

This division of the LT crosses mostly state and some private land. Camping is allowed only at shelters. Small wood fires, although discouraged, are permitted at the shelters' established fire rings. Refer to Leave No Trace principles (pages 11 to 12) to minimize your impact.

Note: Atlas Valley Shelter is not intended for overnight use, and wood fires are prohibited.

12

Group Use

Groups hiking this division of the LT may need a Commercial Use Permit from the Vermont Department of Forests, Parks and Recreation. Group tenting space is available at Hazen's Notch and Jay Camps and Laura Woodward Shelter. Refer to pages 13 to 19 for additional group use guidelines.

Winter Use

The suggested day hikes from Jay and North Jay Passes make good snowshoe trips. This division's terrain is not suitable for beginner or intermediate cross-country skiers. Deep snow often makes the white-blazed route very difficult to discern.

Access to the Long Trail

VT. 58 AT HAZEN'S NOTCH. The LT crosses unpaved Vt. 58 just west of the height of land, 5.3 mi. east of Montgomery Center and 5.2 mi. west of Vt. 100 in Lowell. Limited parking is

Suggested Day Hikes

CARLETON MTN. This hike follows the LT north from Vt. 105, ascending to a lookout. Round trip, 2.4 mi., 1¼ hr. Continuing north to the Canadian border along the ridge offers views into Québec from the boundary clearing at Post 592. Total round trip, 5.2 mi., 3¼ hr.

JAY PEAK. This steady climb on the LT north from Vt. 242 features views from the open summit. Round trip, 3.4 mi., 2½ hr.

HAYSTACK MTN. The LT south from Vt. 58 in Hazen's Notch climbs a steep, rugged route to the spur leading to the summit lookouts. Round trip, 4.0 mi., 2¾ hr.

available on the south side of the road just east of the trail. The road through the notch is not plowed in winter and is part of the Catamount Trail. Refer to Catamount Trail information on page 27.

Vt. 242 at Jay Pass. The LT crosses this highway at Jay Pass, 5.1 mi. west of Jay Village and 6.4 mi. east of Montgomery Center. There is a large parking lot on the south side of the highway.

Vt. 105 at North Jay Pass. This road intersects the LT at North Jay Pass, 5.2 mi. west of Vt. 101 near North Troy and 7.4 mi. east of Vt. 105A near Richford. Parking is on the north side of the road. Overnight parking here is not recommended due to a history of vandalism.

Long Trail Description

From the **Frank Post Trail (0.0 mi.)**, 50 ft. west of **Tillotson Camp**, proceed north and ascend wooded **Tillotson Peak (0.6 mi.)**, passing just east of the summit. Descend into a deep col and climb gradually to **Haystack Mtn. (2.7 mi.)**. A spur leads west 0.2 mi. to the summit knob where there are lookouts. Continue downhill at a moderate, though uneven, grade along the ridge, then drop very steeply to a brook (4.4 mi.) and then to unpaved **Vt. 58 at Hazen's Notch (4.6 mi.)**.

The notch is named for Gen. Moses Hazen who, with Gen. Jacob Bayley, built a military road from 1778–1779. Originally intended to reach Canada, it goes from Peacham to this point. A granite marker just east of the LT commemorates this effort. The south face of Sugarloaf Mtn. rises 700 ft. vertically above the road.

Cross the highway and follow a nearly level grade under the cliffs, then turn right to climb steeply over the west shoulder of Sugarloaf Mtn. Cross the west slope of Sugarloaf and descend moderately to a spur **(6.1 mi.)** leading west 0.1 mi. to **Hazen's Notch Camp**. Built by the Long Trail Patrol (LTP) in 1948 at a site just below the highway, the camp was dismantled, hand-carried, and reassembled by the VYCC with GMC volunteer support in 1997. There are bunks for eight. The water source is

12

a small brook crossed by the spur leading to the camp; it may go dry during droughts. The camp features a view north to Bruce Peak, Buchanan Mtn., Big Jay, and Jay Peak. **Tillotson Camp to Hazen's Notch Camp, 6.2 mi., 10.0 km., 4 hr. (SB 4½ hr.).**

Proceed north from the spur and cross several ravines where there may be water. Ascend to the skyline at **Bruce Peak (7.5 mi.).** Continue along the ridge to the summit of **Buchanan Mtn. (8.4 mi.),** named in honor of Prof. Roy O. Buchanan of Burlington, longtime GMC Trails and Shelters chairman and leader of the LTP. Formerly called Old Splatterfoot, this mountain has a view of Jay Peak and Big Jay. Bruce Peak is named for Bruce Buchanan who helped his brother Roy scout the final miles of the LT from Jay Peak to Canada in 1930.

Continue north from Buchanan Mtn. to **Chet's Lookout (8.6 mi.)** on a boulder to the right reached by a ladder, with views north of the ridge. The lookout is named for one of Roy O. Buchanan's sons who worked with the LTP in the 1930s and continued to help with trail projects into the 1980s. Drop into a saddle and then climb to the summit of **Domey's Dome (9.6 mi.),** named for Capt. R. H. Domey of St. Albans, longtime local trail maintainer. Just south of this summit, pass an opening with views to the east and south. Descend to a sag (10.2 mi), then climb to the south summit of **Gilpin Mtn. (10.6 mi.).** Formerly called Double Top, it is named for the Gilpin brothers, northern Vermont newspaper editors. Follow the ridge, then descend steadily to the west, and after passing a spring on the right, arrive at **Vt. 242 at Jay Pass (11.4 mi.).**

Cross the highway and pass **Atlas Valley Shelter** on its north embankment. *Use caution when crossing Vt. 242; traffic moves at high speeds.* This small structure, not intended for overnight use, was built in 1967 by a plywood company that owned the

WEATHER CHANGES

The weather can change quickly. Always be prepared for rain, cold, and wind.

adjacent timberlands. There is no outhouse, and wood fires are prohibited. Proceed north to the south end of **Jay Loop (11.5 mi.)**, leading 0.2 mi. west to **Jay Camp**. The Catamount Trail shares the south part of Jay Loop. Jay Camp, built in 1958, is a frame cabin with bunk space for ten. It was renovated in 2009 by the Northern Frontier Section led by Ferdinand Lauffer. The site includes a tent platform and a moldering privy. The water source is a spring 50 ft. in front of the camp. Jay Loop continues north uphill 0.2 mi. to rejoin the Long Trail. **Hazen's Notch Camp to Jay Camp, 5.7 mi., 9.2 km., 4¼ hr. (SB 4¼ hr.).**

Ascend to the north end of **Jay Loop (11.7 mi.)** and then climb steadily on the southeast shoulder of Jay Peak. Bear left at the ridge's saddle, and continue uphill, steeply at times, to a ski trail (12.9 mi.). Cross a snow-making pipeline and pass through a snow fence. Proceed directly across the Vermonter ski trail, re-enter the stunted woods, then emerge into the open and climb to the rocky summit of **Jay Peak (13.1 mi.)**. In bad weather, the open summit may be by-passed by turning left onto the Vermonter ski trail, bearing right at the next ski trail junction, and ascending to the Jay Peak Tramway Station, which is located just below the summit. Hikers should not count on finding refuge from bad weather at the summit tramway station because it is sometimes locked.

The summit features views in all directions. In the immediate foreground to the west are Big Jay and Little Jay and to the northwest, the Black Falls Basin and the Stanhope Ridge. These features are all on the 5337 acres acquired by the GMC and added to the Jay State Forest in 1993 and 2001. To the south, the Green Mountains are visible to Camel's Hump, with the White Mountains to the southeast and the Adirondacks to the southwest. To the north is the Green Mountain ridge to the border, as well as Canada's Sutton Mountains, culminating in Round Top. To the northwest, the foreground ridge is Stanhope Ridge, which forms the northern rim of the Black Falls Basin, acquired by GMC and added to Jay State Forest in 2001. Beyond, Mt. Pinnacle stands alone. To the northeast are Sugarloaf, Owl's Head, and Bear Mtn., over which the border passes. The international waters of Lake Memphremagog lie beyond Bear Mtn.

12

From the tramway station, drop northeast on a ski trail, then turn left and cross another ski trail at right angles (13.3 mi.). Pass through a snow fence and cross a water pipeline, then enter the woods and turn right to descend steeply to Ullrs Dream ski trail. This ski trail drops 1.0 mi. east to the Jay Peak Ski Area base lodge and Vt. 242. Bear left to follow the north edge of this trail and then reenter the woods (13.8 mi.). Descend near the top of the ridge to **Laura Woodward Shelter (14.6 mi.)**. Originally built in 1956, this three-sided post-and-beam shelter, which sleeps six, has been replaced twice, most recently by Tom Abbott and son with GMC volunteers in 2001. It is named for an early supporter of the LT. Water is located at a spring west of the trail. **Jay Camp to Laura Woodward Shelter, 3.1 mi., 5.0 km., 2½ hr. (SB 2¼ hr.).**

Continue north along the ridge and climb **Doll Peak (15.5 mi.)**, named for Charles G. Doll (Vermont state geologist 1947–1976) who, with Phillips D. Carleton, both University of Vermont professors, cut the route from Jay Peak to Canada. The official naming of Doll Peak was formally recognized by the U.S. Board on Geographic Names on May 12, 2011. Descend from Doll Peak and follow the ridge uphill to an unnamed peak of the **North Jay massif (16.0 mi.)**. Begin a steady and sometimes steep descent east before crossing a small stream (17.9 mi.), the most reliable water source for Shooting Star Shelter. Follow the ridge north over several low summits to **Shooting Star Shelter (18.9 mi.)**. This post-and-beam shelter was built by Ferdinand Lauffer and Northern Frontier volunteers in 2001 and sleeps six. A display of shooting stars observed by the LTP during the construction of the original shelter in 1934 provided its name. The primary water source is a shallow well with a hand pump, located on a short spur leading west off the LT, 190 ft. south of the shelter. Pump water, like all water along the Long Trail System, should be treated. The quality and quantity of water cannot be guaranteed. In case of pump failure, water might be found 450 ft. east and downhill of the shelter. This source is unreliable. **Laura Woodward Shelter to Shooting Star Shelter, 4.3 mi., 6.9 km., 2¾ hr. (SB 3 hr.).**

From the shelter, ascend **Burnt Mtn. (19.5 mi.)**, where a spur leads west to a lookout. Follow the ridge and descend gradually to cross **Vt. 105 at North Jay Pass (20.7 mi.)**.

North of the highway, turn right past a gated logging road, follow the edge above the top of the road cut, pass under a power line, then turn left. Cross the power line and ascend to the ridge, then climb to the summit of **Carleton Mtn. (21.9 mi.)**, named for Phillips D. Carleton, who helped Charles G. Doll cut the LT from Jay Peak to Canada. A spur leads south to a view of the Jay Mountains. Turn north to descend and then pass over several minor summits to the Journey's End Trail, which leads east 0.5 mi. to Journey's End Camp and 1.3 mi. to Journey's End Road. Continue a few feet beyond the junction to the **U.S.–Canadian border at Line Post 592 (23.3 mi.), the north terminus of the LT.**

The present line post was set in 1907 in accordance with the Webster-Ashburton Treaty, which in 1842 finally settled the U.S.–Canadian boundary. The boundary swath provides views of the Missisquoi River Valley to the west and Québec's Sutton Mountains to the north.

Approach Trail

JOURNEY'S END TRAIL. This is the only approach trail to the north terminus of the LT. From North Troy, follow the gravel North Jay Road west and then south 2.6 mi. to a junction with narrow, unpaved Journey's End Road opposite a dairy barn. Turn right and follow this road west. Or, from Vt. 105, follow the North Jay Road 2.0 mi. north to the same road and turn left.

This rough road leads 1.2 mi. west, mostly uphill, to a log landing where there is plenty of space to park. Bear right and descend 0.1 mi. more on a narrower road to a small trailhead parking area where the road is blocked by boulders. *Use caution on this road, which is sometimes used for local logging operations.* During springtime (through June), road conditions may be poor.

From the trailhead at **Journey's End Road (0.0 mi.)**, continue on the now-abandoned woods road west. Ascend gently

12

to the original site of Journey's End Camp (0.5 mi.), which served LT hikers from 1931 to 2004. Dismantled by GMC staff and volunteers in November 2004, the original camp, built by Roy O. Buchanan in 1931, has been reassembled for viewing on the Short Trail at GMC headquarters in Waterbury Center, Vermont.

Continue west from the small clearing, then bear right to cross a sizable brook, before rejoining the old road again to an old farm settlement evidenced by stone foundations and rock piles. Turn left here and ascend gradually northwest. Pass a spur **(0.8 mi.) leading to Journey's End Camp**. This frame cabin, modeled after the classic "Buchanan era" camps, was built in 2003 by the family and friends of Tyler Robert Green, led by Cary and Julie Poulin with the help of GMC volunteers. It has bunks for eight. The water source is the brook just west of the trail. **Shooting Star Shelter to Journey's End Camp, 4.9 mi., 8 km, 3 hr. (SB 3¾ hr.).** From the spur, continue uphill, crossing several old woods roads, to the border swath. Parallel the border to the **north terminus of the LT (1.3 mi.) at Line Post 592. Journey's End Road to LT, 1.3 mi., 2.1 km., 1 hr. (Rev. ¾ hr.).**

Beechnut seedpod

Appalachian Trail 1
Long Trail at Maine
Junction to Vt. 12

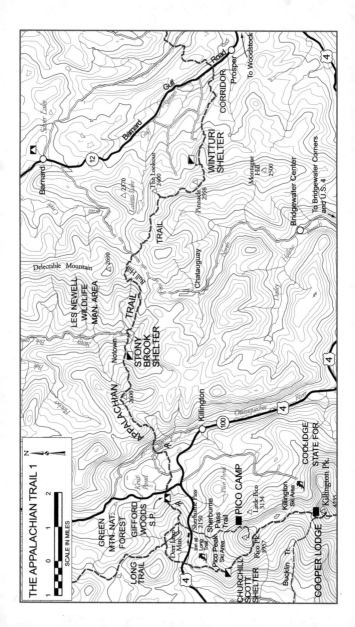

THE APPALACHIAN TRAIL 1

SCALE IN MILES

1 0 1 2

N

Silver Lake

Barnard

To Woodstock

Prosper

Gulf

Barnard

Gulf Stream

WINTTURI SHELTER CORRIDOR

Road

12

4

△2370

Lakota Lake

The Lookout 2400

Pinnacle △ 2568

Delectable Mountain

△3690

LES NEWELL WILDLIFE MAN. AREA

Manasque Hill △ 2500

To Bridgewater Corners and U.S. 4

Bridgewater Center

Chataauguay

TRAIL

Notown

Bull Hill

STONY BROOK SHELTER

North Br.

APPALACHIAN

TRAIL

3600

Killington

100

Ottauquechee River

4

4

GREEN MTN. NAT. FOREST

GIFFORD WOODS S.P.

Long Trail

Inn at Long Trail

Sherburne Pass 2150

Sherburne Pass Trail

Kent Pond

Thundelt River

LONG TRAIL

4

Deer Leap Mtn.

Pico Peak Ski Area

PICO CAMP

Pico Pond

Little Pico 3134

CHURCHILL SCOTT SHELTER

Pico Pk. 3957

Killington Ski Area

Bucklin Tr.

COOLIDGE STATE FOR.

COOPER LODGE

Killington Pk. 4235

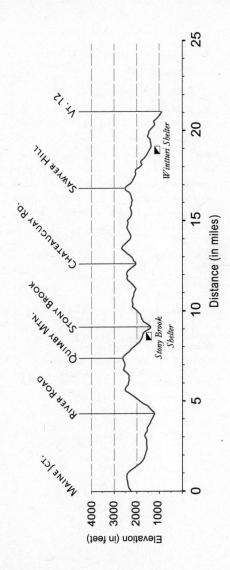

AT 1 Profile

Elevation (in feet)

Distance (in miles)

MAINE JCT.

RIVER ROAD

QUIMBY MTN.

STONY BROOK

CHATEAUGUAY RD.

SAWYER HILL

Vt. 12

Stony Brook Shelter

Wintturi Shelter

Long Trail at Maine Junction to Vt. 12

miles north-bound	▲ NORTH	elevation at Trail (feet/meters)	miles south-bound
22.7	Vt. 12; Gulf Stream bridge	882/269	0.0
18.9	Wintturi Shelter, 0.2 mi N via spur	1900/579	3.8
16.5	The Lookout, 300 ft N via woods road	2320/707	6.2
14.8	Lakota Lake Lookout	2640/805	7.9
13.7	Chateauguay Road	2000/610	9.0
11.6	Height of land	2260/689	11.1
9.8	Stony Brook bridge	1360/415	12.9
9.0	Stony Brook Shelter, 250 ft S via spur	1760/536	13.7
7.9	Height of land on Quimby Mtn.	2550/777	14.8
4.7	River Road	1214/370	18.0
2.4	Kent Brook bridge	1580/482	20.3
2.3	Vt. 100	1580/482	20.4
2.0	Gifford Woods State Park, upper camping area	1660/506	20.7
1.2	Ben's Balcony, 50 ft S via spur	2220/677	21.5
0.9	Deer Leap Trail south end to Deer Leap Overlook via Overlook Spur, 0.6 mi; Sherburne Pass Trail north end: to Sherburne Pass and Inn at Long Trail, 0.5 mi S; to Long Trail/Appalachian Trail at Jungle Junction, 3.4 mi S	2440/744	21.8
0.1	Deer Leap Trail north end to Deer Leap Overlook via Overlook Spur, 1.1 mi S	2290/698	22.6
0.0	Maine Junction at Willard Gap; Long Trail to U.S. 4, 1.0 mi	2250/686	22.7

SOUTH
▼

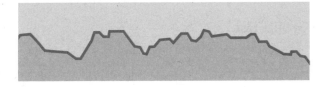

Appalachian Trail 1
Long Trail at Maine Junction to Vt. 12

Vermont's Appalachian Trail (AT) leaves the Long Trail (LT) at Maine Junction, 1.0 mi. north of U.S. 4 and 104.9 miles north of the Massachusetts state line and bears east 44.6 miles to the Connecticut River at Norwich and from there continues north over the White Mountains toward Mt. Katahdin in Maine.

A new relocation of the AT off of Thundering Brook Road providing access to Thundering Falls opened in 2007. This relocation culminating efforts dating back to federal corridor acquisition in the 1980s replaced the road walk on Thundering Brook Road and features a 900-foot wheelchair-accessible boardwalk from River Road to the foot of one of Vermont's highest waterfalls, crossing the floodplain of the Ottauquechee River.

Camping and Fires

Much of this trail is on state land and a narrow strip of federal land surrounded by private property. Camping is allowed only at shelters. Small wood fires, although discouraged, are permitted at the shelters' established fire rings. Refer to Leave No Trace principles (pages 11 to 12) to minimize your impact.

Group Use

Groups hiking this portion of the AT may need an Outfitter-Guide Special Use Permit from the Green Mountain National Forest. Gifford Woods State Park Campground, where the AT crosses Vt. 100, and Silver Lake State Park Campground, north of the AT off Vt. 12 in Barnard, are available for base camp hiking. Refer to pages 13 to 19 for additional group guidelines.

Access to the Appalachian Trail

Vt. 100. The AT crosses this highway at the Gifford Woods State Park maintenance driveway on Vt. 100, 0.5 mi. north of the westernmost junction of Vt. 100 and U.S. 4. Parking is available at the Kent Pond boat landing on the east side of the highway.

River Road. To access the south end of River Road from U.S. 4, turn north at 2.0 mi. east from the westernmost junction of Vt. 100 and U.S. 4. Continue on this road 1.6 mi. to the trail crossing just north of its junction with Thundering Brook Road. To access the north end of River Road from Vt. 100, turn east onto River Road approximately 2 mi. north of Gifford Woods State Park, or 6 mi. south of Pittsfield. The AT crossing is 2.4 mi. from Vt. 100.

Vt. 12. The AT intersects this highway 4.2 mi. north of Woodstock and 12.2 mi. south of Vt. 107 in Bethel. Parking is available on the west side of the highway.

MINIMIZE CAMPFIRE IMPACTS
Build fires only where permitted and only in established fire rings; use a portable stove.

Appalachian Trail Description

From **Maine Junction at Willard Gap (0.0 mi.)**, turn right and leave the LT. Proceed south, passing the north end of the **Deer Leap Trail (0.1 mi.)**. Continue southeast, slabbing the east side of Deer Leap Mtn. and pass the south end of the **Deer Leap Trail** 200 ft. before reaching the north end of the **Sherburne Pass Trail (0.9 mi.)**. This side trail descends 0.5 mi. to U.S. 4 and the Inn at the Long Trail.

Bear left from the trail junction, climb a low ridge, then descend to a **spur (1.2 mi.)** leading south 50 ft. to **Ben's Balcony**, a vista with views of Pico and Killington Peaks. Descend steadily to the upper camping area of **Gifford Woods State Park (2.0 mi.)** and pass through the camping and picnic areas to reach **Vt. 100 (2.3 mi.)** south of the park entrance and 0.5 mi. north of U.S. 4.

Gifford Woods State Park provides open shelters, tent sites, and picnic tables. Make reservations for the use of overnight facilities through the park office (Killington, Vermont 05751; 802-775-5354). Gifford Woods itself, located elsewhere within the park, is one of the few remaining stands of virgin hardwood forest in Vermont.

Cross Vt. 100 and parallel it south a short distance to Kent Pond Fishing Access, 0.4 mi. north of U.S. 4. Traverse the entry drive for the parking lot and reenter the woods. Cross a footbridge over **Kent Brook (2.4 mi.)**, bear left along the brook, and descend to the shore of Kent Pond (2.5 mi.). Follow the shore through the woods, then pass through a field to the gravel Thundering Brook Road (3.0 mi.). Cross the road and ascend to a height of land. Descend through the woods to the road again (4.2 mi.). Cross the road and descend through a hemlock forest to the Thundering Falls wheelchair-accessible spur trail, which leads to the base of the waterfall. The AT switchbacks down to the Ottauquechee floodplain and crosses 900 ft. of boardwalk.

Cross **River Road (4.7 mi.)** and ascend through mixed hardwood forest to an old logging road. Turn left to continue climbing on the road, then bear right to leave it. Continue to climb, in part on old woods roads, to a vista (5.5 mi.) with late

AT 1

fall and early spring views of the Ottauquechee River Valley and the Coolidge Range.

From the vista, follow a logging road, level out, then begin to ascend via switchbacks to the summit of an unnamed hill (6.0 mi.). From the summit, descend to a ridge, and follow it to a power-line clearing (6.5 mi.). Continue along the ridge, cross a woods road (6.8 mi.), and begin an ascent to an unnamed summit (7.1 mi.). Drop again before ascending to the north shoulder of **Quimby Mtn.** Descend to a shallow saddle, and then climb to a **height of land (7.9 mi.)**, the watershed divide between the Ottauquechee River and Stony Brook.

Beyond the height of land, descend to a **spur (9.0 mi.)** leading south 250 ft. to **Stony Brook Shelter**. This shelter, a frame lean-to with space for six, was built by Erik and Laurel Tobiason and friends and Ottauquechee Section volunteers in 1997. It is dedicated in honor of the section volunteers who relocated the AT between Vt. 100 and Vt. 12 from 1980 to 1990. Water is from a brook that crosses the AT 300 ft. north of the spur. **Churchill Scott Shelter** to **Stony Brook Shelter, 12 mi., 19.3 km., 7¼ hr. (SB 7¼ hr.).**

Descend steadily to the valley below, using a ladder to negotiate one ledge (9.2 mi.). Cross **Stony Brook** on a bridge installed by GMC Ottauquechee Section volunteers with the Volunteer Long Trail Patrol in 2006 **(9.8 mi.)** and turn left to reenter the woods before Notown Clearing, which is used for logging operations. Rock hop across Mink Brook and climb, via

---

DRESS IN LAYERS, LIKE AN ONION

Wear wicking underwear, an insulating layer, and a wind- and waterproof shell. Rather than cotton, wear wool or synthetics, like pile or polypropylene. Regulate body temperature by adding and removing layers. Strip layers before you overheat; add layers before you chill.

switchbacks at first, to a ridge. Follow the ridge across several knolls to a **height of land (11.6 mi.)**. Pass a small pond and continue to a sag. Descend from the sag, crossing an intermittent brook and several logging roads. Climb over several small hills, winding just north of Bull Hill. There are occasional views to the west. Drop via switchbacks to the gravel **Chateauguay Road (13.7 mi.)**.

Cross the road and, just beyond, Locust Creek. After climbing over a low hill, cross another brook (14.1 mi.). Switchback up a steep evergreen-covered hillside. Reenter a mixed hardwood forest as the grade moderates and cross an intermittent brook (14.6 mi.). Continue to ascend through a stand of paper birches, passing a southwestern view, before reaching **Lakota Lake Lookout (14.8 mi.)**. Lakota Lake is below with the White Mountains in the distance.

From the lookout, follow the ridge with gradual elevation changes, cross an old woods road, and reach a woods road **(16.5 mi.)** leading north uphill 300 ft. to **The Lookout**, located on private property outside the AT corridor. Please respect this property.

At the junction, turn right to follow the old woods road, which continues to the Lookout Farm Road (17.3 mi.). Cross this road and continue to the King Cabin Road (17.4 mi.). Turn right and follow this road for a short distance, then turn left (17.6 mi.) off the road and gradually ascend the south slope of the Pinnacle, to a southwestern view (18.2 mi.) of Killington and Pico Peaks. Continue to ascend to the height of land on Sawyer Hill (18.3 mi.). Begin a gradual descent, cross a woods road, and reach a **spur (18.9 mi.)** leading north 0.2 mi. to Wintturi Shelter. **Wintturi Shelter**, a frame lean-to with room for six, replaced an older shelter of the same name and was built by Erik and Laurel Tobiason and friends in 1994. It is named in honor of longtime trail maintainer Mauri Wintturi. A spring 300 ft. north of the shelter provides water. **Stony Brook Shelter to Wintturi Shelter, 10.1 mi., 16.3 km., 6 hr. (SB 6 hr.)**.

From the Wintturi Shelter spur, follow the contour of a wooded slope, then descend to an old road (19.7 mi.). Beyond the road, climb to the crest of a low ridge (19.9 mi.), where a spur leads right to a view of North Bridgewater. Descend to a woods road (20.5 mi.),where an old cellar hole and stone chimney to the north are all that remain of a past dwelling. Continue along the contour, then climb to an open ridge (21.3 mi.), with views of Mt. Ascutney. A second bald hilltop with panoramic views (21.5 mi.) is a short distance beyond.

Reenter the woods, make an abrupt left turn, and descend through an open area. Continue through the woods with minor changes in elevation and reach the edge of a hillside clearing where a wooden stile crosses an electric fence. Descend through two more fields with stiles, which provide pastoral views of the valley and hills beyond. Cross **Gulf Stream** on a footbridge constructed by Ottauquechee section volunteers and enter the parking lot at **Vt. 12 (22.7 mi.).**

Hobblebush leaf

Appalachian Trail 2
Vt. 12 to the
Connecticut River

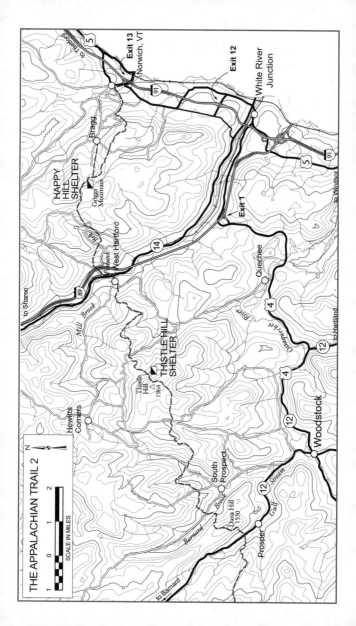

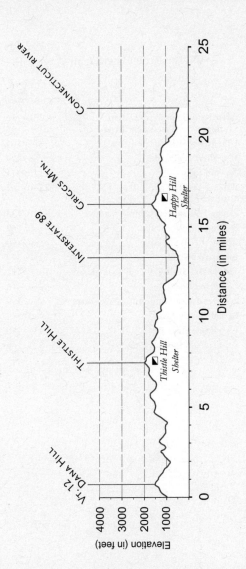

AT 2 Profile

Vt. 12 to the Connecticut River

miles north-bound	▲ NORTH	elevation at Trail (feet/meters)	miles south-bound
21.9	Enter New Hampshire; Ledyard bridge over Connecticut River	380/116	0.0
20.9	U.S. 5; Norwich Village Green	537/164	1.0
20.1	Elm Street trailhead	750/229	1.8
18.2	Newton Lane	1120/341	3.7
16.8	William Tucker Trail to Happy Hill Road, 0.8 mi E	1320/402	5.1
16.6	Happy Hill Shelter, 0.1 mi S via spur	1420/433	5.3
14.0	Podunk Brook	860/262	7.9
12.6	Bridge over White River; Vt. 14	390/119	9.3
9.3	Joe Ranger Road	1280/390	12.6
7.8	Thistle Hill Shelter, 0.1 mi S via spur	1480/451	14.1
5.5	Cloudland Road	1370/418	16.4
3.7	Pomfret–South Pomfret (County) Road	980/299	18.2
3.0	Bartlett Brook Road	980/299	18.9
1.5	Woodstock Stage Road	820/250	20.4
0.0	Vt. 12; Gulf Stream bridge	882/269	21.9

SOUTH
▼

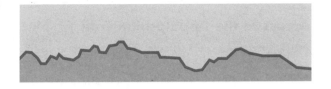

Appalachian Trail 2

Vt. 12 to the Connecticut River

The Appalachian Trail (AT) between Vt. 12 and the Connecticut River is maintained by the Dartmouth Outing Club (DOC). See address information on page 248. The AT from Vt. 12 south to the Vermont-Massachusetts state line is covered in Appalachian Trail 1 and Divisions 1 through 6.

AT 2

Camping and Fires

Most of this trail is on a narrow strip of public land surrounded by private property. Camping is allowed only at shelters. Small wood fires, although discouraged, are permitted at the shelters' established fire rings. Refer to Leave No Trace principles (pages 11 to 12).

Group Use

Groups hiking this portion of the AT may need an Outfitter-Guide Special Use Permit from the Green Mountain National Forest. Group tenting space is available at Happy Hill Shelter. Silver Lake State Park Campground, north of the Appalachian Trail off Vt. 12, is available for base camp hiking. Refer to pages 13 to 19 for additional group use guidelines.

Access to the Appalachian Trail

Vт. 12. Refer to directions on page 232 in Appalachian Trail 1.

Woodstock Stage Road. The AT crosses this road 0.9 mi. north of South Pomfret and 4.1 mi. north of Woodstock.

Pomfret–South Pomfret (County) Road. The AT crosses this road 1.3 mi. north of South Pomfret and 4.5 mi. north of Woodstock. There is parking available at a small pull-off on the west side of the road.

Vт. 14. The AT joins this road at the bridge over White River in West Hartford, 6.9 mi. north of U.S. 4 and U.S. 5 in White River Junction.

U.S. 5. The AT joins this highway in Norwich Village across from the village green, 4.6 mi. north of Vt. 14 in White River Junction.

Appalachian Trail Description

Cross **Vt. 12 (0.0 mi.)**, pass through a small field, and reenter the woods. Ascend steadily, reaching a hilltop field on Dana Hill, with views of the surrounding countryside. Descend from Dana Hill, easily at first and then more steadily, to the paved **Woodstock Stage Road (1.5 mi.)**. Cross the road and then a footbridge over Barnard Creek and gradually climb through a field. Enter the woods, continue uphill to a sag between Totman and Breakneck Hills, and then descend. Bear right at an obvious fork, and cross a narrow road.

Ascend through a field past some foundations to a height of land, then take a right-hand fork downhill. Follow woods roads downhill to a field and meet the gravel **Bartlett Brook Road (3.0 mi.)**. Cross the road and then a small creek, and follow an old fencerow through woods and fields before descending to cross Pomfret Brook and the paved **Pomfret–South Pomfret (County) Road (3.7 mi.)**.

From the road, climb steeply through mixed woods to a field with views. At the edge of the field, turn left and follow an old woods road. This is a remnant of the old Kings Highway, which used to be a major thoroughfare through Pomfret (the trail crosses another section of this old road near Bunker Hill). Continuing on the woods road, pass an old four-way junction and climb a small hill before descending to the east. Leave the former highway at a spur (4.6 mi.), which leads south uphill 50 ft. to an unreliable spring. Ascend to the top of DuPuis Hill, a bald summit with panoramic views, and then descend gradually through the woods to the gravel **Cloudland Road (5.5 mi.)**.

Turn right onto the road for 200 ft., then left into a field north of a house. Follow the south side of the field, then cross it to a gap in the stonewall. Pass through this gap and enter the woods. Ascend through woods, passing under a power line. After crossing over the top of Thistle Hill (7.5 mi.), reach a spur **(7.8 mi.)**, which leads 0.1 mi. south to **Thistle Hill Shelter**. Thistle Hill Shelter, with space for eight, was built by the DOC in 1995. Ample water is available in nearby streams. **Wintturi Shelter to Thistle Hill Shelter, 11.9 mi., 19.2 km., 6¾ hr. (SB 6¾ hr.).**

From the spur, descend to cross a small brook, and then climb to an open field atop Arms Hill, with views. Follow a woods road to a second field, with views to the north and northeast. Continue to drop via switchbacks to the unpaved **Joe Ranger Road (9.3 mi.)**. Cross Joe Ranger Road by a small pond with a stone dam, and then climb via switchbacks to the wooded summit of Bunker Hill. Descend Bunker Hill and cross an old town road (10.0 mi.) by a cemetery and several hilltop pastures with views to the southeast. Traverse an old farm road before descending through a stand of pines and bearing left through a sag, then climb to another hilltop pasture with views of the White River Valley. From the field (11.6 mi.), descend steadily through open hardwoods. Cross a small swampy area and puncheon, and turn left onto the paved Quechee–West Hartford Road. Follow this road to cross an iron bridge over the **White River to Vt. 14 (12.6 mi.)** in the village of West Hartford.

Turn left (north) on Vt. 14, passing a store, and follow it to Tigertown Road (13.0 mi.). Follow Tigertown Road to the right, cross railroad tracks, and bear left at a fork. After passing under Interstate 89, reach a road junction with Podunk Road. Turn right onto Podunk Road (13.2 mi.) and then left into the woods.

AT 2

Climb through overgrown pasture and woods before descending back to Podunk Road. Cross the road, then **Podunk Brook (14.0)**, before ascending and crossing a woods road. Make a sharp left turn across a brook and several old town roads, and then traverse the south shoulder of Griggs Mtn. (16.1 mi.) to reach a spur **(16.6 mi.)** that leads 0.1 mi. south to **Happy Hill Shelter**. This shelter, a stone structure with double-deck accommodations for eight, was built by the DOC in 1997–1998. **Thistle Hill Shelter to Happy Hill Shelter, 9.0 mi., 14.4 km., 5 hr. (SB 5 hr.).**

From the shelter, descend on an old road to a junction with the **William Tucker Trail (16.8 mi.)**, where the old road leads 0.8 mi. to a gate at Happy Hill Road. From the junction, bear to the right and follow the south side of the ridge and cross **Newton Lane (18.2 mi.)**. Wind through hardwood forest and pass under a power line (19.5 mi.) on the north flank of Mosley Hill. From the utility clearing, descend, cross a small stream, and follow the hill's contour to a two-car **trailhead on Elm Street (20.1 mi.)**. Bear right on Elm Street and descend, passing Hickory Ridge Road on the right, and follow the street to **U.S. 5 (20.9 mi.)** on the Norwich Village Green. A grocery store and the Norwich post office are to the left. Turn right and proceed south on U.S. 5 and then east on Vt. 10A under Interstate 91, enter **New Hampshire**, and cross the **Ledyard bridge over the Connecticut River (21.9 mi.)**.

Side Trail

WILLIAM TUCKER TRAIL. This trail provides an alternative route to the AT and the highlands around Griggs Mtn. from Norwich. From its junction with Dutton Hill and Meadow Brook Roads, 0.5 mi. west of the Norwich Village Green, Bragg Hill Road leads 1.3 mi. to a crossroads. The trailhead is another 0.5 mi straight ahead on the gravel Happy Hill Road beyond this junction. There is a turn-around with very limited parking. From the turn-around (0.0 mi, 1100 ft.), follow an old woods road uphill to the Appalachian Trail (0.8 mi., 1320 ft.).

Public Campgrounds
Near the Long Trail

Divisions 1 and 2
Woodford State Park, Woodford
- (802) 447-7169 or Jan. to May 800-658-1622
- From Bennington: 10 mi. east on Vt. 9
- From Bennington: 10 mi. east on Vt. 9, then 1 mi. north on USFS Rd. 274

Divisions 2 and 3
Grout Pond, Stratton (U.S. Forest Service)
- (802) 362-2307
- From Stratton: 2.5 mi. west on Arlington–West Wardsboro Rd., then south on USFS Rd. 262

Divisions 3 and 4
Emerald Lake State Park, North Dorset
- (802) 362-1655 or Jan. to May 800-658-1622
- On U.S. 7 in North Dorset

Hapgood Pond, Peru (U.S. Forest Service)
- (802) 362-2307
- From Vt. 11 in Peru: 2.0 mi. north on Hapgood Pond Rd.

Division 5
Coolidge State Park, Plymouth
- (802) 672-3612 or Jan. to May 800-299-3071
- From junction of Vt. 100 and Vt. 100A in Plymouth Union: 3.0 mi. north on Vt. 100A

Divisions 5 and 6
Gifford Woods State Park, Killington
- (802) 775-5354 or Jan. to May 800-299-3071
- From junction of U.S. 4 and Vt. 100: 0.5 mi. north on Vt. 100

Divisions 6 and 7

Branbury State Park, Brandon
- (802) 247-5925 or Jan. to May 800-658-1622
- From junction of Vt. 73 and Vt. 53: 6.0 mi. north on Vt. 53

Moosalamoo, Ripton (U.S. Forest Service)
- (802) 388-4362
- From junction of Vt. 73 and Vt. 53 in Forest Dale: 1.6 mi. east on Vt. 73, then left on USFS Rd. 32 for 5.3 mi., and left again on USFS Rd. 24

Chittenden Brook, Chittenden (U.S. Forest Service)
- (802) 767-4261
- From the junction of Vt. 100 and Vt. 73: 5.2 mi. west on Vt. 73, then 2.5 mi. south on USFS Rd. 45

Divisions 8, 9, and 10

Little River State Park, Waterbury
- (802) 244-7103 or Jan. to May (802) 479-4280
- From the northern junction of U.S. 2 and Vt. 100 in Waterbury: 1.5 mi. west on U.S. 2 to Little River Rd., then right (north) for 3.5 mi.

Division 10

Underhill State Park, Underhill
- (802) 899-3022 or Jan. to May (802) 879-5674
- From Underhill Center: 1.0 mi. north on Pleasant Valley Rd., then east 2.7 mi. on the Mountain Rd. (Town Highway 2)

Divisions 9, 10, and 11

Smugglers Notch State Park, Stowe
- (802) 253-4014 or Jan. to May (802) 479-4280
- From Stowe: 8 mi. north on Vt. 108

Divisions 10 and 11

Elmore State Park, Lake Elmore
- (802) 888-2982 or Jan. to May (802) 479-4280
- From Morrisville: south 5 mi. on Vt. 12

Post Offices and Stores

The communities listed below are those nearest the Long Trail and its side trails. Each has at least one grocery or general store. Those in boldface are larger communities offering more goods, services, and accommodations. Communities without a postal zip code following the name do not have a post office. Address hiker mail sent to post offices: "General Delivery, hold for Long Trail hiker, arriving [date]."

Division 1
North Adams, MA 01247; Greylock, MA; Williamstown Station, MA; Williamstown, MA 01267; Stamford, VT; **Bennington** 05201

Division 2
East Arlington 05252; Arlington 05250; West Wardsboro 05360

Division 3
Peru 05152; **Manchester Center** 05255; Manchester 05254

Division 4
Danby 05739; South Wallingford; East Wallingford 05742; Wallingford 05773

Division 5
Cuttingsville 05738; North Clarendon 05759; Killington 05751; **Rutland** 05701

Division 6
Chittenden 05737; Rochester 05767; Forest Dale 05745; **Brandon** 05733

Division 7
Hancock 05748; Ripton 05766; East Middlebury 05740; **Middlebury** 05753; Granville 05747

Division 8
Warren 05674; Lincoln; Bristol 05443; **Waitsfield** 05673

Division 9
Huntington 05462; Jonesville 05466; **Richmond** 05477; **Waterbury** 05676

Division 10
Moscow 05662; Underhill Center 05490; **Stowe** 05672; Morristown Corners; Morrisville 05661

Division 11
Johnson 05656; Waterville 05492; Belvidere Center 05442; Eden 05652

Division 12
Lowell 05847; Montgomery Center 05471; Westfield 05874; Jay; North Troy 05859; Richford 05476

Useful Addresses

Green Mountain Club
4711 Waterbury-Stowe Rd., Waterbury Center, VT 05677
(802) 244-7037; www.greenmountainclub.org

Appalachian Trail Conservancy
New England Regional Office
P.O. Box 264, South Egremont, MA 01258
(413) 528-8002; atc-nero@appalachiantrail.org

Appalachian Trail Conservancy
799 Washington St., P.O. Box 807, Harpers Ferry, WV 25425
(304) 535-6331; www.appalachiantrail.org

Catamount Trail Association
1 Mill St., #350, Burlington, VT 05401
(802) 864-5794; www.catamounttrail.org

Dartmouth Outing Club
Outdoor Programs Office
P.O. Box 9, Hanover, NH 03755
(603) 646-2428; opo@dartmouth.edu
www.dartmouth.edu/~opo

Green Mountain National Forest
Forest Supervisor's Office
231 N. Main St., Rutland, VT 05701
(802) 747-6700; www.fs.fed.us/r9/gmfl

Vermont Department of Forests, Parks and Recreation
Vermont Agency of Natural Resources
103 S. Main St., Waterbury, VT 05671-0301
(802) 241-3655; www.anr.state.vt.us

Vermont Department of Tourism and Marketing
One National Life Drive, 6th Floor
Montpelier, VT 05620-0501
(800) VERMONT; (802) 828-3237
www.vermontvacation.com

Index

abbreviations, xiv
Abraham, Mt., 146–47
Adam's Apple Trail, 188, 200
Airport Lookout, 103, 104
Allis Lookout, 166
Allis Trail, 161, 162
alpine areas, 8: on Camel's Hump,
   160; on Mt. Abraham, 146, 147;
   on Mt. Mansfield, 183, 187
Alpine Trail, 162, 163, 166–67, 168
Amherst Trail, 187, 197
animals, 9; and rabies, 25
Appalachian Gap, 145, 149
Appalachian Trail, 18, 42, 119, 123,
   231–36, 241–44: North Adams
   approach, 49, 51
Appalachian Trail Conservancy, xvi,
   39, 42
Arms Hill, 243
Atlas Valley Shelter, 219, 222

Babcock Trail, 211, 212, 213
Babcock Trail Extension, 212, 213
Baby Stark Mtn., 149
Baker Peak, 86, 89, 94
Baker Peak Trail, 89, 94–95
Bald Mtn., 65
Bald Mtn. Trail, 48, 63, 65–66
Bamforth Ridge Shelter, 163
Bartlett Brook Road, 242
Barton Trail, 148
Basin Brook, 211
Battell, Joseph, 133, 159
Battell Shelter, 146
Battell Trail, 146, 150
Beacon Hill, 103, 105
Beane Trail, 149, 150, 160
Bear Hollow Shelter, 191
Bear Mtn., 104
Beaver Meadow, 180–81
Beaver Meadow Lodge, 190

Beaver Meadow Trail, 190, 202
Belvidere Mtn., 208, 214
Belvidere Saddle, 212
Ben's Balcony, 123
Big Black Branch, 91
Big Branch Picnic Area, 95
Big Branch Shelter, 91
Big Branch suspension bridge, 89
Big Branch Wilderness, 86, 94
Big Muddy Pond, 213
Big Rock, 64
Bigelow Spring, 75, 79
Birch Glen Camp, 149
Black Brook Bridge, 64
Black Swamp Trail, 109, 110
blazes, trail, 2–3
Bloodroot Gap, 121
Bloodroot Mtn., 121
Bolton Mtn., 165, 166, 184
Bolton Notch Road, 159, 165
Bourn Pond, 75, 79
Bowen Mtn., 211
Boyce, Mt., 134
Boyce Shelter, 134
Branch Pond Trail, 76, 79, 80
Brandon Gap, 121
Breadloaf Mtn., 135
Breadloaf Wilderness, 130, 134, 137,
   138, 146
Broad Brook Trail, 54
Bromley Mtn., 72, 77
Bromley Brook, 77
Bromley Shelter, 77
Bruce Peak, 222
Buchanan, Bruce, 33
Buchanan, Roy O., 33, 34, 38, 41
Buchanan Shelter, 165
Buchanan Mtn., 222
Bucklin Trail, 108, 110–11
Burnt Hill Trail, 134, 137
Burnt Mtn., 225

Burnt Rock Mtn., 161
Burrows–Forest City connector, 170
Burrows Trail, 163, 168, 170
Butler, Mabel Taylor, 185
Butler Lodge, 185, 196
Butler Lodge Loop, 180
Butler Lodge Trail, 185–86, 193–94
Butternut Mtn., 211
Camel's Hump, 159–60, 162–63
Camel's Hump Hut Clearing, 163
Camel's Hump State Forest, 148, 149
campfires, 3, 12
camping, 3–4; equipment for, 20–21; sites for, 3–4, 14, 16–17, 18, 21, 28. See also Leave No Trace
campsites. See camping, sites for
Cantilever Rock, 199
Cantilever Rock Trail, 199
Canyon North Extension, 187, 198
Canyon North Trail, 198
Canyon Trail, 198
caretakers, 4–5, 14–15, 34–35
Carleton, Phillips D., 33
Carleton Mtn., 220
Castlerock chairlift, 147
Catamount Trail, 27
Chateauguay Road, 235
Chet's Lookout, 222
Chilcoot Pass, 190
Chilcoot Trail, 190, 202
Chin, Mt. Mansfield's, 188
Chittenden Brook Trail, 118, 121, 124
Churchill Scott Shelter, 109
Clara Bow Trail, 193
Clarendon Gorge, 103, 104
Clarendon Shelter, 105
Clark Brook Trail, 135, 138
Clark, Mt., 184
Cleveland, Mt., 136
Cliff Trail, 187, 197–98
Cloudland Road, 243
Codding Hollow Road, 209, 210
Cold River (Lower) Road, 102, 105
Congdon, Herbert Wheaton, 53

Congdon Shelter, 53
Consultation Peak, 52–53
Cooley Glen Shelter, 136, 146
Cooley Glen Trail, 136, 138
Cooper Lodge, 108
Corliss Camp, 211
Couching Line Farm, 169
County Road, 49
Cowles Cove Shelter, 160
Cutts Peak, 147
Dana Hill, 242
David Logan Shelter, 121, 123
David Morse Memorial Bench, 166–67
Davis Neighborhood Trail, 213
Day Hiker's Guide to Vermont, 8
day hikes: equipment for, 20; group size guidelines for, 13. See also hiking
Dean, Howard, 37
Dean Cave, 149
Dean Trail, 162, 167–68
Deer Leap Trail, 118, 122
Devil's Gulch, 211
distances, hiking, xiii
divisions: summaries, xiii; maps, key to, xv
division summaries, how to read, xiii
dogs, 5, 8, 10, 12, 194
Doll, Charles G., 33, 224
Doll Peak, 224
Domey's Dome, 222
Drift Rock, 187
Duck Brook, 165
Duck Brook Shelter, 165
Duxbury Road, 159, 164
Duxbury Window, 156, 164

Eagle Pass, 188
Eden Crossing, 209, 212
Elbow Road, 120
Elephant's Head Cliff, 189
Elephant's Head Trail, 189, 201
elevation profiles, xiv
Ellen, Mt., 144, 147
Emily Proctor Shelter, 135

Emily Proctor Trail, 135, 137–38
end-to-end, of the Long Trail, 31, 34
Eph's Lookout, 51
equipment, for hiking, 20–21
Ethan Allen, Mt., 149, 156, 161

fall and spring hiking, 6–8, 132
Farr Peak, 121
federal lands, 3, 18–19
fires, 3, 12
fire towers: on Belvidere Mtn., 208, 212, 214; on Bromley Mtn., 72, 77; on Glastenbury Mtn., 63; on Stratton Mtn., 72, 74–75
Forehead, Mt. Mansfield's, 186
Forehead By-Pass, 186, 187, 195
Forest City Trail, 162, 167, 170
Forester's Trail, 212, 214
Frank, Joseph E., 38–39
Frank Post Trail, 212, 213–14, 221
Frenchman's Pile, 287
Frost Trail, 194–95, 196
General Stark Mtn., 148
Giardia lamblia, 5
giardiasis, 5, 164
Gifford Woods State Park, 118, 233
Gillespie Peak, 133
Gilpin Mtn., 222
Glastenbury Lookout, 63
Glastenbury Mtn., 63
Gleason Brook Bridge, 164
Glen Ellen Lodge, 148
Goddard, Ted, 63
Goddard Shelter, 63
Gorham Spring, 163
Gould Brook, 107
Governor Clement Shelter, 107
Grant, Mt., 146
Great Cliff, at Mt. Horrid, 130, 133
Green Mountain Club (GMC), 29–42: headquarters of, 31, 37–38; history of, 32–25; information and education provided by, 31; and managing the Long Trail, 39–41; membership in, 30; publications of, 30; mission of, 35–37; Second

Century Campaign of, 38–39; sections of, 30, 33–34, 40; volunteers and, 40–41
Green Mountain National Forest, 18–19
Green Mountain News, 33
Green Mountain Parkway, 35
Green Mtn., 86, 95
Green Mtn. Connector, 95
Green Mtn. Trail, 92, 95
Green Road, 120
Greenwall Shelter, 92
Greenwall Spur, 92
Griffith Lake, 88, 93
Griffith Lake Tenting Area, 88
Group Notification System, 15
group hiking and camping, 13–15; permits for, 18–19; planning trips, 14–15
group use campsites, list of, 16–17
Guide Book of the Long Trail, 33
Gulf Stream, 236

Hagerman Overlook, 190
Halfway House Trail, 187, 196, 199
Happy Hill Shelter, 244
Harmon Hill, 53
Harrington's View, 156, 165–66
Haselton Trail, 187, 197
Hazen, Moses, 221
Hazen's Notch, 220, 221
Hazen's Notch Camp, 221
Haystack Mtn., 220, 221
Hedgehog Brook Trail, 161, 166
Hell Brook Cutoff, 188, 201
Hell Brook Trail, 188, 200–201
Hell Hollow Brook Bridge, 62
hiking: distances, xiii; day, 20; group, 13–15; overnight, 20–21; permits for, 18–19; planning, 19–21; spring and fall, 6–8, 132, 128; winter, 25–27
Holt Hollow, 147
Homer Stone Brook Bridge, 92
Homer Stone Brook Trail, 92, 95–96

Horrid, Mt., 130, 133; Great Cliff of, 130, 133
Hump Brook Tenting Area, 162, 167
hunting, 10, 94
Huntington Gap, 160
hypothermia, 22–23

insects, 24–25
International Paper (IP) Road, 74
Ira Allen, Mt., 149

James P. Taylor Winter Series, 31
Jay Camp, 223
Jay Loop, 223
Jay Pass, 221
Jay Peak, 220
Jerusalem Trail, 150
Joe Ranger Road, 243
Jonesville, 164
Journey's End Camp, 226
Journey's End Road, 225
Journey's End Trail, 225–26

Keewaydin Trail, 92, 96
Kelley Stand Road, 65, 74, 76
Kent Brook, 233
Kent Pond, 233
Kid Gore Shelter, 64
Killington Peak, 103, 110
Killington Ski Area nature trail, 110
Killington Spur, 110
Killington View, 136
Kirby Peak, 134

Ladder Ravine, 161
Lake Brook, 93
Lake Mansfield Trail, 184, 192–93
Lake Pleiad, 130, 134
Lake Trail, 94
Lakeview Trail, 196
Lakota Lake Lookout, 235
Laraway Lookout, 208, 210
Laraway Mtn., 210
Laura Cowles Trail, 187, 195, 200

Laura Woodward Shelter, 224
leaders, of groups, 13
Leave No Trace, 11–12
lightning, 24
Lincoln Gap, 145, 146
Lincoln Gap Road, 145, 146
Lincoln Peak, 147
Little Abe, 147
Little Hans Peak, 135
Little Killington, 107
Little Pond Lookout, 62
Little Pond Mtn., 62
Little Rock Pond, 86, 91, 95
Little Rock Pond Loop Trail, 91, 95
Little Rock Pond Tenting Areas, 86
Little Rock Pond Shelter, 91
Logan, David, 121
Long Trail, the, xvi, 2: access to, 27–28; camping and fires on, 3–4, 14; caretakers of, 4–5; end-to-end hiking of, 31, 34; and the GMC, 29, 32–37, 38–41; history of, 32–35; management of, 39–41; markings on, 2–3; side-to-side hiking of, 32; transportation to, 27–28. See also shelters, on the Long Trail
Long Trail End-to-Ender's Guide, 21, 28
Long Trail News, 33
Long Trail Patrol (LTP), 41
Long Trail Protection Campaign, 36–37
Lost Pond Shelter, 89
Lower Lip, of Mt. Mansfield, 187
Lydia's Rest, 64
Lye Brook Trail, 75, 76, 78
Lye Brook Wilderness, 72, 76, 78–79, 80
lyme disease, 24

Mackaye, Benton, 42, 74
Madonna Peak, 190
Mad Tom Notch, 78
mail delivery, 21, 164

Maine Junction, 119
Mansfield, Mt., 182–83; Summit
   Station, 186, 196, 197, 198, 199;
   Visitor Center, 186
Mansfield Traverse, 190
Maple Hill, 62
Maple Ridge, 194
Maple Ridge Trail, 186, 194, 195–96
maps, xii; key to, 0
Marvin B. Gameroff Hiker Center, 31
Mayo, Mt., 179, 184
Medicine for the Backcountry, 23
Melville Nauheim Shelter, 62
Mendon Lookout, 109
Middlebury Gap, 134
Middlebury Snow Bowl, 134
Minerva Hinchey Shelter, 104
Molly Stark's Balcony, 144, 149
Molly Stark Mtn., 149
Monroe, Will S., 169
Monroe Trail, 163, 169–70
Montclair Glen Lodge, 161–62
Morse Mtn., 190
Mt. Mansfield Toll Road, 186
Mt. Mansfield Visitor Center, 186
Muddy Pond, 213
mud season, 6–8, 132

Nancy Hanks Peak, 147
National Park Service, 39
Nebraska Notch, 180
Nebraska Notch Trail, 185, 193
Needle's Eye, 186
New Boston Trail, 121, 123
Newton Lane, 244
North Jay Massif, 224
North Jay Pass, 221
North Shore Tenting Area, 76, 79,
   80
North Shore Trail, 76, 79–80

Old Bennington–Heartwellville
   Road, 53
Old Job Shelter, 93
Old Job Trail, 89, 93–94
Old Little Rock Pond Shelter, 92

Old Rootville Road, 76
Orvis Lookout, 148
Outfitter-Guide Special Use Permit, 18
Overlook Spur, 122
overnight hiking and camping:
   equipment for, 20–21; for groups,
   14–15; permits for, 18–19; sites,
   3–4
Oxbow Ridge, 165

parking, at trailheads, 28
Patch Hollow, 104
peregrine falcons, 9
permits, 18–19
Peru Peak, 88
Peru Peak Wilderness, 88
Peru Peak Shelter, 88
Pico Camp, 108
Pico Circuit, 103
Pico Link, 112
Pico Peak, 112
Pine Cobble, 48, 51
Pine Cobble Trail, 51–52
Pinnacle, the, 235
plants, in alpine areas, 8, 146, 147,
   160, 183, 187
Plot Road, 209
Podunk Brook, 244
Pomfret–South Pomfret
   (County) Road, 242
Porcupine Lookout, 60, 62
primitive camping, 3
private lands, 2, 3, 18, 36–37, 39
Profanity Trail, 187, 188, 200
Prospect Rock (Div. 3), 76
Prospect Rock (Div. 11), 210
Puffer Shelter, 184
public campgrounds.
   See camping, sites for

Quimby Mtn., 234

rabies, 25
Rail Trail, 191
Ritterbush/Big Muddy Pond Loop,
   208

Ritterbush Lookout, 211–12
River Road, 232, 233
Roaring Branch, 48, 52
Roaring Brook Bridge, 93
Rock Garden Trail, 186, 195, 196
Rock Refuge, 161
Rolston Rest Shelter, 120
Romance Gap, 133
Romance Mtn., 133
Roosevelt, Mt., 130
Roundtop Shelter, 210
Russell Hill, 109
safety, 21–25, 106
sanitation, 4, 11
Sawyer Hill, 235
Second Century Campaign, 38–39
Seth Warner Shelter, 52
shelters, on the Long Trail, 3–4:
   camping between, 3; distances
   between, xiii; and groups, 14;
   history of, 34; management of, 4,
   40–41; and winter, 25, 26
Sherburne Pass Trail, 108,
   111–12, 122–23
Sherman Brook Primitive
   Campsite, 49
Shooting Star Shelter, 224
Short Trail, the, 37–38
South Link, 196
Shrewsbury Peak, 103, 107, 109
Shrewsbury Peak Shelter, 110
Shrewsbury Peak Trail, 107, 109
side-to-side certification program, 32
Silent Cliff Trail, 134, 136–37
Sink Hole Brook, 112
skiing. See winter hiking
Skylight Pond Trail, 134–35, 137
Skyline Lodge, 135
Smugglers' Notch Picnic Area,
   189, 201
Smugglers' Notch State Park Camp-
   ground, 181, 183, 189
snakes, 25
Snowden Peak, 108
snowshoeing. See winter hiking
South Link, 187

Split Rock, 60, 62
spring and fall hiking, 6–8, 132
Spring Lake Clearing, 104
Spruce Knob, 164
Spruce Ledge Camp, 211
Spruce Peak, 72, 77
Spruce Peak Shelter, 76
Stark's Nest, 148
state lands, 3, 6, 19, 39
Sterling Pond, 180
Sterling Pond Shelter, 189–90
Sterling Pond Trail, 201-2
Stony Brook Shelter, 234
Story Spring Shelter, 64
Stratton–Arlington (Kelley
   Stand) Road, 60–61, 74
Stratton Mtn., 72, 74
Stratton Pond, 75, 79
Stratton Pond Trail, 75, 78
Stratton Pond Shelter, 75
Stratton Pond Trail, 75, 78
Stratton View Spring, 79
Styles Peak, 86, 88
Subway, the, 187, 198
Sucker Brook Shelter, 133
Sucker Brook Trail, 133, 136
Sucker Pond Outlet Brook, 53
Summit Station, of Mt. Mansfield,
   186, 196, 197, 198, 199
Sunrise Shelter, 121
Sunset Ledge, 146
Sunset Ridge Trail, 187, 195, 199

Taft Lodge, 184, 188
Taylor, James P., 32, 74, 184
Taylor Lodge, 184
Telephone Gap, 120
Theron Dean Shelter, 148–49
Thistle Hill, 243
Thistle Hill Shelter, 243
Tillotson Camp, 212, 221
Tillotson Peak, 221
Trail and Shelter Adopter Program,
   41
trails: access to, 27–28; descriptions,
   how to read, xiii; markings of, 2–3

transportation, to the Long Trail, 27–28
Trip Leader's Handbook, 13
trip planning, 19–21
Tucker-Johnson Shelter, 119
TV Road, 185
Twin Brooks Tenting Area, 185
265-Mile Club, 37

Upper Lip, of Mt. Mansfield, 187
Upper Road, 107
U.S. 2. 158
U.S. 4. 102–3, 119
U.S. 5. 242
U.S. Forest Service, 18, 28, 39, 41
USFS Road 10. 87, 91
USFS Road 21. 87, 88
USFS Road 30. 87
USFS Road 71. 64

vandalism, 28
Vermont Department of Forests, Parks and Recreation, 19, 183
Volunteer Long Trail Patrol, 41
volunteers, and the GMC, 40–41
Vt. 9. 49
Vt. 11. 73
Vt. 12. 236
Vt. 14. 242
Vt. 15. 182
Vt. 17. 145, 149
Vt. 30. 73
Vt. 58. 220–21
Vt. 73. 119, 131
Vt. 100. 232
Vt. 103. 102
Vt. 105. 221
Vt. 108. 182
Vt. 118. 208, 212
Vt. 125. 131
Vt. 140. 87, 102
Vt. 242. 221

Walker's Guide to Vermont, 8
Wallace Cutoff, 185, 193
Wampahoofus Trail, 186, 196

waste, management of, 11, 164
water, 5
Waterproof Hiking Map of Vermont's Long Trail, 22
Watson Camp, 201
weather, 22
West Ridge Trail, 63, 65
Wetmore Gap, 121
Whiteface Mtn., 191
Whiteface Shelter, 190–91
Whiteface Trail, 190, 202
White Rocks Cliff, 96
White Rocks Cliff Trail, 92, 96
White Rocks Mtn., 92
White Rocks National Recreation Area, 88, 93
White Rocks Picnic Area, 93, 96
wildlife, 9, 10, 12; and rabies, 25
Wilderness Areas, 8–9
Willard Gap, 119
William B. Douglas Shelter, 76, 80
William D. MacArthur Memorial Bridge, 61
Williams, Ephraim, 51
William Tucker Trail, 244
Willis Ross Clearing, 75
Wilson, Mt., 135
Wind Gap, 162, 167
Winhall River, 76
Winooski River Bridge, 164
Wind Gap, 162
winter hiking, 25–27, 50
Woodstock Stage Road, 242
Worth Mtn., 134
Worth Mtn. Lodge, 131, 134